Tacoma's Shul
Talmud Torah — Sinai Temple

Including 212 Biographical Sketches

Deborah K. Freedman

and Harold G. Friedman

ISBN: 9798422073832

Cover design by Chris Fiala Erlich

Front cover photo: Sinai Temple south exterior in 1964
Courtesy of Tacoma Public Library Richards Studio D141770-15
Enhanced by Clif Taylor

Back cover congregational photo: Henry Bell Torah dedication, November 21, 1937
Courtesy of the Farber Family

Back cover building photo: Sinai Temple sanctuary interior in 1964
Courtesy of Tacoma Public Library, Richards Studio D141770-2

Tacoma newspaper clippings used with personal permission of Stephanie Pedersen, president and editor of *The News Tribune*, granted February 28, 2022

Acknowledgments:
Individuals: Jim Farber, Steph Farber, Herman Kleiner, Jackie Rye, Jay Schupack, Clif Taylor and Jack Warnick

Institutions: Ilona and Spencer, staff of Tacoma Public Library's Northwest Room; Leslie Bright, Andy Mauer and staff of Tacoma's Temple Beth El; Tracy Rebstock, Washington State Archives; Ruba Sadi, Special Collections Division, University of Washington Libraries

Special kudos to Suzanne Leichman and Dale R. Wirsing for their editing and friendship

Disclaimer: The authors have compiled biographical sketches to the best of their abilities using available sources, often without the assistance or collaboration of relatives. Errors and omissions are probable and corrections are welcomed. We apologize in advance for any families we may have missed. We have carefully tried to respect the privacy of the living.

Mrs. Harry Rotman (Lena Lamken)
(Left) October 1937, (Right) October 1984

Dedication:

This book is dedicated to my grandmother, Lena Rotman, an immigrant from Sassmacken, Russia (now Valdemarpils, Latvia) and a devoted member of the Jewish community about which we write. By teaching and living the value of community, she made a special name and place for herself in the life of Tacoma, the adopted Jewish home she loved.

(Harold G. Friedman)

Mrs. Harry Rotman

HONORED BY CONGREGATION

It requires the contributions of many, the efforts, the work, the thought of a whole congregation to put into action and successfully conclude an undertaking so vast as the one we are here celebrating this night.

Among those who have worked without thought of personal glory, without seeking thanks, is one of the Congregation Talmud Torah's favorite daughters, Mrs. Harry Rotman, who, by her own efforts, brought in more than a score of ads, and sold many tickets.

But this was not the only time that Mrs. Rotman has come to the aid of the Congregation in time of need. The records are replete with her benign efforts. And there has been no year in the annals of the Congregation's history which does not prove her an ardent and capable worker. To Mrs. Rotman, the Congregation pays tribute in acknowledgment of her unselfish contribution in time and effort given when effort and time were sorely needed.

1944 Talmud Torah Anniversary Banquet Program

Table of Contents:

Table of Biographical Sketches

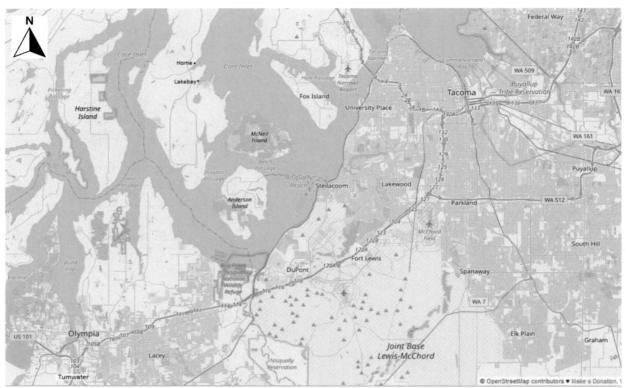

(Above) Tacoma and South Puget Sound region, OpenStreetMap.com
(Below) Downtown Tacoma changing street names, by Chris Fiala Erlich

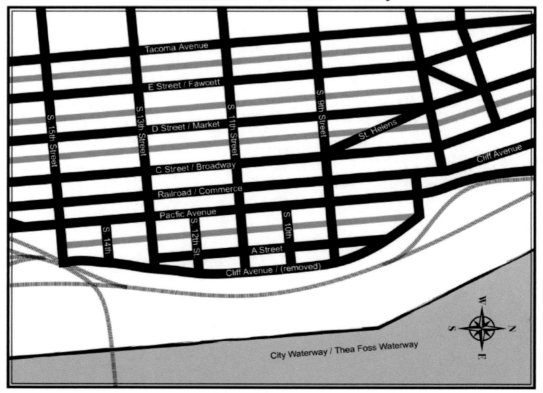

Shul/Temple Locations

1. **Chevra Talmud Torah School** (1907-1910), Samson Hotel, South 13th and E, 1152 South E Street (now Fawcett Avenue)

2. **Chevra Talmud Torah** (1910-1925), 1529 Tacoma Avenue South

3. **Talmud Torah Synagogue/Sinai Temple** (1925-1960), South 4th and I, 901 South 4th Street

4. 1st **Temple Beth Israel** (1893-1918), South 10th and I, 921-923 South I Street

5. 2nd **Temple Beth Israel** (1922-1960), North 4th and J, 324 North J Street

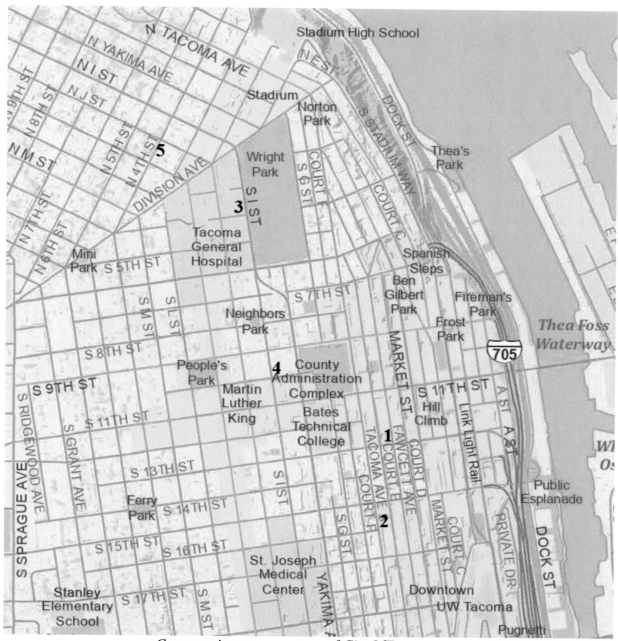

Current city map courtesy of CityOfTacoma.org

> **Shul**: Yiddish for synagogue, pronounced *shool,*
> from an old High German word for school

Introduction:

The Shul. One word, one syllable, yet the word carries so much meaning. A synagogue by definition is a house of worship, study, and assembly. The Shul was not just the synagogue building. It was the heart of the Jewish community. It was where friends and relatives met to worship, to learn, to discuss, to laugh, to cry, and to eat. Every meeting included refreshments, nearly every service was followed by a social hour with food, and every major event included a banquet.

The formation of Tacoma's Orthodox Jewish community is interwoven with the development of the city and its rollercoaster economics. It began with waves of desperate immigration, shadowed by Eastern European pogroms and revolutions. It is no wonder families clustered with others from their homeland (*landsmen* in Yiddish,) forming a tightly knit community, a Chevra. The Shul began as a simple minyan of ten men gathering for daily prayers. In the early 1900s they hired a teacher and kosher butcher, then purchased a building. Growth as a result of the First World War enabled them to build a synagogue. By the Thirties the Chevra had grown into a respected congregation with an ordained scholarly rabbi and a stately brick synagogue building that served as a true communal center. Children thrived, went to college, and came home to marry and take their place as community leaders. The congregation transitioned from Orthodox to Conservative. As events in Europe continued to impact Tacoma's Jews they sent their boys off to another war, their dollars to humanitarian aid, and their prayers to G-d. (And encouraged their daughters to welcome visiting soldiers.) The Fifties brought more changes that led to an historic merger and a new beginning.

Although the building is gone and the families are scattered, many memories remain. This work hopes to capture some of those memories, reminders of a place of worship and study and assembly, of a Shul.

A note about pronunciation:
The letter "a" in the Yiddish word *landsmen* is pronounced "ah," as in papa.
The "ch" in the Hebrew word *chevra* (or *chevrah*) is not the "ch" of checkers or Chevrolet, but the Hebrew "ch" as in Chanukah. When in doubt, Hanukah.

It is said that the first immigrant generation just wants to make a living. The second generation wants to forget they were immigrants. Yet the third generation wants to remember. This work is for those who have listened to their grandmothers' stories, for those who had no one to ask, and for the fourth and fifth generations.

Chapter One: Tacoma Jewish Beginnings

Reform Pioneers

Tacoma's earliest Jewish pioneers by necessity (or perhaps by choice) lived outside of strict Jewish observances and dietary laws. Only a handful of Jewish merchants lived in Steilacoom in the 1860s, all related by marriage. Another cluster of families moved to Tacoma in the 1870s, attracted by the announcement of the coming of the Northern Pacific Railroad via Oregon. Together these families joined with the Jews of Olympia to form a Jewish burial society in nearby Tumwater. They traveled to Portland, Oregon; or Victoria, British Columbia; to participate in High Holy Day services and to be married by a rabbi.

Tacoma was booming by the 1880s as a new Northern Pacific route across the Cascades connected Tacoma directly to eastern cities. Tacoma's Jewish community also boomed. In the fall of 1885 it was necessary to publish newspaper mentions of the observances of Rosh Hashanah and Yom Kippur in rented halls. In part, the articles informed the members of Tacoma's expanding Jewish community of service details and locations. Primarily, the notices warned shoppers that many of Tacoma's leading stores would be closed on those days.

Tacoma's Jews began to organize and formed their own cemetery association in 1888. 1890 brought a social Harmony Club, a women's Judith Montefiore Society, and a men's B'nai B'rith Lodge #406. Published menus from their banquets included ham, oysters, and chicken in cream sauce, indicating that many of Tacoma's Jews were embracing the growing Reform style of Judaism. However, it is unlikely that the observances were unanimous. While we know what was served, we don't know who was willing to actually eat it.

The development of Reform Judaism is typically associated with German Jews. Many of Tacoma's prominent Jews in the 1880s were active in the Germania Society and maintained a strong German identity. In February of 1892 the majority of Tacoma's Jews organized Congregation Beth Israel. They adopted a constitution and by-laws in March and filed articles of incorporation in July, taking vital steps in the path to building a temple. Those by-laws identified the congregation as Reform worshippers, driving a wedge into Tacoma's fledgling Jewish community.

Landsmen

While many of Tacoma's pioneer Jews had roots in central Europe, a cluster of Jews had begun emigrating from the Courland region of what is now Latvia. They spoke Yiddish, gathered together for daily prayer minyans, and would heavily intermarry. In the fall of 1892 the "Hebrew Orthodox of Tacoma" publicly announced separate High Holy Day services. Tacoma's Jewish population had grown large enough to openly divide, and would remain so for nearly seventy years.

ANNOUNCEMENTS.

THE HEBREW ORTHODOX OF TA-coma will commence their services for Yom Kippur this (Friday) evening, at 7 o'clock, at the Elks' hall, corner of Twelfth and A streets.

Tacoma Daily Ledger Friday September 30, 1892

Orthodox Worshippers

Who were the "Hebrew Orthodox of Tacoma" who worshipped together in 1892? Fewer than ten men have been identified who stayed to affiliate with other Orthodox Jews in the next decade. That would imply that for every man listed below, two or three more have been lost to history. Or perhaps, many who had helped form Beth Israel were personally more traditional in their practices, but soon after left Tacoma.

Adolph Friedman

Adolph was born in Bauske, Courland, Russia; now Bauska, Latvia. In 1892 he was a bachelor in his sixties or early seventies.

Julius Samuel Stusser wrote a letter of family recollections in 1958. He stated that his great-uncle, Adolph Friedman, had arrived in Steilacoom, Washington, in 1845. At that time the Hudson's Bay Colony was still part of British Columbia. That date led historians to declare that Adolph was the first Jew to arrive in the entire Pacific Northwest, including British Columbia. While that arrival date has not yet been verified, the rest of the letter told a compelling tale of Adolph's later activities in Pierce County.

Adolph's 1911 obituary was perhaps more accurate, stating that he had come to California as a teen. There he joined the Masons in San Francisco in 1860, specifically the Clay Lodge No. 101. That clue significantly narrowed the Friedman paper trail, as the Clay Lodge was located in Dutch Flat, in Placer County, not far from Reno, Nevada.

Adolph was naturalized in October of 1860 in Nevada City, California. In 1863 he was enrolled as a senior student in the College of the Pacific. He operated stores in a series of small towns in the 1860s, paying taxes on liquor sales and a billiards table. Adolph registered to vote in Nevada County in 1867 and was appointed postmaster at Meadow Lake (now part of the Tahoe National Forest.) The following year he was quoted in a newspaper interview saying he had tired of opening temporary saloons along the railroad construction route and was content to stay in Meadow Lake. However, he moved on to Nevada and places unknown. There is a gap in his history over the next fifteen years.

> The Mexico arrived in port Sunday evening at 5 o'clock with the following passengers for Tacoma:
> Mrs Douglas and children, Mrs Rosa Levy, H B Pelham, A Friedman, E F Cameron and eleven others.

Tacoma Daily Ledger October 28, 1884

Adolph Friedman arrived in Tacoma at the dock of what is now Old Town on the steamer *Mexico* at 5 p.m. on October 26, 1884. On that same Sunday many from Tacoma's Jewish community had gone to Seattle to celebrate the 100th birthday of Sir Moses Montefiore.

Adolph initially worked with Meyer Kaufman, and the following year purchased Meyer's dry goods and grocery business. Both had been in San Francisco in 1860, both had worked near Reno, Nevada, in the 1870s, and both invested in Tacoma's fledgling real estate market. Sales in Adolph's American Lake Park development in the 1890s encouraged other Friedman family members to join him in Tacoma. Late in life Adolph would marry his niece, Mascha Stusser, sister of Jennie Stusser.

Julius Friedman

Family members relate that Julius Friedman emigrated around his 18th birthday, but mistakenly took transportation to the wrong Washington. He had to work on the East Coast to earn funds to travel west. Although his name didn't appear in the Tacoma city directory until several years later, his store letterhead proclaimed "Established in 1892." His arrival likely helped establish the minyan of ten men needed for separate prayer services.

In 1899 Julius Friedman would marry his second cousin, Augusta Stusser, daughter of Hugo Stusser. Their extended families would form the nucleus of Tacoma's first Orthodox community. His 1906 real estate success likely served as incentive for other Friedman relatives to join him from their temporary homes in New York, directly leading to the formation of Chevra Talmud Torah. Julius would play a vital leadership role, serving multiple times as president and leading building efforts. He also provided jobs and housing for new arrivals and assisted them through the citizenship process.

Isaac "Ike" Moses

Isaac was born in Davinsk, Russia; now Latvia. In 1892 he was a bachelor, and had just turned seventeen.

Ike was closely connected with the Winkleman family. He probably moved to Washington Territory with them from New York around 1888 and worked in their family junk business. In 1895 he would briefly partner with Julius Friedman in a secondhand clothing store. In 1908 he would be an incorporator of Chevra Talmud Torah, but would later belong to Temple Beth Israel.

Frank S. Rosenberg

Frank sold fruits and cigars in Tacoma in the early 1890s, an industry with one of the city's cheapest business licenses. His store was near that of Julius Friedman, and he would be a guest at his wedding.

Hirsch "Herman" Stusser

Herman was born in Libau, Courland, Russia; now Liepaja, Latvia. He was possibly the same Hirsch Stusser who arrived in New York in December of 1891. In 1892 he lived in Tacoma with Adolph Friedman, and his siblings Jacob Julius and Mascha Stusser. At the time he was 35 and had a wife and four children in Libau. He worked as a tailor, dyeing and pressing clothing. Herman would return to Europe, have four more children with his wife, Betty, and come again to Tacoma in 1901.

Hirsch "Hugo" Stusser

Hugo was born in Libau, Courland, Russia; now Liepaja, Latvia. He likely emigrated in 1891, joining his brother-in-law Jacob Julius Stusser. Hugo had married his cousin, Jennie, and had seven children ages two through twelve. In 1892 he was in his mid-thirties and worked as a tailor. Hugo was remembered as a leader of daily prayer minyans in his store for those saying Kaddish after the death of a family member.

Jacob Julius Stusser

Jennie's brother, Jacob Julius, was also born in Libau, Courland, Russia; now Liepaja, Latvia. He emigrated as a teenager and became a citizen in 1890. In 1892 he was 24 and living in Tacoma with Adolph Friedman, along with his siblings, Herman and Mascha. Jacob worked as a shoemaker.

Jacob would marry California native Edith Hirschfeld, daughter of Tacoma merchant Sigmund Hirschfeld. Dozens of other relatives would join the Stussers in Tacoma.

Raphael Winkleman

Raphael was born in New York in 1881. His parents, Henry Philip and Lottie (Raphael) Winkleman, came to Washington Territory about 1888. His family operated a junk business and later manufactured burlap bags. Raphael would be an incorporator of Chevra Talmud Torah in 1908, likely the only charter member born in the United States.

To Tacoma via Devil's Lake, North Dakota

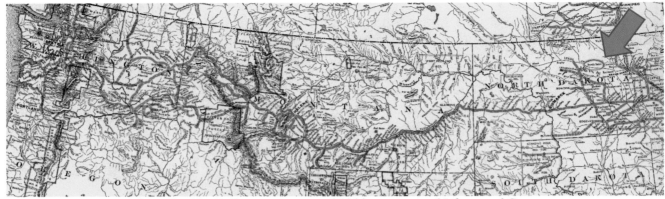

Northern Pacific Railway routes as of 1900, courtesy of Library of Congress

The Lithuanian/Bremerton Friedmans

While Adolph Friedman was initiating an immigration of Latvian families to Tacoma, another Friedman family was taking a very different route to the Pacific Northwest. Jacob B. Friedman arrived in New York from Russia on December 23, 1881, with his sons, Joseph and Julius. His wife, Jennie (Kaplan) Friedman, followed him with their daughters Lena, Anna, and Mary. Jacob's brothers, Aron and Herman, also emigrated in the 1880s, eventually joining Jacob in St. Paul, Minnesota.

The brothers took advantage of land opportunities in Devil's Lake, North Dakota, in a Jewish farm colony. By 1890 all three had filed land patents and applied for citizenship. The harsh realities of severe weather, crop failures, and social isolation led them to sell their farms and move to cities.

Aron and his wife moved to Chicago with their four children. After Mindel's death Aron joined another brother, Samuel, in Jaffa, Palestine. Aron died there in 1916.

Jacob and Herman took advantage of the nearby railroad to travel nearly as far west as they could. By 1892 both were living in Seattle, Washington. Most of the family members stayed in Seattle, but Jacob's daughter, Anne, married S.N. Witenberg and moved to Tacoma around the turn of the century.

A younger brother, Abraham M., joined Anne in Tacoma in 1911. His wife, Gittel, died in childbirth in Tacoma in 1914. After her death Abraham became known as the "Father of the Bremerton Friedmans." His great-granddaughter, Debra Friedman, would return to Tacoma in 2011 as chancellor of the University of Washington Tacoma. Abraham's son, Charles, resumed the family's original surname of Pelin.

Olswang and Sussman from Sassmacken

Another set of brothers, Jacob and Peter "Pit" Alswang/Olswang, also found their way from Devil's Lake to Seattle. They were joined by siblings Herman, Ben, Abe, Shabse, and Johanna. The four eldest brothers all married in Seattle in the 1890s. Peter and his wife, Rebecca (Sussman) lived in Seattle and Bellingham before moving to Tacoma about 1904. Shabse Olswang lived in Tacoma in 1918 when he informed the draft board that he served as "reverend of Talmud Torah." In 1922 Shabse also moved to Palestine, taking the surname Boruch. Ben's son, Henry, married Alice Kahan, daughter of Louis Kahan, another Devil's Lake farmer who had moved to Seattle.

The Olswang and Sussman families were from Sassmacken, now Valdemarpils, Latvia. Again, many Sassmacken relatives and landsmen followed them to the Pacific Northwest. The Sussman brothers came to Tacoma in 1903. Five years later young Lena Lamken lived briefly in Seattle before marrying Harry Rotman and adopting Tacoma as her home and the Jewish community as her family.

Reform Congregation Beth Israel

In the spring of 1893 the members of Tacoma's new Reform Congregation Beth Israel took out a mortgage and hired an architect to draw plans. May third brought approval of a building permit for construction of a two-story wooden synagogue on the corner of South 10th and I Streets. The timing couldn't have been worse. Two days later a series of business failures in the East rippled to create a national banking panic. With no way of foreseeing the severity of the situation, Tacoma's Reform Jews went ahead with building construction.

Tacoma's booming economy stalled. Over the summer half a dozen of Tacoma's Jewish merchants closed their businesses in default. The city's former mayor committed suicide in financial ruin. Tacoma's Jews came together in September of 1893 to dedicate the new building, then again went their separate ways. Over the next several years, as land values plummeted and more businesses failed, Tacoma lost nearly half of its population, including the majority of the pioneer Jewish merchants. Congregation Beth Israel would not hire a rabbi until a decade later, when the mortgage was paid off. He would stay only one year. The members of Congregation Beth Israel would spend twenty-five of their first twenty-six years without a rabbi and often without holding regular weekly services.

Congregation Beth Israel postcard from the Freedman Collection

Tacoma's Failed Economy

The effects of the 1893 Banking Panic devastated the finances of the city of Tacoma for nearly two decades. Historian Murray Morgan noted that Tacoma was perhaps the hardest-hit city in the nation. In part the impact was due to timing, as Tacoma had been on a wild rise of real estate values. Brokers in the late 1880s claimed that their clients could buy a property in the morning and sell the same in the afternoon for a large profit.

More importantly, the city had been spending beyond its means. Bond sales financed construction of roads and bridges, a new city hall, and the purchase of Charles Wright's water and power system. Council members assumed that property taxes would continue to provide a steady revenue stream to cover the five million dollars of indebtedness.

A third element made Tacoma's city finances particularly vulnerable: fraud. Not one, but two city treasurers were sentenced to the penitentiary at Walla Walla, as bank examiners eventually discovered a system of graft, corruption, and creative financing.

The result was a city in default, struggling even to make interest payments on its loans or to pay its employees. Merchants loaned funds for salaries for firemen, in order to preserve their store insurance policies. The city council paid teachers and other employees in warrants, a series of IOUs that created a All but a handful of Tacoma's banks failed and depositors lost their savings.

Tacoma's city finances were still in a legal nightmare when news came of fabulous gold fields in the Klondike in 1897. More importantly, Seattle transportation companies had exclusive contracts in place so that gold seekers could only get to Alaska via Seattle. Seattle merchants reaped the benefits and Seattle's economy and population exploded. Tacoma would never again catch up. The same would be true of its Jewish population.

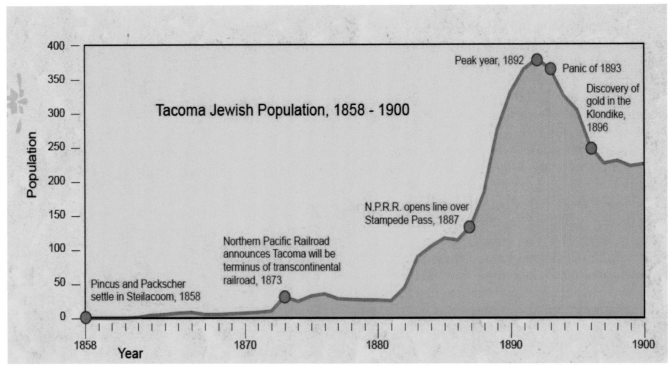

Population graphic designed by Chris Fiala Erlich for Tacoma Historical Society

Jacob Julius Stusser married Edith Hirschfeld in Tacoma in January of 1897. The event didn't merit a mention in the newspaper's Society pages, an indication of their lack of social and community status and his limited advertising budget. During the height of the Yukon gold rush stampede (1897-1898) some prosperity returned to Tacoma, as merchants worked to outfit prospectors at prices lower than those in Seattle. Conditions in Tacoma improved mostly through taking advantage of coal and other natural resources in the state. Lumbermen formed the Weyerhaeuser Company in Tacoma in 1900, leading to nearly a century of economic growth through the timber industry. However, Tacoma's economy didn't fully recover until the First World War.

What Could Be Worse?

The exodus of prominent pioneer Jewish merchants left a void in Tacoma's downtown business district. The next wave of Jewish merchants had to adapt to the depressed economy. They operated secondhand stores and pawnshops. They offered shoe repair and clothes dyeing services, and often lived at their stores. Many clustered on Commerce Street, one block uphill from the fashionable main thoroughfare, Pacific Avenue.

Who in their right mind would choose to move to Tacoma in this period? Perhaps someone who was joining other family members, someone who recognized the opportunities of a depressed economy, or someone who was coming from an even worse situation.

One intermarried family of Friedmans and Stussers would meet all three of those criteria. They would bring a steady stream of relatives to join them. And unlike most of their predecessors, they would stay in Tacoma for generations to come.

Chapter Two: Chevra Talmud Torah

In 1899 when Julius Friedman married Augusta Stusser, the *Tacoma Daily Ledger* published the full guest list. The prominence of the Friedman and Stusser families from Courland had begun.

A pretty wedding took place last Sunday afternoon in Walhalla hall, when Miss Augusta Stusser, daughter of Mr. and Mrs. H. Stusser, was married to Mr. Julius Friedman by Rabbi Brooks of the Hebrew temple in Seattle. The hall was handsomely decorated for the occasion, and the ceremony was most impressive and beautiful. The bride was dressed in white silk with chiffon trimmings and carried white chrysanthemums. After the ceremony an elaborate spread of wedding delicacies was partaken of by the large company and a reception followed. Mr. and Mrs. Friedman left on the night train for Portland. Those present at the wedding were Mr. and Mrs. Ramelsburg, Miss Ella Winkleman, Mr. and Mrs. J. Jacoby, Mr. and Mrs. M. Schmidt, Mr. John Schmidt, Mr. and Mrs. John Schultz, Mr. and Mrs. S. Zelinsky, Mr. and Mrs. George Simon, Mr. and Mrs. Hirschfield, Mr. and Mrs. Shapeero, Mr. Sam Simon, Mr. and Mrs. Eckstein, Mr. and Mrs. Morris Gross, Mr. and Mrs. Guy K. Llewellyn, Mr. and Mrs. S. Jacoby, Miss Mollie Jacoby, Mr. and Mrs. Winkleman, Mr. and Mrs. John Schock, Miss Rose Hirschfield, Mrs. Rob and son, Mr. and Mrs. Kaufman, Mr. and Mrs. McNichel and family, Mrs. Koons, Mrs. Lipscomb, Mrs. Gleedan, Mr. and Mrs. Bloom, Misses Ella and Emma Bloom, Mr. Nat Bloom, Mr. Frank Rosenberg, Mr. B. Yondelson, Mr. and Mrs. Wittenburg, Mr. Friedman, Mr. Knob, Mr. Rudnick, Miss Mabel Jackson, Mr. Oileer, Mr. W. Oileer, Mr. John Oileer, Mr. Fisher, Mr. and Mrs. Chilberg, Mr. William Behler, Mr. and Mrs. N. Blosberg of Seattle, Mrs. H. Friedman of Seattle, Miss Mary Friedman of Seattle, Miss Esther Friedman of Seattle.

Tacoma Daily Ledger December 10, 1899

Courland

In 1881 nearly 48,000 Jews lived in the Courland area of what is now Latvia, making up over eight per cent of the population. Most were concentrated in urban areas. Bauske's population was nearly sixty per cent Jewish. Those Jews had grown up in a period of relative tolerance.

However, the murder of Alexander II in the spring of 1881 brought an outburst of antisemitism. The situation was made worse by resentment against 20,000 Jewish refugees arriving in Courland in the 1880s from what is now Ukraine, Belarus, and Poland. The strikes and riots of the Revolution of 1905, beginning with "Bloody Sunday" in January, contributed to a flood of emigration.

A cluster of those immigrants found safety and opportunity in Tacoma. Several members of the Friedman and Stusser families had already come to Tacoma from Courland. Others followed, bringing cousins and in-laws. Unlike many of their predecessors, they upheld a strong Jewish identity and maintained an Orthodox style of Jewish practice. They prayed together daily. Their children would intermarry with the Sussmans, Lamkens, and other Courland Jews, forming a community of landsmen with a shared history and a common goal. They sought to provide an Orthodox Jewish education for their children in a proper house of study, worship, and assembly. A Shul.

It is impossible to overstate the significance and sheer numbers of the family relationships that connected Tacoma's Courland Jewish immigrants. Jehuda "Yudel" Friedman's daughter, Mollie (Friedman) Stusser, had twelve children. Jehuda's son Zalman's two sons also fathered twelve children each. Jehuda's grandchildren and great-grandchildren would account for three dozen adults living in Tacoma by 1906.

Jehuda/Yudel Friedman

Jehuda's son
Solomon/Zalman Friedman

Solomon married twice and died in Latvia in 1890

Jehuda's son
Adolph/Avram Friedman

Adolph married his niece Mascha Stusser late in life and died in 1911 in Tacoma without children

To US 1845 or 1855, Tacoma 1884

Jehuda's daughter
Mollie/Malca Friedman

Mollie married Abraham Stusser and both died in Latvia

Stusser

Friedman

Solomon's son
Jacob/Yankel 1834-1917

Married 1st in 1863 to Rebecca/
Rivka Rolov (1834-1880)

Jacob to US Dec 1905, Tacoma bef 1908

Friedman

Solomon's son
Philip B/Feivish 1847-1917

Married about 1875 to Rose/
Roche Landsman (1854-1939)

To US June 1906, Tacoma abt 1914

Mollie & Abraham's children:
1. Yudel 1852-1866
2. Bluma 1854-1920
   - Married PJ Yudelson about 1883
   - Seven sons died in Latvia
   - PJ to Tacoma November 1901
   - Bluma to Tacoma August 1902
   - Five daughters married in Tacoma
3. Herman/Hirsch 1857-1921
   - Married Betty Ulman in 1879
   - To Tacoma in May 1901, Betty in 1902
   - Eight children married PNW
4. Itsek/Itsev 1858-?
   - At least six children by 1900
   - Stayed in Latvia
5. Jennie/Sheina 1861-1928
   - Married cousin Hugo Stusser
   - Seven children born 1880-1890
   - Hugo to US & Tacoma December 1891
6. Betty 1863-?
7. Shalom 1864-?
8. Mascha 1865-1950
   - To Tacoma before 1894
   - Married uncle Adolph Friedman
9. Solomon 1866-1949
   - Married Yetta Kahn in 1888
   - To NY July 1906, to Tacoma bef 1910
10. Jacob Julius 1868-1941
    - To US abt 1884, to Tacoma bef 1892
    - Married Edith Hirschfeld in 1897
11. Gutman 1869-1890
12. Esther 1871-1957
    - Married Max Jacobson in 1896
    - To Tacoma abt 1903, Seattle abt 1914

Jacob and Rebecca's children:
1. Jennie/Passa 1869-1939
   - Married Abraham Tone abt 1893
   - To US & Tacoma as widow August 1913
2. Rachel/Roche 1870-1952
   - Married Chaim Bender abt 1889
   - Entire family to Seattle January 1921
3. Julius 1872-1937
   - To US abt 1890, Tacoma before 1892
   - Married Augusta Stusser Tacoma 1899
4. Sarah 1873-1959
   - To Tacoma July 1898, Seattle 1900
   - Married Nathan Blasberg 1899
5. Olga/Golda 1877-1945
   - To US & Tacoma September 1900
   - Married Harry Morris Wowa 1907
6. Anna/Chane 1880-1956
   - Married Louis Levinthal abt 1897
   - To US & Tacoma Aug 1907 from London
7. Jennie/Sima 1880-1942
   - Married Morris Levinson abt 1898
   - To US 1905 from London, Tacoma 1907

Philip and Rose's children:
1. Yankel Ruben 1875-1877
2. Israel 1877 - abt 1905
3. Nathan 1880-1947
   - To US April 1903, Tacoma before 1907
   - Married Betty Yudelson in 1909
4. Joseph 1882-1945
   - To US Sept 1902, Tacoma about 1907
   - Married Sarah Shoffer in NY 1905
5. Morris J 1883-1947
   - To US March 1904, Tacoma in 1907
   - Married Rose Carp in 1914
6. Harry H 1886-1958
   - To NY Dec 1905, Tacoma in 1910
   - Married Dorothy Eichenwald 1918
7. Bessie 1890-1952
   - To NY Dec 1905, to Tacoma abt 1912
   - Married Samuel Reibman NY 1910
8. Jennie 1891-1949
   - To US Dec 1905, to Tacoma bef 1910
   - Married William Forman in 1913
9. Celia 1891-1971
   - To NY June 1906, stayed in NY
   - Married Abe Lichtenstein in 1914
10. Mary Leona 1893-1986
    - To NY June 1906, Tacoma before 1913
    - Married Samuel Friedman in 1913
11. Fannette 1896-1968
    - To NY June 1906, Tacoma abt 1914
    - Married 1st Samuel Chernis 1921
    - Married 2nd Ike Levinson
12. Zalman Lipman 1900-1900

Jacob married 2nd to Leibe Schneider (1848-1910) in 1881,
Both to US Dec 1905, Tacoma bef 1908

Jacob and Liebe's children:
1. Isaac 1882-??
2. Philip Bernard 1884-1920
   - To US Sept 1901, Tacoma Jan 1907
   - Married Rose Schneider in 1907
3. Samuel Isadore 1886-1969
   - To US August 1902, Tacoma 1904
   - Married Mary L Friedman in 1913
4. Rose 1888-1965
   - To US November 1904, Tacoma 1907
   - Married Bernard Rackmil in 1910
5. Zalman 1891-1891

Math word problem:

If three of Jehuda's descendants each have 12 children, how many descendants live in Tacoma in 1907?

Answer:

Enough to form a congregation.

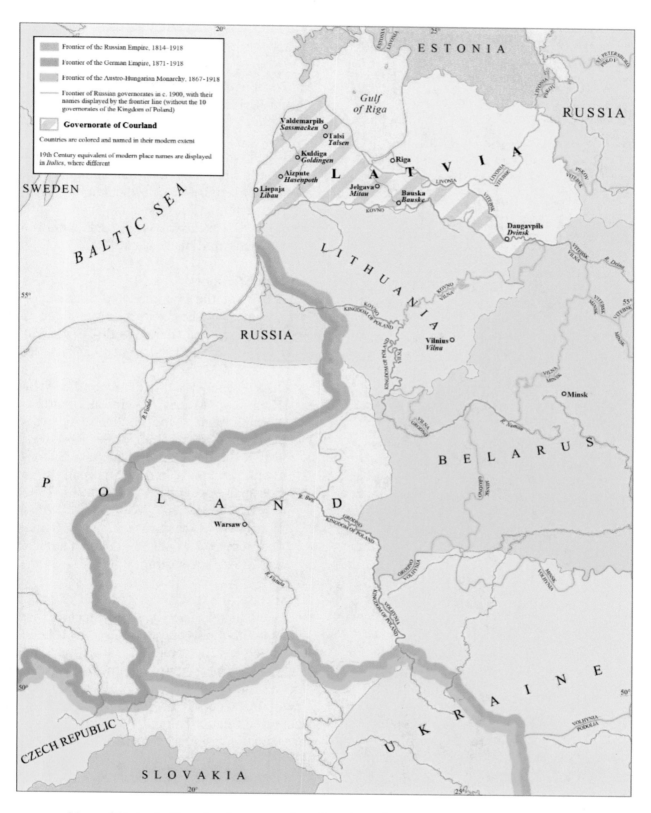

Map of historic Courland over modern Latvia and vicinity. Map by Andras Bereznay

Organizing Chevra Talmud Torah 1906

The Day of Atonement commenced last night for the orthodox Jews at 6 o'clock. The services were held in Fawcett hall, South Fifteenth and C street. There were present several rabbis of Tacoma, besides two from Seattle. Professor Carl Bach, Dr. L. Levin and H. Stusser assisted in the chorus. Services open at 7 o'clock in the morning at the hall and will be continued throughout the day.

Tacoma Daily Ledger September 29, 1906

As Tacoma's economy stabilized, the Orthodox Jewish community grew. By 1906 they again held Yom Kippur services in a rented hall, advertised in the local newspapers. However, the term "rabbi" likely referred to respected lay leaders. Lesser Levin was a pioneer barber known as "Doc." Hugo Stusser, was a tailor. Carl Bach was a non-Jewish professional musician who later served two terms in the state legislature.

Tacoma's Orthodox Jews then formally organized, taking the name Chevra Talmud Torah. The name meant a tightly knit group of friends (Chevra) united through the study (Talmud) of Jewish law (Torah.) It was time for a school and a teacher.

Samson Hotel, 1152-1156 Fawcett, in 1927
(1152 on far right)
Courtesy of Tacoma Public Library BU 18898

Rabbi Meier Elyn

The congregation advertised in New York for a teacher and *shochet*, a kosher butcher. Rabbi Meier Elyn answered the call. His family joined him in November of 1907. They initially lived in the Samson Hotel at 1152 E Street, now Fawcett Avenue. The Hebrew school met in the same building. The location on the corner of South Thirteenth was near the homes of many of the Jewish families. Rabbi Elyn continued through 1912 as the Chevra's teacher and worked as a butcher until his death in 1921.

Known Members

While the Friedman and Stusser families were numerous, they were far from alone. Other known members affiliated with Chevra Talmud Torah who were in Tacoma in 1907 included:

Jack Bender, Max Jacobson, Ben Klegman, Morris Levinson, Abraham Lyon, Isaac Moses, Peter Olswang, Abraham Rose, Frank S. Rosenberg, David Shafer, Barney and Sam Shapiro, Frank Spigal, Charles Sussman, Frank Sussman, Joseph A. Sussman, Robert Tone, Emanuel Waldocks, Morris Werbisky, Raphael Winkleman, Samuel and Bernard J. Witenberg, Peter Yudelson, and Max Zuckerkorn.

By 1908 Chevra Talmud Torah was included in the Tacoma city directory listings under both schools and churches. It was helpfully described as a "Russian Orthodox Hebrew Church." The group approved articles of incorporation in December of 1908 and filed them in January of 1909. The documents identified Chevra Talmud Torah of Tacoma as an organization created "for the furtherance of the Orthodox Hebrew religion." The agreement to incorporate made it clear that "under no circumstances will any man or boy be allowed in place of worship with head uncovered."

20

AGREEMENT TO INCORPORATE

This Agreement, Made this _15th_ day of _December_ A. D. _1908_

Witnesseth:

FIRST, That we, the undersigned _Philip B. Friedman, Max Zuckerhorn, Samuel Friedman, Joe Sussman, Nathan Friedman, Chas. Stusser, Julius Friedman, Ike Moses, M. Jacobson and H. Stusser and R. Winkleman_

subscribers hereto, have associated and do hereby associate ourselves for the purpose and with the intention of forming a corporation under the provisions of an act of the legislature of the State of Washington, entitled "An act to provide for the incorporation of associations for social, charitable and educational purposes, approved by the Governor of Washington on the 21st day of March, 1895."

SECOND, The name of the said corporation shall be _Chevra Talmud Torah_

THIRD, That the objects for which said corporation is formed are and shall be: _To further the Orthodox Hebrew Religion — To acquire suitable place or places in which to conduct worship of same; To rent or lease real and personal property; To acquire, purchase or otherwise obtain real property, upon which to erect buildings for worship, and for burial purposes. To erect buildings; To mortgage or transfer any property it may acquire; To acquire real or personal property to further said purposes: Under no circumstances will any man or boy be allowed in place of worship with head uncovered._

Generally to do all other things necessary or expedient to further the Orthodox Hebrew Religion only.

Purchasing a Building

Orthodox Jews held High Holy Days services in rented facilities for two more years. Rosh Hashanah and Yom Kippur services in 1909 took place at the newly remodeled Fraternity Hall, 1117 ½ Tacoma Avenue. Rabbi Falk came from Columbus, Ohio, to lead services. He was assisted by Max Jacobson, brother-in-law of Hugo and Jennie Stusser.

Rabbi M. Goldman of Seattle officiated at the 1910 services, again observed in Fraternity Hall. In attendance were members of the Harris Warnick family. They had recently moved to Tacoma from Portland, Oregon, where Harris had been recruited to work in the plywood industry. While they were at services their home was vandalized.

While the Warnick residence at 3502 South Fifteenth street was deserted yesterday, during the time the family was at church attending the Jewish New Year's ceremonies, tramps broke in and tore things around in the house, as if they were celebrating, and as a climax set the house on fire this morning. Neighbors who saw the flames rushed to the burning building, and succeeded in getting it out before much damage was done. It has not yet been determined how much if anything was stolen.

Tacoma Times October 5, 1910

One month later, the officers of Chevra Talmud Torah completed the purchase of a building and two lots at 1529 Tacoma Avenue South. Constructed in 1885, it was previously home to the Norwegian-Danish Methodist Church, and then the First German Baptist Church. It had been for sale for several years and had most recently housed a Japanese mission. The sellers were pioneer attorneys, Marshall K. and Bertha (Denton) Snell.

406 M K Snell and wf to Chevra Talmud Torah L 15-16 B 1511 T 1

Tacoma Daily Ledger November 18, 1910
(Not 1914 as noted in previous histories)

Programming

In February of 1911 the group obtained a permit for nearly $600 worth of building alterations. After these improvements Chevra Talmud Torah began hosting concerts and special events.

NOTED CANTOR SINGER SPEAKS HERE SUNDAY

Rev. A. A. Rosenbloom Will Give "Song Sermon" in Orthodox Synagogue in Connection With Sacred Concert.

Rev. A. A. Rosenbloom of Minneapolis, one of the best known operatic cantor singers and composers of Hebrew sacred music of his nationality in this country, will appear for the first time in Tacoma Sunday night, occupying the pulpit of the Orthodox synagogue at 1529 Tacoma avenue for the evening service.

Mr. Rosenbloom's effort is described as a "song sermon" and will be given in connection with an elaborate sacred concert, the whole constituting a typical Hebrew "mariv." Among the songs will be selections in Hebrew of national, Zionistic, historical and critical songs.

Tacoma Daily Ledger June 24, 1911

Families joined in a Chanukah festival on December 17, 1911. The following July, Chicago's Rabbi Adolph Steiner delivered a guest sermon. The program included several opera selections, some of which were sung in Hebrew.

Another key development would come in 1912. Sam Andrews' proposal to add exclusionary language to the by-laws of Tacoma's Reform Temple Beth Israel coincided with yet another division.

"The services in Temple Beth Israel shall be of strict Reform with Union Prayer Book and no hats shall be worn by the male members of this congregation during the service and no hats shall be worn by any male person attending services and the Trustees are herby empowered to enforce the new bylaw."
1912 Temple Beth Israel minutes

Chapter Three: Lost to History

Polish Landsmen

In Russian-controlled Poland, anti-Semitism and pogroms were rampant in the 1880s. Economic recessions in the early 1900s led to protests and strikes, culminating in the bloody Lodz insurrection in 1905. Socialist groups emerged, including the formation of the Ostrowiec Republic in the winter of 1905. These factors, and many more, contributed to a steady flow of emigration.

Numerous Warsaw and "Ostrower" families made their way to Tacoma. They would replicate the Friedman and Stusser pattern of chain migration and intermarriage.

Barney Shapiro left Ostrow, Poland, in the 1890s. By 1905 he was working as a shoemaker in Tacoma. His first mention in the press was when his teenage son, Jake, was involved in a traffic accident caused by a team of startled horses. Barney's wife, Dora, and daughter, Sadie, joined him the next year. Sadie married in November of 1908, a month before her sister, Ethel, was born. Barney was soon joined in Tacoma by his brother, Sam Shapiro; Dora's brother, Isadore Kraft and his wife Anna (August); and several other relatives. When Barney and Dora celebrated their 25th wedding anniversary in 1913 the published guest list included the names of dozens of friends and relatives. Reflecting their recent immigrant status and language challenges, nearly all of the names were spelled incorrectly.

Young Sadie's groom was **Abraham Rose**. Unlike others whose stories have been lost, Abe gave a charming newspaper interview on the 50th anniversary of his 1905 arrival in Tacoma. He recalled that as a teenager he had served briefly in the Czar's army before escaping to England in 1898. From there he made his way to New York and San Francisco, where he served as an officer in the garment makers' union.

In Tacoma Abe operated his own pawn shop. His first storefront was a seven-foot by seven-foot cubicle on Pacific Avenue. He nearly lost his license and his livelihood when he was arrested in 1906, charged with receiving stolen property. He was accused of buying stolen watches, pilfered by Sam Andrews' young clerk. Sam owned a long-established pawn shop and jewelry business and was prominent in Tacoma's Temple Beth Israel. Abe managed to keep his license because it was his first offense, but he likely spent much of his first year's income paying his $50 fine, attorney fees and court costs. It was not the last time the two would be on opposite sides.

Rabbi **Meier Elyn** brought his own cluster of Polish/Russian in-laws to Tacoma:
- Meier's sister, Libby Elyn, married Nochem Anches
- Meier's sister, Goldie Elyn, married Solomon J. Farber
  - Goldie's daughter, Lena Farber, later married Bert Baruch Treiger

Solomon J. Farber's siblings:
- S. J.'s sister, Ida, married Solomon Epstein
- S. J.'s sister, Sadie, married Ben Rashbam

Solomon's brother, Joseph, later married Rose August, half-sister of Mrs. Isadore Kraft; looping back to Dora Kraft, wife of Barney Shapiro.

Poland map by Andras Bereznay
(See page 19 for legend)

23

Scrap Metal and Junk

The classic Jewish immigrant career path began with peddling. A relative or friend helped the newcomer to obtain a backpack of merchandise. The peddler sold door-to-door, expanding his emerging English vocabulary. Advancement came by earning enough to afford a horse and wagon. Success brought the stability of a fixed storefront.

In the early 1900s Tacoma's Jewish peddlers worked a bit in reverse, going on rounds and gathering scrap metal and unwanted items. These they passed on to friends, family, and employers who operated metal yards and secondhand stores. Some of the junk dealers operating in Tacoma at the time were:

- Milwaukee Junk: Isaac Moses and Victor Lamken, and later Arthur Lamken
- Tacoma Junk: Charles, Frank, and Joseph A. Sussman
- Tacoma Secondhand Store: Frank Spigal and Louis Drill
- Winkleman Junk: Henry and Raphael Winkleman

In addition, many of the smaller Jewish clothing and jewelry stores carried mostly secondhand and pawned merchandise. These merchants fit well in Tacoma's depressed economy.

At the same time, Tacoma's city officials were trying to catch petty thieves by going after the dealers who bought from them. Storekeepers were required to submit daily reports to the police, identifying each item purchased. If the item turned out to be stolen, the merchant lost his investment and risked arrest. Morris Levinsons' 1910 petition for naturalization was denied because his witness, Max Zuckerkorn, had such an arrest record.

Organizing Chevrah Ahavas Israel

Through working long hours, and buying low and selling high, Tacoma's Polish/Russian Jewish community grew and thrived. In 1912 they took the ambitious step of forming their own Orthodox congregation. The High Holy Days were celebrated in Tacoma by *three* Jewish groups, one with the name Chevrah Ahavas Israel.

JEWISH HOLIDAY SERVICES PLANNED

New Year's, September 11, Will Be Observed Here With Worcester, Mass., Rabbi in Charge.

Tacoma Daily Ledger September 3 & 4, 1912

The new rabbi was Abraham August, son of Yakov Yosef and Lena Augustower, and brother-in-law of Solomon J. Farber and Isadore Kraft. The extended August family had recently moved from Worcester, Massachusetts, to the

REV. ABRAHAM AUGUST.

Northwest. Many would become part of Bikur Cholim in Seattle. After leading High Holy Day services in Tacoma "Rabbi" August also moved to Seattle, where he worked as a tailor. He briefly married Esther Hytowitz in Seattle in 1917, then made ugly headlines when he refused to give her a *get*, a Jewish divorce. Abraham died in 1935 at the age of 55.

Tacoma Daily Ledger September 8, 1912

David Shafer was the first president of Chevrah Ahavas Israel. His brother, Julius Schofowich/Shafer, was an 1895 trustee of Seattle's Chevra Bikur Cholim, identified in 1901 newspapers as a "Polish Jewish Church." Unlike many of the other founders of Chevrah Ahavas Israel, David Shafer had lived in Tacoma for nearly two decades. He operated a prominent clothing store on Pacific Avenue. David and Hugo Stusser had challenged Tacoma's Sunday closure laws in 1905, albeit unsuccessfully.

Kiev-born Harris Warnick was the first vice president, while Abraham Rose served as the first secretary and treasurer. Both were vital positions, as the new group had big plans.

HEBREWS OF TACOMA TO HAVE SYNAGOGUE

DEDICATE NEW SAFER HATORCH.

Funds Raised at Meeting to Finance Building; Seattle Brethern Give Aid.

Many prominent Hebrews of Tacoma and Seattle were present at the dedication of the new Safer Hatorch by the Chevra Ahavas Israel of Tacoma last Sunday at Eagles hall. H. Kesler of Seattle was chairman of the evening.

Addresses were made by Dave Schafer and H. Warnick of Tacoma, president and vice president, respectively, of the Chevra, Rabbi Geanss and President I. Shneider of the Chevra Mishnies of Seattle, and by Chairman Kesler.

After the speaking, a considerable sum of money was raised by selling final initials, which will be placed in the building fund that will soon be used to purchase a synagogue. Refreshments and a dance followed the business session.

Necessity for Organization.

The theme that most of the speakers dwelt on was the necessity for organization to perpetuate the Hebrew spirit in Tacoma. Many prospective members who had not attended the former meetings of the Chevra were present and expressed a willingness to push the work forward. One of the prominent members of the Tacoma Chevra at the conclusion of the meeting said:

"On the whole the affair was replete with marked enthusiasm. Never before was the necessity for organization more clearly demonstrated. The Hebrew spirit is yet alive in Tacoma."

Tacoma Daily Ledger January 26, 1913

In the fall of 1913 the Chevrah filed articles of incorporation. Joseph B. Gyle served as secretary, with trustees Hyman Greenberg, Frank Spigal, and Louis Wacholder.

Articles of incorporation of the Orthodox Chevera Ahavas Israel were filed with the county auditor yesterday by the trustees, H. Greenberg, Philip Spiegel and Louis Wacholder; and David Schoefer, president; Harris Warnick, vice president; J. B. Gyle, secretary, and Abraham Rose, treasurer.

Tacoma Daily Ledger September 17, 1913

Chevra Kadisha Cemetery

In July of 1914 many of these same men organized their own Jewish cemetery, named Chevra Kadisha. Nochem Anches, Hyman Greenberg, Barney Shapiro and Solomon Stusser purchased land adjoining the existing Home of Peace Jewish cemetery and applied for a permit. Not surprisingly the trustees of Home of Peace appealed to county officials to stop them. The trustee who spoke out against the new cemetery was Sam Andrews, again causing strife for Abraham Rose. Home of Peace lost its appeal and the new cemetery deed was successfully transferred in November. Chevra Kadisha was incorporated in 1930. The cemetery was operated independently until 1978, then merged into Home of Peace. Many of the families mentioned in this chapter have burials there. Both are located in Lakewood, between Tacoma and Steilacoom.

Lost to History

Worsening conditions in Europe and the threat of war added to the challenges of divided Jewish communities in Tacoma in 1914. All three congregations went quiet. Chevrah Ahavas Israel likely never existed for more than a year or two. Some members moved elsewhere, while most joined Chevra Talmud Torah. The divided Orthodox community was apparently mended. The repair was truly invisible, as none of the published histories of Talmud Torah or Temple Beth Israel mentioned a third congregation. Descendants of founders were dumbfounded to learn of its brief existence.

Tale of a Torah

But what happened to their Torah? It has been hiding right before our eyes, in the ark at Tacoma's Temple Beth El. It is easily identifiable, as it is the largest of the several Torahs and has distinctive decorative handles. Around the wooden disc at the top is a celluloid inset with Hebrew characters. Two words "Tacoma Washington" are clearly written in Yiddish, along with abbreviations representing the Hebrew year corresponding to 1912. More importantly, by turning the Torah and completing the circle, the entire Yiddish phrase properly reads "Chevrah Ahavas Israel Tacoma Washington 5673." What was assumed to be a general phrase about loving Israel, instead describes a Chevrah, a close-knit society of friends with love and solidarity for all Jews. It honors a community of Polish landsmen who formed a burial society and commissioned a Torah. And for more than one hundred years that Torah has carried the memory.

"Turn it and turn it, for everything is in it."   (*Mishnah Pirkei Avot 5:22*)

Torah Scroll Inscription "Chevrah Ahavas Israel Tacoma Washington"

The 1912 date on this Torah disk is possibly what led to the inaccurate assumption that Chevra Talmud Torah was founded in 1912. That error was reinforced when it was included in a timeline of Jewish history, set in tiles along the entrance wall of Tacoma's Temple Beth El.

Chapter Four: Impact of War

Chevra Talmud Torah

Meanwhile, Chevra Talmud Torah continued. Rabbi Adolph Steiner, described earlier in Seattle newspapers as the "singing minister of the Jewish church," led Simchat Torah in October of 1912. Later the inter-war period would be known as the golden age of cantors. Orthodox Jews used the term *Chazzan* for their musical leaders.

> **Kantor A. Steiner of Chicago,** who recently gave a highly successful concert in Seattle, will officiate here October 3 and 4 at the Jewish services of Simax Torah, at the synagogue, 1529 Tacoma av.

Tacoma Times October 2, 1912

Jewish lecturer Jacob Sklover spoke in Yiddish in February of 1913 on the topic of "The Conditions of the Jews in Europe and the Aims of the Jews in America." Julius B. Jaffe of Victoria spoke in March, using the upcoming festival of Purim to highlight the prominence of "the Jewish race" in America. Rabbi Meier Elyn led Passover services in April.

Rabbi Max Aronin

Rabbi Max Aronin led Talmud Torah's celebration of Shavuot in May of 1913. In the fall Dr. Jacobs came from Seattle to lead High Holy Day services. At the same time the Chevra made plans to resume the daily school. Frank Sussman was president, with Nochem Anches as vice president and Joseph A. Sussman treasurer.

Max Aronin and his wife, the former Jennie Kleban, were both from the Minsk area of Russia and had immigrated in 1906. They moved to Tacoma about 1911, and from 1912 to 1914 they lived in the rear of the synagogue building. The following year Max was active in the Jewish Central Relief Committee in Seattle, where he worked as a junk peddler. His wife lived separately with their four daughters in Lakebay.

Today the terms "immigrant" and "Socialist" are sometimes used with derision. Both accurately identified several of Tacoma's refugees around the time of the Russian Revolution. Jennie (and later Max) Aronin, Abe Cohn, Isaac Schneider, and Jacob Shain all lived for a period on Pierce County's Key Peninsula in Lakebay, near the anarchist colony of Home. Many others were active in Workmen's Circle groups throughout their lives. (See page 49.)

War Years

Aronin was not alone in his war relief work. It is likely that in 1914 nearly every person in Tacoma's Jewish community still had friends and relatives in Europe. In October of 1914 Morris Friedman led special services at Chevra Talmud Torah, part of a national Peace Day requested by President Wilson. In May of 1915 the sinking of the *Lusitania* must have been even more shocking to Alice Carrick, Nathan Rabstoff, and Libby Weinstone, all of whom had immigrated on that same ocean liner during the past several years.

Rabbi M. Cohen of Seattle led High Holy Day services in 1915. Significantly, services at Reform Beth Israel included the "confirmation" of thirteen-year-olds Isador Benjamin and Herbert Shafer. Herb was the son of David Shafer, former president of Chevrah Ahavas Israel. David Shafer and his family continued as members of Temple Beth Israel. David served several terms on the board of trustees.

Despite discreet overtures from Temple Beth Israel offering to share the costs of hiring an ordained rabbi, Chevra Talmud Torah continued relying heavily on the leadership of its board presidents.

- 1915: Nochem Anches
- 1916: Henry Zeidell
- 1917: Joseph A. Sussman
- 1918: Nathan Friedman
- 1919-1920: David Klegman

Camp Lewis

In January of 1916 the voters of Pierce County agreed to bond themselves to purchase 70,000 acres on the Nisqually Plain, south of Tacoma. The County then donated the land to the federal government for use as a military base. The huge tract included Adolph Friedman's 1890s American Lake Park development. Most of the lots, considered to be of little value, had gone back to the county in lieu of property taxes,.

American Lake Park

The Plat of this Tract was filed for record in the County Auditor's office July 31, 1889.

Acre lots overlooking the Lake and situated in beautiful groves.

Water front lots of 50 feet front running to the Lake.

Tacoma Daily News August 1, 1889

The U.S. entered the war before the entire land transaction was complete, but site development was rushed forward. Newly named Camp Lewis opened to recruits in September of 1917. It was the only induction center on the West Coast, training new recruits from Washington, Oregon, California, Idaho, Utah, Nevada, Wyoming, and Montana.

Tacoma's population understood the benefits and openly welcomed the influx of temporary residents. Tacoma's citywide Jewish community went one step farther. In December of 1917 they announced that they would lease and furnish a club house for Jewish servicemen. The club would be supported by the regional International Order of B'nai B'rith.

HEBREWS ORGANIZE TO HELP SOLDIERS

WILL ESTABLISH WELFARE HOUSE HERE.

Tacoma Daily Ledger December 10, 1917

International Order of B'nai B'rith

Tacoma's Jewish men had organized B'nai B'rith Lodge #406 in 1890, but later forfeited the charter as a result of the Banking Panic. In 1913 another generation organized Lodge #741, initiating fifty-five members on June 16 at Fraternal Hall. The group's officers came from both congregations, with Beth Israel's Theo Feist as president and Talmud Torah's Julius Friedman as vice president. Nearly 200 people attended a dance afterward at the Tacoma Hotel. Regional officials at the time had been expecting nearly 200,000 Jewish immigrants on the Pacific Coast due to the opening of the Panama Canal. Instead they supported soldiers training for world war.

ORGANIZE LODGE OF B'NAI B'RITH HERE

55 TACOMA JEWS ARE FIRST MEMBERS.

Tacoma Daily Ledger June 15, 1913

Julius Friedman was B'nai B'rith president in 1915 and Philip B. Friedman was president in 1916. S.B. Asia and Theo Feist of Beth Israel succeeded them, establishing a pattern of alternating officers between the Shul and the Temple.

The B'nai B'rith's Servicemen's Club hHuse opened in January of 1918 in the former Monarch Club at 448 Broadway, originally the home of financier Chester Thorne. The club house was formally dedicated in February amid much fanfare. Its dormitory could accommodate 100 men overnight.

The men were joined in the support of the Servicemen's Club House by the women of Destiny Lodge No. 14 Daughters of the Covenant. The auxiliary to the B'nai B'rith was organized in Tacoma in June of 1917. Again, the seventy charter members represented Jewish women from across the city, not just from Talmud Torah. They set up hostess committees at the club house, provided meals twice weekly, and offered a variety of weekend activities.

B'NAI B'RITH OPEN SOLDIERS' CLUB HOUSE

Tacoma B'nai B'rith Thursday night formally opened the soldiers' clubhouse at 6th and Broadway. After election of officers Phil B. Friedman, deputy of the district grand lodge, addressed members of B'nai B'rith present.

Officers installed by B'nai B'rith were: Theo. Feist, president; H. A. Kaufman vice president; I. E. Epstein, secretary; Herman Jacobs, treasurer; H. Warnick, assistant monitor; Jacob Shapiro, warden; F. Spigel, outside guardian; R. A. Rose, M. Friedman and Joe Sussman, trustees; representatives to the meeting of the grand lodge at Fresno, Cal., Phil B. Friedman, Theo. Feist, H. A. Kaufman and S. B. Asia.

Officers of the Ladies' auxiliary: Mrs. Theo. Feist, president; Mrs. Joseph Sussman, vice president; Miss Millie Wheinstone, conductress; Mrs. I. E. Epstein, secretary; Mrs. Joseph Bachrach, treasurer; Mrs. Sarah Miller, guardian; Mrs. Lee Lewis, sentinel; Mrs. Morris Bloom, Mrs. Abe Lamken, Mrs. A. Rose, trustees; Mrs. S. B. Asia, past president.

Tacoma Daily Ledger January 12, 1918

The club house was also a non-sectarian meeting space, hosting school PTA groups and war relief committees. In May of 1918 the Army and Navy Jewish Welfare Board took over governance of the club house. The Destiny ladies' auxiliary continued sponsoring dances and entertainments throughout the summer.

After the war the Welfare Board sold the dormitory furnishings. Temple Beth Israel later bought other furniture. Members met there one more time in January of 1919 for the funeral of Estelle (Heinemann) Epstein, a young mother and victim of a late wave of the influenza epidemic.

Jewish Veterans

At least ten Tacoma Jewish men served in the First World War: Boris Dannenhirsch, Louis Lamken, Harry Levinson, W.D. Meier, Abraham and Samuel Olswang, Max Stern, Robert Thorne, Meyer Winkleman and Leon Witenberg. Robert Thorne would later use his service revolver to kill his step-father, Philip Friedman. (See biographical sketch.) Decades earlier Emanuel Waldocks had served in Alaska, the Philippines, and China during his career as a U.S. Marine.

Jewish War Relief and Zionism Roots

Tacoma Daily Ledger October 19, 1919

With the war ended, relief efforts could begin in earnest. In October of 1919 Talmud Torah members donated $1786 in advance of the city's Jewish Relief campaign. Talmud Torah's list of donors and amounts given was printed in the newspaper, leaving a priceless paper trail for future researchers. Publicizing donation figures was seen as a way of helping others to learn to give. Another list the next week mentioned more donors from both Jewish congregations.

The following month many of those same Jews formed the Tacoma Zionist district. Over the next few years a series of Talmud Torah guests lectured on the land of Palestine. Former Courland residents had seen their homeland emerge as part of the independent state of Latvia. Poland had regained its status as a nation. Was there hope for a Jewish homeland as the 1917 Balfour Declaration promised?

Roll of Honor: Talmud Torah 1919 Jewish Relief Campaign Donors

(With spouses added and spelling adjusted)

Nathan Friedman (Betty Yudelson) and son Cecil	$200
Frank Sussman (Ida Yudelson) and son Philip	$200
Julius Friedman (Augusta Stusser) and sons (Saul, Abe, Sieg)	$160
Witenberg Brothers: S.N. (Anne Friedman) & B.J. (Charlotte Endelman)	$115
David Klegman (Helen Gevurtz)	$65
A(rthur) Lamken (Fanny Sussman)	$50
Hugo Stusser (Jennie Stusser)	$50
E(manuel) Waldocks (Yetta Hoffman)	$50
J(oseph) Weinstein (Hannah Waldocks)	$50
J(oseph A) Sussman (Minnie Benson)	$50
H(arry) Rotman (Lena Lamken) and daughter (Rose)	$30
F(rank) Spigal (Dora Yallon) and son (David)	$30
A(rthur) Meier	$25
M(ax) Meier (Bessie Nagel)	$25
A(braham) Rose (Sadie Shapiro)	$25
P(incos) Lampart (Esther Greenberg)	$25
Charles Sussman (Gustie Stusser)	$25
Joe (S.) Sussman (Rosie Kahn)	$25
Morris Friedman (Rose Carp)	$25
Mrs. Herman Stusser (Betty Ulman)	$25
A(braham) Lyon (Mildred Witenberg))	$25
Lyon sons	$25
Vic(tor) Lamken (Carolyn Goldstein)	$25
H(arry) Richlen (Sarah Singer)	$25
(Ellis Harry) Ruden (Anna Rovsky)	$25
Fashion Craft Tailors	$25
M(orris) Siegel (Ethel Chain)	$25
B(en) Thompson (Esther Nagel)	$25
M(orris) Lyon (Rae Levine)	$20
Julius (Sam) Stusser and sister (Hazel)	$20
S(amuel) Stusser (Birdie Hecht)	$18
Liberty Store, Mrs. (Jacob) Cohen (Sarah Phillips)	$15
D(avid) Kaplow (Dora Metzger)	$25
Harry Friedman (Dorothy Eichenwald)	$15
Jacob Blechman (Anna Tone)	$10
H. Freeman	$10
M(ax) Goldberg (Molly Diamond)	$10
M(ax) Novikoff (Emma Yudelson)	$10
I(sidor) Stusser (engaged to Anne Levy)	$10

Joe Friedman (Sarah Shaffer)	$10
S(amuel) Elyn (bachelor)	$10
Mrs. R(ebecca Haman) (widow of Herman Olswang)	$10
Mrs. Max Cohen (Elizabeth Kaplan)	$10
(Joseph) P. Gevurtz	$10
Mrs. Rabin	$10
Mrs. (Sam) Reibman (Bessie Friedman)	$10
Mrs. (Hyman) Greenberg (Molla Appel)	$10
Mrs. Levinson (Jennie Friedman) (widow of Morris, died May)	$10
M(orris) Warnick (Bessie Yablonovich) and sons (Wray, Jack, Robert)	$6
(Isadore) Rosenbaum (Frances Jacobs)	$5
M(orris) Werbisky (Viola Hecht)	$5
B(oris H) Dannenhirsch (Naval reserve)	$5
M(eier) Elyn (Rebecca Tropp)	$5
H(arry) Bear (later h/o Lillian Lamken)	$5
Ethel Shapiro (dau. of Barney & Dora)	$5
Master (Nathan) Forman (son of William Forman & Jennie Friedman)	$5
A(braham) M. Friedman (Gittel Schapsy)	$5
Kopel Weinstone (Libby Averback)	$5
H(arris) Warnick (Fannie Weinstone)	$5
And son (Robert) Warnick	$5
Mrs. (David) Good (Mildred Weinstone)	$5
F(rank S.) Rosenberg (bachelor)	$5
(Carl) Rubenstein (Dora Tiefenbrun)	$5
Mr. Vogel (formerly Jacob Fogelbaum)	$3
F(roem) Weinstone (Bertha Kurash)	$1
W(ill) Cohen (son of Ruby Weinstone)	$1
Moses Lewinson (Olga Fradenheim)	$2
S(am) Feldman (Alice Shaffer)	$10

Pioneer Losses

Before the decade ended, Tacoma lost several of her Orthodox Jewish pioneers.

March 2, 1911	Adolph Friedman
July 30, 1911	Henry Winkleman
January 26, 1916	Raphael Winkleman
January 11, 1917	Jacob Friedman
August 23, 1917	Philip B. Friedman (Jacob's brother)
May 17, 1920	Philip B. Friedman (Jacob's son)
October 14, 1920	Bluma (Stusser) Yudelson

Chapter Five: True House of Worship

Return to Prosperity

Although all aspects of the war itself were horrific, the Tacoma area benefitted from the thriving wartime economy. In addition to the military presence at Camp Lewis and the Bremerton navy yard, a frenzy of shipbuilding in Tacoma created thousands of jobs. In 1918 the creation of the Port of Tacoma gave Russian families a direct route for immigration to the Pacific Northwest. After the war several Jewish secondhand and junk merchants quickly adapted by converting to military surplus stores. Many business names began with the word "Liberty." Tacoma's population increased by 50% from 1915 to 1925. With all of this growth in Tacoma, the term Roaring Twenties was entirely fitting.

Clergy

Chevra Talmud Torah had continued bringing in clergy to lead High Holy Day services. Jacob Tonitzky came from Portland in 1918 and Mat Levin came the following year. Rabbi Friedman of Seattle officiated in 1920. As economic stability returned, Tacoma embraced the slogan "Tacoma, the City of Hospitality." Tacoma's two Jewish congregations each welcomed full-time rabbis. In 1920 Tacoma's Reform congregation, Temple Beth Israel, brought Rabbi Samuel Margolis to lead their congregation for a year.

In January of 1921 Oxford graduate **Rabbi J.B. Gordon** was introduced as Chevra Talmud Torah's new rabbi. He had formerly worked as a correspondent for the *New York Tribune*. Rabbi Gordon, like many New Yorkers, spent winters in Florida and often lectured in the South. Rabbi Gordon presented several lectures in Tacoma and officiated at a wedding, but then spent Passover in Portland, Oregon. In May Jacob B. Gordon again accepted a new position, this time as rabbi at Portland's Neveh Zedek Talmud Torah. (He didn't stay there either.)

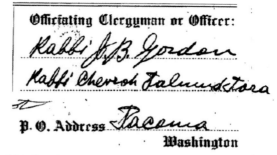

Rabbi Gordon signature on 1921 wedding license of Joseph Farber and Rosie August

City directory listings for Tacoma's Chevra Talmud Torah in 1922 and 1923 still included Gordon as its rabbi, likely as a carryover error.

Rabbi Leib Slotnik

Chevra Talmud Torah brought the next rabbi straight from Latvia. In December of 1921 Morris and Julius Friedman served as witnesses to begin Leib Slotnik's naturalization process. His wife, Lea, and four of his five children joined him in Tacoma the following year. He was still serving as Talmud Torah's rabbi when several large barrels of "sacramental" wine were stolen from his home's basement in 1927.

Tacoma News Tribune April 4, 1927

Leib's daughter, Rhea, married Israel Volotin in Tacoma in 1928. The young couple moved to Seattle, where Israel would serve several times as president of Bikur Cholim. Rabbi Slotnik and his family lived in Tacoma through 1932, then joined Rhea in Seattle.

After graduation from the University of Washington, Leib's son Jack formed the LeRoy jewelry firm with Tacoma's Irving Farber. Two more adult children, twins Myer and Cecille, moved with their parents to Philadelphia, Pennsylvania. According to his 1966 obituary, Rabbi Yehuda Leib Slotnik had been rabbi to Philadelphia's Congregation B'nai Abraham.

Moving North

By the early 1920s the building at 1529 Tacoma Avenue was starting to show its age. Renovations in 1922 required a building permit. More importantly, as Tacoma's Jewish families became more established they left the immigrant district along South E Street and moved to Tacoma's fashionable North End. Proximity to the Shul was essential for Orthodox worshippers.

This northern migration was the same in Tacoma's Reform Temple Beth Israel. In 1918 the congregation sold their temple building at South 10th and I Streets to a church. From 1918 through 1921 the Reform congregation rented Triangle Hall for High Holy Day services. In 1922 they dedicated a new Temple Beth Israel, built on the corner of North 4th and J Streets. It would be their place of worship for over forty years. Many of the Orthodox members attended club meetings there.

Chevra Talmud Torah arranged to sell their Tacoma Avenue building just two years later. The structure eventually housed a "Negro Elks Lodge." A rare image of the building is from the cover of a worn 1929 booklet that called it Elks' Rest. It was demolished in 1958.

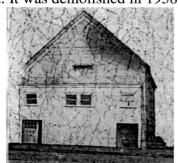

1529 Tacoma Avenue South in 1929
Tacoma Public Library

Members of Chevra Talmud Torah took a huge leap of faith in the spring of 1924 when they purchased three building lots in Tacoma's North End. President Julius Friedman, who had organized the initial committee, made the public announcement just after Passover.

SYNAGOGUE TO BE BUILT ON I STREET

Chevra Talmud Torah Buys Site Near Wright Park From Freiday

Through the firm of Albert C. Philips & Co., realtors, Tacoma building, Chevra Talmud Torah acquired last week from Jacob A. Freiday three lots at South 4th and I streets for the immediate erection of a synagogue. Cost of construction of the synagogue has been estimated at between $30,000 and $35,000.

The former home of Chevra Talmud Torah at Tacoma avenue and 15th street was sold by the same realty firm to the Busby Horn Company.

The site of the new synagogue is techcnically described as lots 10, 11 and 12, block 318, map of New Tacoma. It was obtained from Jacob A. Freiday for a consideration reported at $5,500.

The new synagogue, construction of which will begin immediately upon the completion of the campaign for building funds, will face Wright Park.

Julius Friedman, president of the corporation, announced Saturday that construction will be started within the next 60 days. An architect will be retained immediately, he said, and bids let for the building of the structure at the earliest possible date.

Tacoma Daily Ledger April 20, 1924

The same issue carried an invitation for friends to attend the "confirmation" of Harris Warnick's 13-year-old son, Robert Warnick, at Talmud Torah.

AWARD CONTRACT FOR NEW TEMPLE

Knoell and Westerfield Will Build New Home for Congregation

The contract for the new Temple Chevra Talmud Torah, to be constructed at South 4th and I streets, was let this week to Knoell & Westerfield. The cost of the ne wbuilding is to be $35,000.

Plans for the new temple were drawn by Hill & Mock, architects, and were completed some time ago. The edifice is to be in adapted Romanesque style. It will be built of concrete and brick with a cast-stone trim. The lower story will be of concrete, while the second story will be brick.

The ground story is to contain a large social room with kitchen in connection. At one end is to be a large stage with dressing rooms in connection. Men's and women's retiring rooms will be provided near the entrance. Oo this floor also will be the heating plant and quarters for the caretaker.

The main story will include the main auditorium, class rooms and cloak rooms.

The building is to be 42 by 118 feet. The Chevra Talmud Torah is the local orthodox Jewish congregation.

Tacoma Daily Ledger January 25, 1925

The Chevra issued the contract for construction of the new synagogue in January of 1925, to the same firm that had built Temple Beth Israel. The basic plans were also the same, but the results were strikingly different. Talmud Torah adjoined Wright Park and was clad in stately brick. It included an additional school room on the west end, had a pillared stone entrance, and featured a curved sanctuary ceiling twinkling with painted gold stars.

It was time for a few last parties in the old building. In March of 1925 the students celebrated the festival of Purim and Samuel Klegman celebrated his bar mitzvah. The next ceremonies would be to set the new cornerstone. There were many more young men studying.

Dinner Will Be Given In Cathedral

In honor of their young son Samuel, Mr. and Mrs. Dave Klegman are giving a dinner to 100 guests this evening in the Scottish Rite Cathedral. It will celebrate young Samuel's confirmation in the tenets of the Hebrew faith solemnized with impressive services yesterday at the Jewish synagogue.

Elaborate preparations have been made for the dinner, and guests will be here from Spokane, Seattle and Portland. Included in the evening's hospitable program will be speeches, toasts proposed by Samuel Friedman, who has been asked to preside as toastmaster, readings by Rose Rotman, a talented young girl studying with Mrs. Frederick Dean, and violin music by Hilda Malen, a young student of music in the membership of Mrs. C. E. Dunkleberger's Ensemble Violinists' Club.

Mr. and Mrs. Klegman's son is just 13, the confirmation age, and has completed with credit the course of study required in the church of his faith.

The dinner follows an established custom in Jewish families and in appointment and hospitable interest is anticipated among the family friends as one of the most attractive of the year in synagogue circles.

Tacoma Daily Ledger March 15, 1925

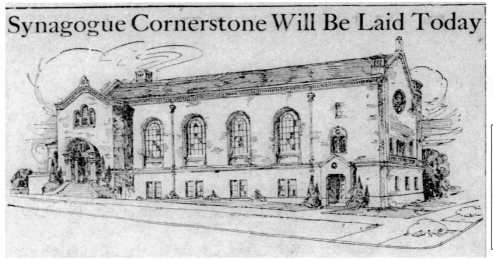

Synagogue Cornerstone Will Be Laid Today

(Above) Temple Beth Israel, the architectural template for Talmud Torah Synagogue

Tacoma News Tribune May 22, 1942

(Above left) Talmud Torah sketch, Tacoma Sunday Ledger April 19, 1925
(Below) Tacoma News Tribune September 18, 1925
Photo now at Tacoma Public Library, Richards A1362-0, enhanced by Clif Taylor

Talmud Torah Synagogue Ready for Dedication

The Building Layout

The primary entrance to the synagogue building was on the southwest corner, up a short set of stone steps with gently curving sidewalls. An elaborate arched stone lintel crowned the massive wooden doors.

(Right) Main entrance

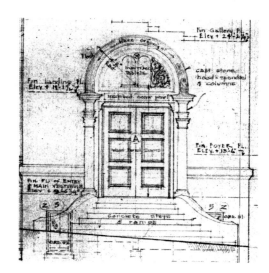

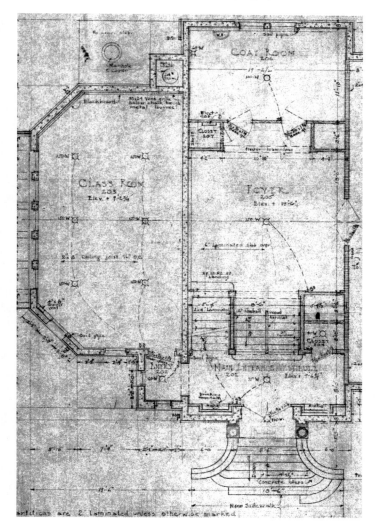

The exterior stairs opened into a vestibule. The sunny one-story school room, or *cheder*, was accessed from the left side of this entry. Slate blackboards lined the northern classroom wall.

(Left) Main vestibule, foyer, and class room

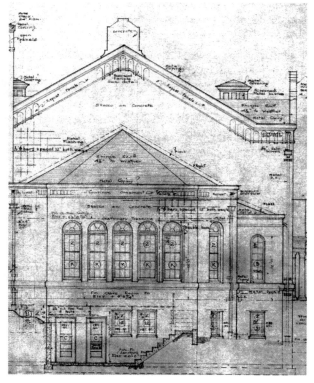

Ornate stairs from the front vestibule led either down to the basement level, or up to the main foyer and coat room. Doors on the right side of the foyer opened to the large sanctuary.

(Right) West elevation

Hill & Mock Architects' blueprints courtesy of
Tacoma Public Library Northwest Room
Enhanced by Clif Taylor

The rabbi's study was located in the northeast corner of the sanctuary, to the left of the *bimah*, or raised speaker's platform. Stairs on the right side of the sanctuary led to the social hall below, and to an exterior doorway that opened directly to street level on the southeast corner of the building.

(Right) East end of sanctuary

Downstairs were mechanical rooms, storage, restrooms, and a large social hall capable of seating nearly 400 people. The kosher kitchen was on the northwest corner, under the upstairs coat room. Somehow the women of the congregation prepared and served meals with one range and one sink, and no automatic dishwasher. They did have three north-facing windows above the sink.

(Below) Kitchen

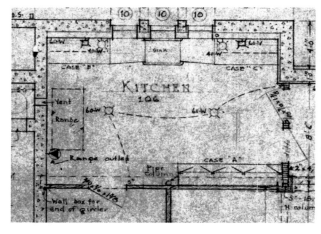

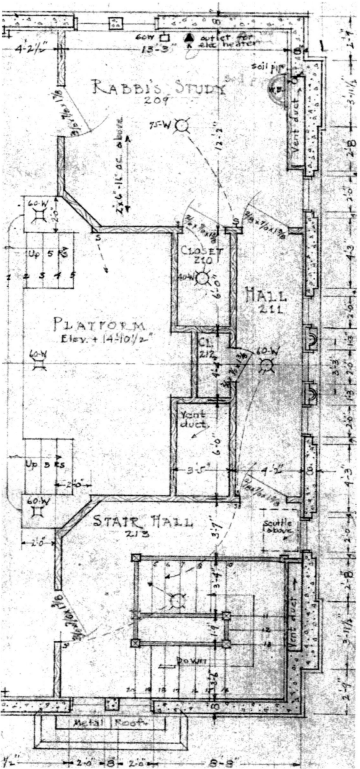

Hill & Mock Architects' blueprints courtesy of Tacoma Public Library Northwest Room Enhanced by Clif Taylor

The eastern wall of the social hall featured a stage, complete with footlights and a dressing room on the left. A stairwell on the right gave access to the sanctuary above, or to an exterior doorway that offered easy egress to the park next door.

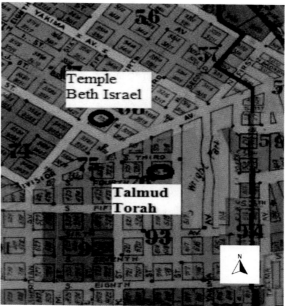

1950 Sanborn insurance map
Courtesy Library of Congress

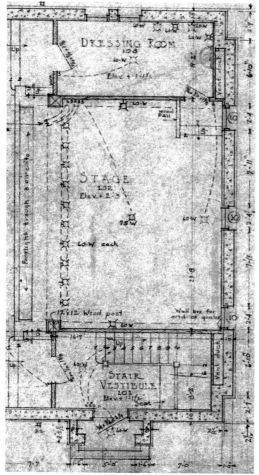

Stage and dressing room

Wright Park

Wright Park postcard, courtesy of MetroParks

The new synagogue was strategically located. First and foremost, the building was situated so that worshippers in the main sanctuary faced east, towards Jerusalem. They also faced Wright Park, just across South I Street. The twenty-seven acre park was created around a parcel of land donated for that purpose by the Tacoma Land Company in 1886. The tree-filled park was named for the company's president, Charles Wright, and contained statuary, walking paths, and the Seymour Botanical Conservatory.

The main driving road through the park was closed to vehicular traffic about the time the synagogue was built, as use of automobiles increased. At the same time a public bandstand was created from an enormous cedar stump and used for public celebrations. Many Talmud Torah students later recalled slipping over to the park to play despite wearing their best clothing.

Tacoma's Jewish congregations were not alone in their progress. Other churches under construction were First Methodist, First Baptist, First Presbyterian, St. Luke's, First United Presbyterian, First Church of Christ Christian Scientists, First Congregation, and Holy Rosary.

The plans for the building included signage that said Temple Chevra Talmud Torah, but the word Chevra slipped from usage. The signage that was installed on the east side of the building read Talmud Torah Synagogue.

Male Leadership

The congregation dedicated the new synagogue building at Rosh Hashanah, as they welcomed the Hebrew year of 5656. The leadership team was equally dedicated.

Julius Friedman, now in his fifties, again served as president. He noted that the decade-long effort was the work of fifty families, clearly understating his own integral role.

> The synagogue represents nearly a decade of planning and preparation on the part of the Jewish community of Tacoma, and is considered a somewhat more remarkable undertaking than the average church edifice by the fact that the congregation it will accommodate comprises only 50 families.

Julius Friedman   B. Thompson
Tacoma Sunday Ledger April 19, 1925

His vice president was Benjamin Thompson, brother-in-law of Max Meier. Also in his fifties, Benjamin had emigrated from Sebezh, Russia, in late 1903 as Baruch Tomczynski. His Latvian wife, the former Esther Nagel, joined him two years later with their four young children. They had two more sons in New York before heading west in 1910. In Tacoma they had two more daughters, but their young son, Sanford, died of appendicitis in 1913. Like many others, Benjamin operated a secondhand store in the 1300 block of Commerce Street. He would move to Portland in 1932, joining more of his wife's family.

Julius' younger half-brother, Samuel I. Friedman, was secretary of Talmud Torah in 1925, when he was not quite forty. He had lived in Tacoma for over twenty years and had partnered with cousins Joseph and Morris in operating several clothing stores, including the Hub Clothiers. Samuel married their sister, Mary Friedman, in 1913. The couple had four young children. At his death in 1969 Samuel would be noted as the last surviving charter member of Talmud Torah and Tacoma's B'nai B'rith.

Frank Sussman was treasurer and also chaired the executive committee, likely supervising construction. Frank's sister, Rebecca (Sussman) Olswang, had been among the first Jews to arrive in the Pacific Northwest from Sassmacken. The extended Sussman family had lived in Tacoma since 1903. Frank and his brothers, Joseph A. and Charles, operated Tacoma Junk. Frank became sole owner in 1910, just before his marriage to Ida Yudelson. He formed the Frank Sussman Company in 1920, specializing in scrap iron and demolition work. Frank and Ida had three children before 1925, when Frank was 45. In 1929 he would build a substantial building at 21st and Pacific Avenue that still bears his name across the upper facade.

Frank was joined on the executive committee by his younger brother Joseph A. Sussman, his brother-in-law and clothier Nathan Friedman, plywood manufacturer Harris Warnick, and glove-maker Bernard J. Witenberg. All were in their mid-forties and parents of several young children. Among the fifty families were the leaders of the next decades.

Chapter Six: Emerging Leadership

Female Leadership

The new social room, kitchen, and stage would soon become busy places in the beating heart of the Orthodox Jewish community. The women had been busy for decades.

The Ladies' Auxiliary

Dozens of Tacoma's churches, unions, and fraternal organizations were supported by a Ladies' Auxiliary. Talmud Torah was no exception. The group quietly hosted numerous social events, likely with an element of charitable fundraising. Behind every Passover meal was a team of women preparing, serving, and cleaning up afterward.

Mrs. Charles Sussman was remembered as the first Ladies' Auxiliary president, elected in 1914. The former Gustie Stusser was the daughter of Herman and Betty (Ulman) Stusser, and at the time had two young children.

Give Entertainment.

The ladies auxiliary to the congregation of Talmud Torah, 1529 Tacoma evenue will entertain mothers and children of the congregation at 7:30.

Tacoma Daily News October 18, 1916

Many of the women joined the citywide auxiliary to the Order of B'nai B'rith in 1917, supporting the Servicemen's Club House as members of Destiny Lodge No. 14.

Despite the intense publicity around the servicemen's club house, very few women from the Orthodox Jewish community were noted by name in Tacoma's Society columns during the Teens. Many had lived in the U.S. less than a decade and were still becoming acclimated. That changed during the Twenties, although the women were identified in the press only by their husband's names, preceded by Mrs. or the collective term Mesdames. Seattle's *Jewish Transcript* began weekly publication in April of 1924 and carried a Tacoma column.

Synagogue construction publicity in 1925 acknowledged "substantial assistance from the Ladies' Auxiliary, headed by Mrs. Nathan (Betty) Friedman." The women also managed the celebratory dinner dance in October.

In celebration of the near completion of the Synagogue Talmud Torah, the Womens' Auxiliary announces a dinner dance in the new vestry rooms on October 14th. Mrs. Arthur Meier is chairman and will be assisted by Mrs. Chas. Sussman, Mrs. Max Meier, Mrs. S. Brotman, Mrs. Sam Friedman, Mrs. L. Lamken and Mrs. H. Richelin. Dinner will be served from 6 to 8 o'clock and a three-piece orchestra will play for dancing after dinner.

Jewish Transcript October 9, 1925
Courtesy of Seattle Public Library

Mrs. David Good (Mildred Weinstone) was Auxiliary president in 1927. By 1929 enrollment was up to eighty, led by Mrs. Morris Warnick.

Talmud Torah Auxiliary Announces Opening of Autumn Sessions

Women linked in the interest of the Talmud Torah Synagogue auxiliary are beginning their season of service Wednesday, October 16, at 2 o'clock in the vestry rooms.

Eighty are now enrolled for the support of the social and educational life of the congregaiton and for help in the daily Hebrew school. Frequent dinners and card parties fill each season, and to make plans for a series of such entertainments those gathered in the coming week are called by Mrs. M. Warnick, the president.

Associated with Mrs. Warnick are Mrs. E. Klegman, and Mrs. Samuel Friedman, vice presidents; Mrs. Frank Sussman, treasurer; Mrs. Harry Friedman and Mrs. Nathan Friedman, secretaries.

Tacoma News Tribune October 11, 1929

Council of Jewish Women

The National Council of Jewish Women held its first convention in New York in 1896, presided over by Hannah Solomon of Chicago. Tacoma's first chapter was organized in February of 1903, led entirely by women of Temple Beth Israel. The group met weekly at the Temple every Thursday for three years, then faded.

During 1918 the Seattle chapter offered several programs to Jewish servicemen in Tacoma. Beth Israel's Mrs. Theophil (Jessie Levy) Feist served as president in 1920 when the Tacoma chapter was reorganized. The group held its first dance at Triangle Hall, since Temple Beth Israel had sold its building in 1918.

Jewish Women

The Council of Jewish Women will hold a regular meeting Tuesday afternoon at 1529 South Tacoma avenue. The business meeting will be followed by an interesting program. A full attendance is desired.

Tacoma Daily Ledger February 12, 1922

In 1922, while Beth Israel's new temple was under construction, the Tacoma Council of Jewish Women met several times at 1529 Tacoma Avenue South. Although the officers were all from Beth Israel, the board of trustees included Mrs. Isadore (Frances Jacobs) Rosenbaum, Mrs. Peter (Rebecca Sussman) Olswang, and Mrs. Frank (Ida Yudelson) Sussman. Committee heads included Mrs. Morris (Bessie Yablonovich) Warnick and Mrs. Nathan (Betty Yudelson) Friedman. Mesdames Friedman, Weinstein, Shafer and Lamken welcomed guests at a dance in March. In October, after Temple Beth Israel's new building was dedicated, the Council began holding meetings there. Study groups met in private homes.

The Council often participated in citywide campaigns with other women's clubs and had representation in Tacoma's powerful Presidents' Club. Programs typically included musical selections and card games. The club's annual luncheon in 1924 drew approximately 100 Jewish women from across the city. Children provided the December 1924 entertainment, including Dorothy and Wilbur Meier and Rose Rotman. Even after Talmud Torah's new synagogue was dedicated in the fall of 1925, the Council still held meetings at Temple Beth Israel.

Members of Council to Meet Today

Mrs. Joseph A. Sussman has called for today at the Tacoma hotel a meeting of the executive board of the Tacoma Council of Jewish Women. She is president of the Tacoma branch and has arranged a luncheon in one of the smaller rooms of the hotel suite to precede a business conference of the officers and board members. After the formal session, tables will be arranged for bridge.

The board members include beside Mrs. Sussman, Mesdames Robert Friedman, Lee Lewis, A. Burnett, Morris Kleiner, Saul Friedman, Bernard Comber, Harry Warnick, Bernard Witenberg, Samuel Sondheim, I. F. Jacobs, David Klegman, Samuel J. Friedman, Peter Olswang, Herman Jacobs and Miss Elizabeth Warnick.

Tacoma Daily Ledger April 8, 1927

In 1926 Michigan native Mrs. Joseph A. (Minnie Benson) Sussman was elected chairman. She kept a detailed scrapbook of the Council's activities. 1927 elections brought more Orthodox women into leadership roles. The group ended 1929 with a mother and daughter luncheon at the historic Tacoma Hotel.

Hadassah

The Women's Zionist Organization of America, now known simply as Hadassah, was founded in New York in 1912 by Henrietta Szold. In 1923 the Jewish women of Seattle formed several local chapters. The women of Tacoma formed a chapter three years later. Although the organization's name honors the Biblical name of Queen Esther, in the 1920s its slogan was "Hadassah Means Health."

JEWISH GROUP UNITES

"HADASSAH means health in Palestine to Jew, Christian and Arab. It is the work of a united Jewish womanhood."

With this as their goal, 40 women formed a Tacoma chapter of the Hadassah in the home of Mrs. Morris Friedman, mid-week, with Mrs. Friedman as the unanimous choice for their president; Mrs. P. Olswang, vice president; Mrs. H. Barde, secretary, and Mrs. Arthur Meier, treasurer.

Their meetings, as announced by Mrs. Friedman, will be held in the synagogue every second Thursday of the month, when the entire day will be given to sewing and business matters. Tacoma will thus take her place in the ranks of those cities where Hadassah has proved its worth to the world and to "Jews, Christians and Arabs" of the Promised Land, now desolate.

Tacoma News Tribune May 15, 1926

Mrs. Morris Friedman, the former Rose Carp of Milwaukee, called for an organizational meeting at her home in May of 1926. Forty women attended and chose her to be president of the "Ada Strauss" (sic) Chapter of Hadassah. (Ida

Blun Straus was the wife of Isador Straus, co-owner of Macy's department store. Both were victims of the *Titanic* disaster. Ida was noted for choosing to stay aboard with her husband.) In 1926 Hadassah had 25,000 members and 234 chapters doing welfare work for Jewish refugees and hospitals in Palestine. Secretary was Mrs. Hymie (Annette Hurwitt) Barde, with Mrs. Arthur (Berdie Tat) Meier as treasurer. (Twenty years later Berdie's neice, Adelyne Meier; and Annette's nephew, Warren Barde; would marry in Tacoma.)

Mrs. Peter Olswang, the former Rebecca Sussman, chaired the organization's first public benefit in November. Guests from across the city were invited to the evening card party. In 1927 the group held a "hospital shower," requesting that guests bring donations of needed items.

AFFAIR WILL AID HOSPITAL

In behalf of the Palestine hospital a shower will be given by the Ada Strauss chapter of Hadassah in the synagogue, South 4th and I streets, at 2:30 p. m. Tuesday. Admission will be by donations of towels, baby clothes or bed linen. Tables for cards will be arranged and refreshments will be served after playing.

On the committee for the shower are Mrs. Nathan Friedman, chairman, and Mesdames Harry Richelin, J. Robinson, Michael Green, Joseph Buckner, Arthur Meier, K. Weinstone, B. Etsekson and A. Lanzen.

Tacoma Daily Ledger February 27, 1927

Mrs. Arthur (Berdie Tat) Meier was elected president in 1927. Under her leadership the Tacoma Hadassah chapter organized a sewing circle, sponsored a bridge luncheon, and helped support an orphanage in Palestine. The group hosted another hospital shower in March of 1928, then became silent after Berdie moved from Tacoma. In the 1930s welfare work for Palestine was done by Tacoma's Council of Jewish Women.

Youth Leadership
Young Hebrew Moderates

While their parents were forming local chapters of national organizations, Talmud Torah's youth created their own Jewish social club. Before the mortar was dry on the brick of the new synagogue, Talmud Torah's teens formed a club they called Young Hebrew Moderates. They began with twenty-eight charter members in July of 1925. Samuel I. Friedman and Harris Warnick served as their advisors, representing the B'nai B'rith. The group was open to Jews between the ages of fourteen and twenty.

NEW SOCIETY IS ORGANIZED

Recently there was formed the Young Hebrew Moderates, only Jewish young people's society in Tacoma. The purpose of the new organization is to engage in activities which develop mind and body and promote sociability among the members. Already there are 28 charter members and as many more are expected to be initiated within the next few weeks. The new club is receiving enthusiastic support from the older Hebrew societies.

The officers are: Jack Warnick, president; Alec Cohn, vice president; Dorothy Shain, secretary; Max Shain, treasurer; Ben Levinson, sergeant at arms. The following names are on the club roster: Louis Berlin, Harold Brotman, Morley Brotman, Minnie Carrick, Leon Diamond, Morris Elyn, Irving Farber, Cyrus Finegold, Morris Finegold, Sybil Finegold, Cecil Friedman, Charles Friedman, Julius Friedman, Siegfried Friedman, Agnes Lazerson, Isador Masher, Morris Plotkin, Rose Polisky, Morris Richman, Lester Seinfeld, Ethel Shapiro, Jack Slotnik and Robert Warnick.

Tacoma Daily Ledger July 12, 1925

Over the next several months the teens met temporarily at Temple Beth Israel. They brought in speakers on Jewish welfare and debated the pros and cons of child labor. Temple Beth Israel's Rabbi M.N.A. Cohen wrote in an editorial to the *Jewish Transcript* that while he wished the young Orthodox men had formed a chapter of the Y.M.H.A., he admired their innovation.

The Ladies' Auxiliary hosted the first gala in the new building on October 14. The Young Moderates followed with their own dance on October 17, chaired by Rose Polisky and Morris Plotkin. Minnie Carrick, Max Shain, and Sam and Morrie Rabstoff made up the orchestra. Miss Mary Friedman and Miss Bella Lazerson presided over the punchbowl.

Harold "Hal" Brotman was elected president in 1926, with Marie Sussman vice president, Dorothy Shain secretary, Lester Seinfeld treasurer, and Alex Cohen sergeant at arms. Morris Elyn and Jack Slotnik made up the rest of the executive committee. The Young Moderates' fundraising efforts in February benefited the synagogue's library.

The teens continued sponsoring social events, including summer picnics at DeKoven Inn on the shore of Lake Steilacoom. In 1928 they formed a basketball team and joined Tacoma's intramural Church League. The following summer their golf team of Klegman, Olswang, Sussman and Meier proudly defeated Seattle's AZA quartet. The Young Moderates' last publicized event was in November of 1929, just two weeks after the Black Tuesday stock market crash.

Hebrew Moderates Plan Jubilee

Elaborate preparations are being made for the success of the jubilee entertainment which is to be given Saturday evening by the Young Hebrew Moderates at Talmud Torah synagogue, South 4th and I streets. A record attendance is indicated and the program of vaudeville numbers, games and dancing is arranged for both young people and their elders. Before supper there is to be fortune-telling by mysterious strangers.

Tacoma News Tribune November 8, 1929

Jewish Juniors

While the young men gravitated toward sports and summer entertainment, the young ladies were modeling the leadership roles set by their mothers. Many did so under the umbrella of the Tacoma Council of Jewish Women.

The Tacoma Chapter of Jewish Juniors was formed in January of 1926. The group met at Talmud Torah and had many Orthodox members, yet their advisor was Beth Israel's reigning spinster, Minnie Pincus. Hortense Shafer chaired their first event, an evening bridge party. Officers in 1926 were Elizabeth Warnick president, Alice Carrick vice president, and Lillian Friedman and Gertrude Polisky secretaries. (Lillian and Hortense would also remain unmarried.)

The group gave dances twice each year, but also made time for community work. In March of 1927 they performed a play and musical selections for veterans at the American Lake Veterans' Hospital. In December of 1929 their dance was a benefit for aid to Palestine.

Many of the same young ladies also assisted in Talmud Torah's classroom and holiday programs. Below, Lillian Friedman is pictured with students at a Purim celebration in 1928. (Identified in the photographer's daybook as Passover, but the boys are wearing party hats and the table is set with loaves of challah.) Ira Funck led Sunday morning classes as school superintendent in May of 1929 when the students honored their mothers. Rabbi Leib Slotnik taught Byron Friedman in 1931.

Lillian Friedman and Talmud Torah students in 1928
Courtesy of Tacoma Public Library Boland-B-18322

Pairs of Events

Sometimes significant events occur in pairs. Two young men celebrated their bar mitzvahs in 1927. Both would graduate from the University of Washington and become caring and influential adults, serving their communities throughout their lives.

**INVITE FRIENDS TO CONFIR-
MATION**

Mr. and Mrs. Samuel I. Friedman, of 424 Borough Road, are inviting relatives and friends to the Bar Mitzwah (confirmation) of their son, Leonard Martin Friedman, Saturday morning at 9:30 o'clock.

The ceremony will be held in the Talmud Torah Synagogue, South 4th and I streets.

Tacoma News Tribune April 15, 1927

Leonard Friedman, son of Samuel and Mary Friedman, went on to become a lawyer and respected judge, known for his professional manner and literary abilities.

Leslie Sussman, son of Joseph Aaron and Minnie (Benson) Sussman, worked with his father in founding Tacoma Steel. Later he headed General Metals of Tacoma and Jet Equipment and Tools. His parents donated an ark curtain at the time of his 1927 bar mitzvah.

Incident to the recent confirmation of their son, Leslie, on his 13th birthday, Mr. and Mrs. Joseph A. Sussman were hosts at a large reception for his young friends and an elaborately appointed dinner for older family friends.

For the reception friends assisting Mrs. Sussman were Mesdames P. Olswang, Bernard Witenberg, Samuel Friedman, Bernard Comber, A. Lamken and I. F. Jacobs.

The dinner, in the spacious vestry hall at the Talmud Torah temple, was for 225 guests assembled from the city, Olympia, Seattle, Everett and Bremerton.

Tacoma Daily Ledger December 25, 1927

The first of two 1928 weddings, that of Rhea Slotnik and Israel Volotin, perhaps contributed to Rabbi Slotnik's departure to Seattle. The second, between Lena Farber and Bert Treiger, would influence the future rabbi to come back to Tacoma in a few years.

Wedding Is Solemnized In Tacoma

In the presence of 300 friends and relatives the marriage of Miss Rhea Slotnik, daughter of Rev. and Mrs. L. Slotnik, and Israel Volotin was solemnized by Rabbi Shapiro of Seattle at Talmud Torah synagogue Sunday afternoon, March 25.

Tacoma Daily Ledger April 1, 1928

Miss Farber Is Bride of Portlander

The marriage of Miss Lina Farber, daughter of Mr. and Mrs. S. Farber, and Bert Treiger of Portland, Ore., was solemnized Sunday, May 27, at 5 o'clock in Talmud Torah synagogue. Guests numbered 350 and many came from out of town for the service.

Tacoma Daily Ledger June 10, 1928

Jennie Stusser died at the end of 1928, and her husband, Hugo, died just nine months later.

44

Chapter Seven: Community Center

Lumber Capital

Tacoma's Chamber of Commerce promoted the city in 1930 as the "Lumber Capital of America." The lumber industry created jobs in Tacoma, "making doors swing around the world." The same industry brought several Jewish families to Tacoma.

Morris Kleiner came to Tacoma via Poland and then Canada, where he had married Pauline Weinfield in 1919. He operated Liberty Lumber and later Model Lumber. The Kleiners supported both congregations, although they belonged primarily to Temple Beth Israel. All three of their children participated in Talmud Torah youth activities. Morris often led B'nai B'rith installations at Talmud Torah and maintained friendships among many Tacoma Jews.

The lumber industry also brought the extended Warnick and Weinstone families to Tacoma. Harris Warnick had lived in Glasgow, Scotland; and in Montreal, Canada; and then trained in Portland, Oregon. That skill brought him to Tacoma to work for the Wheeler-Osgood Company. In 1919 he opened his own company, Puget Sound Manufacturing. Like Morris Kleiner, Harris Warnick was active in the B'nai B'rith and was respected in both congregations. Harris had been vice president of the short-lived Chevrah Ahavas Israel, but again took a leadership role in Talmud Torah.

1930 Rededication

Although Talmud Torah's synagogue building had been in use for nearly five years, portions were not completed or decorated until the spring of 1930. Once again congregational president Julius Friedman "was chiefly responsible" for the project's success. He had helped organize it, he had worked to get it built, and he would see it finished. Harris Warnick was credited with a substantial financial contribution.

Congregation Prepares To Dedicate Synagogue

Julius Friedman

Talmud Torah synagogue, South 4th and I streets, will be formally dedicated Sunday, March 30, at 5 p. m. by Tacoma Jewry. Morris Friedman, chairman of the dedication, will preside.

Julius Friedman, 523 North E street, president of the congregation and a Tacoma pioneer, was chiefly

Harris Warnick

responsible for bringing about the completion of the synagogue and Harris Warnick, 3218 North 19th street, by contributing a substantial sum, was another of the congregation to those efforts the new building can be attributed.

In the picture above Julius Friedman is shown at the left and Mr. Warnick at the right.

Tacoma Daily Ledger March 23, 1930

Morris Friedman served as chairman of the dedication committee and hosted guests from across the Pacific Northwest. As part of the event Mrs. Edward (Jennie Waldocks) Nudelman of Portland presented a menorah in memory of her father, charter member Emanuel Waldocks. Mrs. Harris (Fannie Weinstone) Warnick chaired the team of hard-working women responsible for the accompanying banquet.

DEDICATE JEWISH SYNAGOGUE SUNDAY

Expecting an assembly composed of several hundred members, friends and guests, the Jewish leaders of the Tacoma Talmud Torah synagogue, South 4th and I street, have arranged for the dedication of the synagogue Sunday, at 5 p. m.

Tacoma Daily Ledger March 29, 1930

Tacoma Hebrew School
Dr. Itzehak Ivar Spector

Russian-born Dr. Itzehak Spector began lecturing in Tacoma in the fall of 1929. He had just completed his doctoral dissertation at the University of Chicago. While in Tacoma he taught at the College of Puget Sound (later the University of Puget Sound).

Dr. Spector also became the head of the Tacoma Hebrew School. The school held classes at Talmud Torah, but operated independently. Classes were open to all, regardless of affiliation. In 1930 under Dr. Spector's leadership the daily Tacoma Hebrew School had 55 pupils enrolled, even more on Sundays, and had started a confirmation class.

President Samuel L. Nudelman led the board of education. Goldie (Elyn) Farber was vice president, with secretary Betty (Yudelson) Friedman and treasurer Morris Kleiner.

Samuel Nudelman operated a women's clothing store on Broadway. (At the time the women's shops were clustered on Broadway, two blocks above the men's stores on Pacific Avenue.) In 1924 he had married Tacoma native Tillie Witenberg, daughter of S.N. and Anne (Friedman) Witenberg. Due to the Depression Samuel closed his Tacoma store at the end of 1931 and moved to Astoria, Oregon.

Dr. Spector moved to Seattle about the same time and taught at the University of Washington. He would visit Tacoma in 1937 for his wedding to fellow scholar Margaret Marion Mitchell, and frequently lectured throughout the area. He became a respected authority, writing dozens of texts on Russian language and Russian history. At least four young men trained for their bar mitzvahs under Dr. Spector. They learned to chant from Seattle's Samuel E. Goldfarb.

- Philip Byron Friedman, son of Morris and Rose
- Myron Herschell Freyd, son of Sol and Lena, grandson of Max and Leba Cohen
- Herman Kleiner, son of Morris & Pauline
- Stanford Shapiro, son of Kate and the late Jacob, grandson of Barney and Dora

Gabriel Agouff

The next teacher was Rabbi Gabriel Agouff, also a Russian refugee and linguist. Before coming to Tacoma he had lived and worked in over a dozen cities across the nation. He had returned to Russia at least three times, living most recently in Riga, Latvia.

Tacoma Daily Ledger March 20, 1932
(Left to right: Herbert Clayman, Annie Lewinson, Claire Boonov, Irving Boonov and Bertha Farber

Rabbi Agouff directed a pageant at Talmud Torah in Tacoma in the spring of 1932, in which the students recited in Hebrew and then translated in English. Julius Friedman and W.D. Meier witnessed his naturalization petition two months after the pageant. Rabbi Agouff left abruptly in October of 1933 to take a position in Portland, Oregon. (Like Rabbi Gordon, he wouldn't stay in Portland either.)

Deep in the midst of the Great Depression the Tacoma Hebrew School slipped away and Talmud Torah was lay-led for three years. The Shul continued, however, to fulfill the definition of the word synagogue, as a house of worship and a communal center.

Communal Center

Courtesy of Josephine (Kleiner) Heiman

Talmud Torah Women's Auxiliary circa 1929
On the front lawn of 810 North J Street (home of Harry and Lena Rotman)
<u>Back row from left:</u> Mrs. Peter (Rebecca Sussman) Olswang, Mrs. Frank (Ida Yudelson) Sussman, Louis Benson (father of Minnie Benson Sussman,) Mrs. Herman (Rose LeBid) Dobry, Mrs. Max (Emma Yudelson) Novikoff, Mrs. Louis (Pauline Edelstein) Benson, Mrs. Joseph S. (Rosie Kahn) Sussman, Mrs. Max (Bessie Nagel) Meier, Mrs. William D. (Anna Brenner) Meier, Mrs. Nathan (Betty Yudelson) Friedman, and Mrs. Morris (Bessie Yablonovich) Warnick
<u>Front row from left:</u> Mrs. Max (Nura Godesoff) LeBid, Mrs. Samuel I. (Mary) Friedman, Mrs. David (Helen Gevurtz) Klegman, Mrs. Harris (Fannie Weinstone) Warnick, Mrs. Louis (Elizabeth Kaufman) Lamken, Mrs. Arthur (Fanny Sussman) Lamken, and Mrs. Harry (Lena Lamken) Rotman.

The "vestry rooms" of Talmud Torah must have been busy nearly every night of the week. B'nai B'rith men held their citywide meetings on Monday nights. Women of Tacoma's Destiny Lodge auxiliary met on Tuesday evenings, sometimes jointly with the men. Talmud Torah's Women's Auxiliary held their programs on Wednesday evenings. Plus, there were meetings for the Tacoma Council of Jewish Women and the Tacoma Council of Jewish Juniors, in addition to synagogue board and committee meetings.

Most club meetings typically included refreshments or late suppers. Officers submitted the names of each meeting's hostess committee members to the ladies' club section of Tacoma's newspapers. The meeting programs often incorporated entertainment or card games.

Several times a year the club groups sponsored dances with live music. Members also gathered for holidays, especially those enjoyed by children. In 1930 Mrs. Louis (Elizabeth) Lamken and her committee planned a Chanukah meal for 300 guests, at a time when dishwashing was done manually and in accordance with kosher rules.

Many of the events had a fundraising element, either to benefit the Hebrew school or other philanthropy. In November of 1930 Talmud Torah members hosted a mass meeting of Tacoma Jews for an Allied Jewish campaign. Their goal was to raise $2500 in cash, particularly for aid to needy Jews in Europe.

TACOMA JEWS TO AID FUND

Tacoma News Tribune November 18, 1930

In April of 1932 the Destiny auxiliary women held a "Hard Times Frolic," complete with prizes for "hard-time costumes." By 1933 their programs offered home-cooked meals, perhaps tactfully helping any members in need.

Frolic Planned By Destiny Group

Saturday evening Destiny auxiliary, I. O. B. B., will be host to members and friends at a hard-time frolic in the vestry rooms of Talmud Torah synagogue. An orchestra of eight pieces will play and a special committee of judges will take note of hard-time costumes and award honors, represented in attractive favors, to the couple appearing in the most unique and fitting mode.

Mrs. J. J. Hurley is chairman for the party and her committee of assistants includes Miss Vallie Lewis, Mrs. Frank Shafer, Mrs. Harry Reiman, Mrs. Israel Sohn, Mrs. J. E. Bukofzer and Mrs. S. Farber.

Tacoma Daily Ledger April 1, 1932

Music

Although Orthodox worship services excluded playing musical instruments, singing was integral. Talmud Torah often hosted concerts of touring musicians, some of whom assisted in leading services.

- May 1926, "the famous European cantor, Rev. G. Ronconi"
- April 1928, "Madame Reinhart performing Jewish folk songs"
- September 1928, "dramatic tenor Cantor Hymmoshe Goldenthal of New York"
- September 1931, "Rev. Leon Karz, formerly of the Minsker Shul"
- October 1933, "composer and singer Solomon (Smulewitz) Small"

Hanukah Operetta

At home the children play with the Hanukah Spinner (Draidle or Trendle). It is customary for parents or Hanukah to give Hanukah Gelt (literally, money, i. e., Hanukah presents) to their children. It is also customary to exchange gifts on Hanukah.

The pupils of the Tacoma Hebrew school will celebrate Hanukah on Sunday, December 21, at 5 p. m. at the Talmud Torah synagogue. One of the features of this celebration will be an operetta entitled "A Unique Hanukah Party," presented by the pupils. The play will be supervised by the composer of this work, S. E. Goldfard of Seattle, assisted by Miss Dorothy Rashbam.

Tacoma Daily Ledger December 14, 1930

In December of 1930 Tacoma's Hebrew pupils presented an operetta, "A Unique Chanukah Party." Their choir teacher was the composer, Samuel E. Goldfarb, then director of music at Seattle's Temple De Hirsch. Goldfarb had composed the Dreidel Song melody in 1927, still little-known at the time. (His brother, Rabbi Israel Goldfarb, wrote a popular Shalom Aleichem melody.) In 1956 Samuel and his second wife would be among the passengers who survived the sinking of the *Andrea Doria*.

Workmen's Circle

Jewish Transcript March 17, 1933

In the Thirties several members of Tacoma's Jewish community gained prominence in the Northwest district of Workmen's Circle. Also known by its Yiddish name Der Arbeter Ring, the organization was formed by Jewish immigrants in New York in 1900 as a mutual aid society. The group promoted Yiddish culture and at one point in its history was closely tied to Socialist ideals.

The group's earliest mention in Tacoma was under the name Workingman's Circle. In May of 1922 the Circle of Branch #578 held a basket social to benefit destitute Russian children. The event was held at Maccabee Hall on 13th and Commerce. The following year the Workmen's Circle brought union leader and Socialist candidate Eugene V. Debs to speak at the Tacoma Theater. The group's secretary, Mrs. Solomon J. (Goldie) Farber, handled the arrangements. Her son, Irving, helped hand out leaflets. On September 14th the *Tacoma Daily Ledger* noted that "1,300 persons filled every seat, packed the stage and stood in the aisles."

Workmen's Circle members joined with the auxiliary groups of both congregations in the spring of 1928 in sponsoring a concert at Talmud Torah to benefit the Los Angeles sanitarium of the Jewish Consumptive Relief Association. The concert featured Jewish performers Madame Fannie Reinhart and Eva Turbow, both touring on behalf of the sanitarium. Gustie (Stusser) Sussman, Mrs. Morris Kleiner, and Mrs. Farber made the arrangements.

In 1931 Tacoma hosted the Northwest district's annual convention, held at Talmud Torah. Delegates came from Oregon, Montana, Washington, British Columbia, and Alberta. Abe Plotkin served as toastmaster. Abe Cohn, Sam Seinfeld, and Joseph Buckner worked on the committee.

Tacoma Daily News September 7, 1931

The following year the convention took place in Seattle. Regional officers included Joseph Rome as district recorder and Abe Cohn as district treasurer. Tacoma delegates to the 1933 convention included Morris Raphalowitz, Arthur Greenblat, and Kopel Weinstone. The following year Abe Cohn was president of the Tacoma branch when the president of the grand lodge spoke at a banquet at Talmud Torah.

In 1939 Abe Cohn was still a district officer, along with Abe Plotkin. Joseph Willner served as secretary of the local branch. The following year Samuel Offerman held that office.

Other memberships were mentioned in obituaries, including those of Abraham and Sadie Rose, Harry Rotman, Anna Shain, and Jacob Wolf.

Today the worldwide non-profit organization goes by the shortened name of Workers Circle. It promotes social and economic justice, and still provides Yiddish education.

Moderates Basketball

The members of the Young Hebrew Moderates were still playing basketball in the Church League in 1933. Now adults, they shortened their team's name to just Moderates. In January of that year the men finally defeated their crosstown rivals from St. Joseph's. Their uniforms left no doubt as to their affiliation.

Bid for Church Basket Title

Here are the members of the Moderates' basketball team of the Church league, considered a title contender following a victory over the powerful St. Joseph's team recently. It was the first time in five years of Church league competition that the Moderates defeated the St. Joe's. Those in the picture are: Back row, left to right—Stanley Friedman, business manager; David Hyman, Max Shain, Robert Warnick Sr., Robert Warnick Jr., Bert Meier. Front row—Isadore Epstein, Edward Olswang, Al Cohn, team manager and coach; Morris Epstein, Henry Epstein. Front center—Jerry Meier, mascot. Photo by Lite-O-Rite Photo service.

Moderates Basketball Team, *Tacoma Daily Ledger January 15, 1933*
Back row, left to right: Stanley Friedman, business manager; David Hyman, Max Shain, Robert Warnick Sr., Robert Warnick Jr., Bert Meier. Front row: Isadore Epstein, Edward Olswang, Alex Cohn team manager and coach, Morris Epstein, Henry Epstein. Front center: Gerald "Jerry" Meier, mascot

Burning the Mortgage

MORTGAGE BURNING TO BE CELEBRATED

In celebration of burning the old mortgage, Talmud Torah synagogue, South 4th and I streets, is holding a grand banquet Sunday at 5 o'clock. The toastmaster of the evening will be P. Allen Rickles, prominent Seattle attorney, and the address will be given by Rabbi Philip A. Langh of Seattle. A group of songs will be sung by Mrs. Eva Finesilver of Seattle. After the banquet dancing will be enjoyed. The burning of this mortgage marks a milestone in the progress of the congegation. The president of the congegation. W. Meier, is in charge of the affair assisted by a group of the women.

Tacoma Daily Ledger March 14, 1935

The hard work and frugality had paid off. The congregation burned the 1925 mortgage after just ten years. During the Great Depression.

William D. Meier was president at the time. He and his older brothers, Max and Arthur, were also active in Tacoma's Jewish community. Their original surname had been Droyan, but like many others they chose a new name after emigrating. Family lore tells that Max saw a Portland, Oregon, building exterior painted with a large ad for the firm of Meier and Frank. He decided then and there that a name that big would make a good name for him.

To Name Rabbi

Talmud Torah synagog men and women announce a joint meeting in the vestry rooms Wednesday at 7:30 o'clock for the purpose of choosing a new rabbi and to elect officers of the two societies. H. Warnick and Mrs. F. Farber are presiding. Supper will follow business.

Tacoma News Tribune May 6, 1935

Hiring a Rabbi

In 1935 congregation Talmud Torah decided then and there that it was time to choose a rabbi. Although a meeting was announced in May for that purpose, the process wasn't immediate. Several guest rabbis spoke in Tacoma over the next year, perhaps as test visits, or perhaps just touring.

Rabbi Hugo Mantel visited in June. He was a graduate of New York's Yeshiva College. "Rabbi Mantel occupies the pulpit at the Jewish community center in Dubuque, Iowa, where conservative, orthodox and reform elements have combined under his leadership." *Tacoma News Tribune June 7, 1935.*

Rabbi David Savitz came in August from the Huntsport Jewish Center. Rabbi Savitz had entered Harvard at thirteen and went on to become the first American-born Orthodox rabbi. However, Seattle's Cantor S. Merpert led the High Holy Day services in 1935. The process would take another year.

Rabbi Aaron Blumenthal spoke at Talmud Torah in February of 1936 and led Friday night services. He was a graduate of McGill University and described as one of the younger rabbis of the country. The congregation was perhaps ready for a young, modern rabbi.

Rabbi Baruch Treiger

Rabbi Baruch Treiger arrived in Tacoma in the fall of 1936 to lead Talmud Torah. Like many of the congregation Rabbi Treiger was born in Russia, where he received no public schooling. He worked his way through remedial school by teaching Hebrew in Portland, Oregon. He became a school principal, both in Portland and in Ontario, Canada. He then earned degrees from Columbia and the (Conservative) Jewish Theological Seminary of America.

Perhaps more importantly, he had married Lena Farber in Tacoma in 1928. She was the daughter of Solomon J. and Goldie (Elyn) Farber, and niece of Rabbi Meier Elyn. He was family. He was 41 and a scholar. He would fit.

Will Occupy Tacoma Pulpit

RABBI TREIGER

New Pastor of Talmud Zorah to Be Welcomed Here

Rabbi Barush Treiger, of Toronto, Canada, arrived in Tacoma Wednesday to occupy the pulpit of Congregation Talmud Torah. A reception for Rabbi and Mrs. Treiger in the synagogue, at South 4th and I streets, Friday evening, September 4, will inaugurate weekly Friday evening services.

Rabbi Treiger is a young, modern rabbi, a graduate of Reed college, Portland, and Columbia university. Ordained at the Jewish Theological Seminary of America, for the past three years he has occupied an important post in Toronto. In inviting him to the Tacoma pulpit, it is the purpose of the congregation to introduce a modern, Americanized form of worship, conserving, however, the beauty and meaning of traditional Jewish service and ritual. The rabbi will present a series of talks on contemporary Jewish and American problems, accompanied by a program of activities along cultural, religious and social lines.

In charge of the reception in honor of Rabbi and Mrs. Treiger, who is the former Lena Farber, daughter of Mr. and Mrs. S. J. Farber of Tacoma, are Morris Friedman, president of the Congregation, and Mrs. Nathan Friedman, president of the Sisterhood.

Tacoma News Tribune August 27, 1936

"It is the purpose of the congregation to introduce a modern, Americanized form of worship, conserving, however, the beauty and meaning of traditional Jewish service and ritual."

Chapter Eight: Rabbi Treiger

A Unifying Force

Rabbi Treiger immediately set to work, beginning with regular Friday night services. He submitted the topics of his weekly sermons to Tacoma's newspapers, along with invitations for the public to attend. His second sermon was "Conservative Judaism as a Unifying Force in Jewry." Other sermons were inspired by current events, such as the 80th birthday of Supreme Court Justice Louis D. Brandeis. Rabbi Treiger frequently included a guest speaker or additional program in the social hour after the service. Seattle's Morris Bender began chanting as a guest cantor.

Modern worship also meant welcoming children and teens beyond the twice-weekly Hebrew School. Yom Kippur afternoon services included a special youth sermon, followed by an evening dance honoring young people. Talmud Torah's new Young People's League (later nicknamed Treiger's Tigers) elected Rhoda Sussman as president in December of 1936. The group often presented a forum of debates and entertainment after Friday services.

In October, "in keeping with the trend of modern adult education," Rabbi Treiger launched a program advertised as the first of its kind in Tacoma, with the lofty title of Institute of Jewish Studies. A month later the adult education classes were moved to Tuesday evening so the men and women of the B'nai B'rith groups could participate, implying that women were welcome in the classes.

Rabbi Treiger also dedicated a sermon to the "Merits of Jewish Women's Organizations" and was the guest of honor at a series of luncheons and receptions. He understood and appreciated the work of Talmud Torah's women. Decades later many of those same women would still speak of him with respect and admiration.

PLAN JEWISH STUDY GROUP

Wednesday evening will mark the opening of the Institute of Jewish Studies for adults ever to be held in this city. At Congregation Talmud Torah, located at South 4th and I streets, courses for adults will begin this evening, Rabbi B. I. Treiger, spiritual leader of the synagogue, announced.

Courses offered will include elementary and advanced Hebrew, Jewish Customs and Ceremonies and Jewish History. Classes will meet once a week, on Wednesday from 8 to 10 p. m., for a period of 20 weeks. A nominal registration fee will be charged. Rabbi Trieger holds degrees from Reed college, Columbia university and the Jewish Theological Seminary. He recently came to Tacoma from Toronto, Canada.

Tacoma News Tribune October 21, 1936

By the time of Rabbi Treiger's formal installation in November, the women were planning a banquet for 400 people. Mrs. Louis (Elizabeth) Lamken led the hospitality committee and Mrs. Nathan (Betty) Friedman was president of the Auxiliary.

To Assist At Installation

MRS. LOUIS LAMKEN   MRS. NATHAN FRIEDMAN

Tacoma News Tribune November 5, 1936

Voice of a Woman

Viewing the activities of the members of Talmud Torah through the lenses of newspaper Society pages perhaps gives a skewed impression. The Shul was primarily a place of worship. The men of the Orthodox congregation were service leaders, participants, and speakers. Traditionally even the voice of a woman, *kol ishah,* was prohibited in the sanctuary. That was about to change in Tacoma.

The National Council of Jewish Women celebrated its 44th anniversary in January of 1937, along with the 79th birthday of one of its founders, Mrs. Hannah Solomon. The women of the Tacoma chapter gathered together on January 11 to listen to a national radio broadcast. On Friday evening, January 22, members of the chapter *participated in services* at Talmud Torah. Mrs. Robert (Phreda Soss) Warnick, president of the chapter, *spoke during services* on the work of the organization. Of course, they also served as hostesses of the following social hour.

JEWISH WOMEN PLAN SERVICES

The 44th anniversary of the founding of the National Council of Jewish Women will be observed Friday evening at Congregation Talmud Torah, when members of the local chapter of the council will participate in services and Rabbi C. F. Treiger will deliver a sermon on: "Jewish Women in America. . .Some Things They Have Accomplished". Mrs. Robert Warnick, president of the Tacoma chapter, will speak on the work of the organization and will participate in the services. Other members who will represent the council in the evening's program are: Mesdames J. Buckner, I. F. Jacobs, Morris Kleiner, and William Spellman. Members of the council will serve as hostesses during the social hour following the devotional services.

Tacoma News Tribune January 22, 1937

Women had many ways of sharing their voices. The Destiny Lodge auxiliary of the B'nai B'rith joined with the men in February to raise funds to support relief efforts after the tragic Ohio River floods. The Talmud Torah Auxiliary continued supporting synagogue programs through rummage sales, basket suppers, and major banquets. They also coordinated huge community meals at Passover.

Plan Talmud Torah Dinner

MRS. S. J. FARBER   MRS. HARRY ROTMAN

Tacoma News Tribune April 28, 1937

"Three hundred guests are expected Wednesday evening...Mrs. Farber, whose daughter is the wife of Talmud Torah's new Rabbi, Baruch Treiger, receives guests as chairman of the evening. Mrs. Rotman, whose devotion to the cause has accompanied all of her 27 years of life in Tacoma, has arranged ticket sales, thus assuring a record attendance for the annual affair."

Mrs. Solomon (Goldie Elyn) Farber and Mrs. Harry (Lena Lamken) Rotman led two major events in 1937, the spring gala and Rabbi Treiger's fall anniversary banquet. In 1934 Mrs. Rotman's daughter, Rose, had married Dr. Abedeaux Friedman, son of Julius Friedman.

1937 brought one more history-making event. Radio station KMO broadcast a special Yom Kippur service on Sunday evening, September 12. Rabbi Treiger spoke, and Miss Belle Ruth Clayman and Mrs. Samuel (Thelma) Klegman performed the melodies of Kol Nidre. Traditional Yom Kippur services were on Tuesday and Wednesday, followed by a dance hosted by the Young People's League.

PLANS SERVICE OF ATONEMENT

Rabbi Baruch I. Treiger of Congregation Talmud Torah, South 4th and I streets, will present Day of Atonement, or Yom Kippur, services over station KMO at 5:30 p. m. today. Mrs. Thelma Klegman and Miss Belle Ruth Clayman will play the traditional melodies of the Kol Nidre. Rabbi Treiger will speak on "The Message of the Day of Atonement."

Tacoma News Tribune September 12, 1937

Miss Belle Ruth Clayman was the daughter of Samuel Clayman and Lena Eichenwald. Her Eichenwald aunts were:
- Bea, Mrs. Henry Zeidell
- Rose, Mrs. Karl Adelberg
- Dorothy, Mrs. Harry Friedman
- Josephine, Mrs. Solomon Becker
- Clara, Mrs. Morris Bender

Belle Ruth was valedictorian of her class at Stadium High School. During the 1937-1938 school year she routinely chanted portions of the Friday evening services. Belle Ruth later graduated from the College of Puget Sound and took graduate work at Northwestern. Before her 1944 marriage to Joseph Witkin, Belle Ruth was one of the Society editors of the *Tacoma News Tribune*. As Dr. Belle Ruth Witkin she would become a prominent university speech educator.

Thelma Korklin was born in Aberdeen, Washington, and grew up in Centralia, daughter of Sarah Weiss and Julius Korklin. She married

Samuel Herman Klegman in 1936, son of Helen Gevurtz and David Klegman. At the time of the radio broadcast Thelma was six months pregnant with her first son, Marvin, who would later be a victim of Tacoma's 1949 Passover earthquake.

Young women participated in Talmud Torah services through their membership in the Junior League of the congregation. The election of officers in conjunction with Sukkot services in 1937 included Gerald Meier, Edward Feldman, Estelle Lamken, Bernard Friedman, and Josephine Kleiner; replacing outgoing officers Rhoda Sussman, Philburn Friedman, and Beatrice Sussman.

Young women also participated in services as part of a synagogue choir, which debuted in December of 1937. Belle Ruth Clayman directed the singers, most of whom were in their teens.

PLAN SABBATH EVE SERVICES

Regular Sabbath eve services will be held Friday at 8:15 p. m. at the Talmud Torah synagogue, South 4th and I streets. Rabbi Treiger has chosen as his sermon topic the timely subject: "Let the Christians Show the Way." The synagogue choir will chant selected portions of the service with the following participating: Belle Ruth Clayman, Phyllis Friedman, Gladys Brodsky, Bluma Novikoff, Bernard Friedman, Melvin Novikoff and Rhoda Sussman.

Tacoma News Tribune December 23, 1937

Confirmation Classes

Dr. Spector had taught a Confirmation group in 1929-1930, and Rabbi Treiger did the same in 1936-1937 and 1937-1938. Each class concluded in the spring with a special program at the holiday of Shavuot, celebrating the receiving of the Torah.

15 PUPILS IN CONFIRMATION

Fifteen boys and girls who have been pupils of the confirmation class of congregation Talmud Torah, South 4th and I streets, will take part in the impressive confirmation service in the synagogue on Sunday at 7 p. m. This service, held in conjunction with the festival of Pentecost or the giving of the law, is in the nature of a service of consecration of these young people to the ideals of Jewish religious and ethical precepts. The religious service includes an interesting exposition by the confirmants of the ethical and religious precepts of the Jewish faith. There will be traditional synagogue melodies and since this festival is associated with the ancient agricultural festival when the first fruits were brought to the temple in Jerusalem, there will be a floral offering. Certificates will be presented the pupils by M. J. Friedman, president of the congregation. Bibles given by the Women's auxiliary will be presented by Mrs. Dave Klegman and Mrs. J. Sussman. Rabbi Baruch Treiger, who has prepared the confirmants for this event, will deliver the charge. Following the service there will be a reception with parents of the confirmants receiving guests. The confirmants are: Florence Barnett, Sidney Blechman, Jerry Donion, Walter Etsekson, Bernard Friedman, Philburn Friedman, Estelle Lamken, Gerald Meier, Jordan Meier, Melvin Novikoff, Simon Rose, Roy Slotnick, Beatrice Sussman, Lorraine Sussman and Rhoda Sussman.

Tacoma News Tribune May 15, 1937

FESTIVAL OF SHEVUOTH TO BE OBSERVED

This Saturday evening at sundown the ancient Jewish Festival of Shevuoth, or the Feast of Weeks, will begin. It will be observed Sunday and Monday. Shevuoth is also known as Pentecost, because it takes place on the 50th day after the second evening of Passover, and is also traditionally associated with the giving of the Torah or Ten Commandments to Moses on Mount Sinai.

At Congregation Talmud Torah, South 4th and I streets, Shevuoth services will be held Saturday evening at 8 o'clock, Sunday morning at 9 o'clock, Sunday evening at 7 o'clock, and Monday morning at 8 o'clock. There will be a memorial service at 9 o'clock Monday morning.

Of especial interest is the confirmation service and ceremony to be held in the synagogue on Sunday evening at 7 o'clock. This is the second annual confirmation service. The class to be confirmed includes Esther Goldberg, Gerald Goldfarb, Leon Meier, Harold Novikoff and Jerry Spellman. The synagogue choir will sing. Miss Belle Ruth Clayman and Ronald Naimark will offer vocal solos. Rabbi Baruch Treiger will deliver the charge to the confirmants. Philip Brodsky, president of the congregation, will award the certificates; Mesdames J. A. Sussman and B. Witenberg will present Bibles on behalf of the women's auxiliary. Following the service there will be a reception in the vestry rooms, with the parents of the confirmants receiving.

Tacoma News Tribune June 4, 1938

May 1937 confirmation class, courtesy of Temple Beth El

Dedication of the Henry Bell Torah November 21, 1937
Courtesy of the Farber Family

Henry Bell Torah

Henry Bell, another native of Riga, Latvia, had immigrated around 1906 and lived previously in San Francisco. He came to Tacoma in 1931, where he operated a secondhand store on Commerce Street and worked as a shoemaker. His ex-wife and five children remained in California.

Henry was so moved by the progress of the congregation that he donated a Torah in memory of his father. Philip Brodsky accepted the donation as president of Talmud Torah. Rabbi Treiger arranged a dedication ceremony that included a final inscription by a Torah scribe, Rev. (Mendel) Baronsky of Seattle.

SIYUM HATORAH COMES SUNDAY

The Siyum Hatorah celebration will take place on Sunday at Congregation Talmud Torah. A new Sefer Torah or Holly Scroll, containing the five books of Moses, written by hand in Hebrew on parchment, has been donated to the synagogue by Henry Bell in memory of his father. Mr. Bell is a member of the Tacoma Congregation. The Sefer Torah will be used by the synagogue for the reading of portions of the law on Sabbaths and festivals. A ceremony of dedication and inscription is being planned by Rabbi Baruch Treiger and the officers of the Congregation for Sunday afternoon. The inscription is to be made by a scribe, specially trained for such work, Rev. Baronsky of Seattle. This is the first ceremony of this sort to take place in Tacoma in many years.

Tacoma News Tribune November 9, 1937

The Torah that Henry Bell donated is likely the one that is now in regular use at Temple Beth El, as it is the newest and least fragile.

Rabbi Means Teacher

Talmud Torah had become a social and communal center during the interim years in the Thirties without a rabbi. Rabbi Treiger brought an increased emphasis on education. Students celebrated the translation of the Bible into more than 1,000 different languages by reciting the Ten Commandments in Hebrew, English, French, German, Spanish, Russian, and Chinese. Many Friday evenings included a guest speaker from the community or academia. Occasionally Rabbi Treiger simply chatted about current events after services. During December he solicited advance questions from members and delivered an "Ask the Rabbi" sermon.

Youth Lecture Series Slated At Synagogue

Tacoma News Tribune February 11, 1938

Rabbi Treiger also created a non-denominational public lecture series. In the spring of 1938 he assembled a team of professionals to discuss problems faced by youth. Eight lectures in early 1939 revolved around the question "Is Civilization Doomed?"

As the situation in Europe worsened, Rabbi Treiger brought in speakers from relief agencies, then went to see the situation for himself. He and Lena were already committed Zionists.

RABBI RETURNS FROM PALESTINE

Rabbi and Mrs. Baruch I. Treiger returned Thursday to their home at 210 North G street, after a three months' trip to Europe and Palestine. Rabbi Treiger is pastor of Talmud Torah synagogue, from which he has been on leave of absence during his extended trip.

Tacoma News Tribune September 10, 1938

Second Annual

LECTURE SERIES

IS CIVILIZATION DOOMED?

A SERIES OF SEVEN LECTURES, ARRANGED ON A NON-SECTARIAN BASIS

CONDUCTED BY

Rabbi Baruch I. Treiger

Auspices of

Congregation Talmud Torah and its Auxiliary Organizations

Monday Evenings, beginning February 20th and concluding Thursday Evening,
April 6th, 1939

at

THE TALMUD TORAH SYNAGOGUE

South 4th and I Streets   Tacoma, Washington

LECTURERS

PROFESSOR RUSSELL BLANKENSHIP, Dept. of English Literature, U. of W.

DR. EDWIN R. GUTHRIE, Psychology Dept., U. of W.

PROFESSOR MELVIN KOHLER, Art Dept., C. P. S.

DEAN EDWARD H. LAUER, Dean of University College, U. of W.

PROFESSOR VERNON A. MUND, Head of Economics Dept., U. of W.

DEAN FREDERICK M. PADELFORD, Dean of Graduate School, U. of W.

PROFESSOR DUDLEY PRATT, Art Dept., U. of W.

PROFESSOR C. J. RATH, History Dept., C. P. S.

DR. MARVIN R. SCHAFER, Head of Sociology Dept., C. P. S.

DR. WARREN TOMLINSON, Head of German Dept., C. P. S.

RABBI BARUCH I. TREIGER, Talmud Torah Synagogue, Tacoma.

DR. FRANK G. WILLISTON, Head of the History Dept., C. P. S.

LECTURE I.
Monday Evening, February 20, 1939
8:15 P. M.

A Symposium by
Dr. Frank G. Williston, Dr. Warren E. Tomlinson, and Professor C. J. Rath of the College of Puget Sound

CAN FORMS OF GOVERNMENT ADVANCE OR RETARD CIVILIZATION?

In a world of threatened Democracies and rising Dictatorships, what are the realizable values of Democracy? Is Democracy more than a mere form of government? Is there an ideal form of political organization? What have been the causes of the retreat of democracies before dictatorships? What Contributions should Society expect from the State?

Lecture brochure from the 1938-1939 scrapbook of Mrs. Bernard (Charlotte Endelman) Witenberg

Rabbi and Mrs. Treiger spent the summer of 1938 traveling in Europe, North Africa, and Palestine. In Palestine they visited cooperative communities and the cities of Haifa, Jerusalem and Tel Aviv. Ever the teacher, Rabbi Treiger brought back movies.

In November of 1938 Tacoma's Jewish community prepared to celebrate the twentieth anniversary of the European Armistice of the First World War, followed by a public showing of Rabbi Treiger's Palestine film footage. But in Germany, the nights of November 9 and 10 erupted in violence against Jews. The Night of Broken Glass, Kristallnacht, was to be the final shattering of Jewish existence in Germany.

CHURCH GROUPS JOIN PRAYER WEEK MEETING

"Christians throughout the United States are joining with their Jewish neighbors in fellowship meetings in the observance of National Prayer week, indicating the solidarity of all civilized humanity against the barbarism of Nazi pogroms and tortures of innocent people during recent weeks," according to Rabbi Baruch I. Treiger, who announces a similar meeting here. "All religious groups in Germany," he points out, "have suffered persecution at the hands of the Nazis and the world conscience has been outraged by recent destruction of Jewis lives."

Tacoma News Tribune November 18, 1938

Talmud Torah immediately joined in observing National Prayer Week. Organizations around the city invited Rabbi Treiger to speak. His summer of travel gave him a personal view of Palestine and Italy. His congregation and his community would need his leadership.

Many of the members of his congregation had relatives in Germany. One of them, Mrs. Samuel (Frieda) Offerman, was waiting to hear from her sister who had been living in Berlin. Frieda's sister, Ruchla Zuckerkorn Gruenbaum, and her husband, Hersz, arrived safely at Tacoma's Union Station on December 28, 1938. They had reached the U.S. on November 8, one day before Kristallnacht. Their reunion would be brief, as Frieda died just ten weeks later. She was buried in the Chevra Kadisha Cemetery co-founded by her brother, Max Zuckerkorn. A few years later Ruchla and Hersz, now Hannah and Harry Greenbaum, joined another brother, Ben, in New York.

Organizing

Tacoma's Jewish women immediately banded together, forming the Hadassah Joint Council of Tacoma. Members came from the Destiny B'nai B'rith Auxiliary, Council of Jewish Women, Sisterhood of Temple Beth Israel, and the Women's Auxiliary of Talmud Torah. Their December 1938 event raised funds to rescue children from central Europe, under the motto "Give a Gift to Save a Life."

Two new youth groups emerged at the same time. The Tacoma Aleph Zadik Aleph (AZA) No. 336, Junior Order of B'nai B'rith, held its first cultural symposium. The group elected Paul Goldfarb to serve as the first president and voted Bluma Novikoff as its first chapter sweetheart. (Paul and Bluma would marry in 1941.) A newly organized Junior Girls' Auxiliary worked with the AZA. Miss Griselda (later known as "Babe") Lyon was the first president, with Josephine Kleiner as vice president, both from Temple Beth Israel.

In April of 1939 Marvin Lowenthal spoke at Talmud Torah. He was the author of the recent book "The Jews of Germany: A Story of 16 Centuries." The topic of his address was "Five Million Jews on a Raft." His count would be short and there would be no raft. Germany invaded Poland on September first and Europe was again at war.

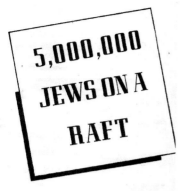

5,000,000 JEWS ON A RAFT

The fate of European Jewry is the most eventful issue in Jewish life today. Hear it discussed by . . .

MARVIN LOWENTHAL

Author of
THE JEWS OF GERMANY
A WORLD PASSED BY
AUTOBIOGRAPHY OF MONTAIGNE
OUR FATHERS THAT BEGAT US
MEMOIRS OF GLUECKEL OF HAMELN

- WORLD TRAVELER
- BRILLIANT LECTURER
- HISTORIAN OF HIS PEOPLE
- "BORN STORY TELLER"

His Appearance Here is Made Possible Through the Cooperation of the

AMERICAN JEWISH JOINT DISTRIBUTION COMMITTEE

TALMUD TORAH SYNAGOGUE
South 4th & I Sts.
Tacoma, Washington
Wed. April 5, 1939
8:15 P. M.

THE WESTERN UNION TELEGRAPH COMPANY

TELEGRAM RECEIVED BY TELEPHONE

Form 3385-B

CHECK AND ACCOUNTING INFORMATION	OFFICE FROM	DATE	FILING TIME
63 NL PR 1989		1938 OCT 14 PM 11 51	

CORDELL HULL

    SECRETARY OF STATE WASHINGTON DC

DEEPLY ALARMED OVER REPORTS ENGLAND PLANNING CONVERT PALESTINE INTO ARAB STATE STOPPING JEWISH IMMIGRATION AND WRECKING GREAT JEWISH CONSTRUCTIVE ENTERPRISE AND DOOMING MULTITUDES OF JEWISH HOMELESS REFUGEES SUCH BETRAYAL JEWISH HOPES VIOLATES BRITISH PLEDGE NOT TO CHANGE STATUS OF PALESTINE WITHOUT CONSULTING AMERICA. JEWRY WILL OWE YOU NEW DEBT OF GRATITUDE IF YOU ACT TO AVERT THREATENED TRAGEDY TO JEWISH LIVES AND HOPES

    MR AND MRS BERNARD WITTENBERG

SIGN	TELEPHONE NUMBER	CLASS OF STATION	SPECIAL INFORMATION
R	2420 NORTH UNION		
	SUBSCRIBER'S NAME		SENDER'S NAME

1938-1939 scrapbook of Mrs. Bernard (Charlotte Endelman) Witenberg, courtesy of Temple Beth El

TALMUD TORAH PREPARES FOR YEAR 5700

Tacoma News Tribune September 13, 1939

Ben Bialostotsky of Seattle chanted High Holy Day services in 1939. High school senior Melvin Novikoff began chanting portions of the reguar Friday evening services. Mrs. Samuel (Goldie Rickles) Cone became president of the Women's Auxiliary and Robert Tone was president of the congregation.

The entire congregation celebrated Rabbi Treiger's fourth anniversary in November of 1939. The anniversary banquets had become an annual tradition, celebrating the beloved rabbi and the congregation's achievements. The banquet programs became treasured keepsakes.

Nearly two dozen men were installed as Talmud Torah board members in February of 1940, representing decades of stability. Incoming President Robert Tone had come to Tacoma as a boy in 1907 with his older Bender cousins. Recently widowed Sam Offerman was vice president. He had lived in Tacoma since 1911 and also served as Workmen's Circle secretary. Clothing merchant Max Meier was treasurer, and Rabbi Treiger's father-in-law, Solomon J. Farber, was financial secretary. The secretary was Samuel Elyn, son of the late Rabbi Meier Elyn. Other board members were Jack R. Bender, Philip Brodsky, Sam Cone, Herman Dobry, Morris J. Friedman, Sam Friedman, Jack Karp, David Klegman, Louis Lamken, W.D. Meier, Harry Rotman, Ben Slotnick, Joseph A. Sussman, Leslie Sussman, Harris Warnick and Bernard J. Witenberg.

Community Lectures

Rabbi Trieger used the power of his pulpit to teach, always inviting the public to attend. During the winter his sermons were a "series of talks exposing libels and unjust defamation of the Jewish people." In January of 1940 he sent telegrams to President Franklin D. Roosevelt and Cyrus Adler, supporting their peace efforts.

> We, as a congregation, stand ready to join with all other men and women of religious groups to further such hopes and plans. May God lengthen your days and strengthen your hands to enable you to carry out the mission which has been placed upon you at this time."

Tacoma News Tribune January 22, 1940

The following month Rabbi Treiger launched yet an even bigger citywide lecture series, held at Talmud Torah on Monday evenings. The optimistic theme "World of Tomorrow" engaged professors from the University of Washington and the College of Puget Sound, plus experts from the fields of education, social work, and a field then called "Mental Hygiene." A session devoted to economics was primary, as the Great Depression was still impacting the community. The Tacoma Public Library created a special bookshelf of related titles.

Educators to Talk on "World Tomorrow" at Talmud Torah

Tacoma News Tribune January 31, 1940

Each program began with musical entertainment, often performed by students from city schools. Perhaps most importantly, the lectures included several speakers with opposing viewpoints. A supportive *Tacoma News Tribune* editorial on February 16 suggested the lectures recalled the "lyceums" and debating societies of old. Rabbi Treiger was cleverly using a technique from the Talmud, the basis of Jewish law, in presenting multiple opinions.

Continuing his anti-defamation theme, Rabbi Treiger gave a series of sermons on great Jewish leaders. He observed the 900th birthday of Rabbi Shlomo Yitzhaki, better known as Rashi. He compared Freud to God and Moses, then moved on to teach about the lives of Hillel and Rabbi Judah, compiler of the Mishnah.

Meanwhile, the Roosevelt administration had been preparing its military. Two months after Germany took over Austria, the federal government took ownership of the Tacoma airfield. Within a month the Federal Works Project Administration applied for a permit to build a suspension bridge across the Tacoma Narrows, essential to connecting the naval yards of Bremerton to Fort Lewis. The Tacoma Narrows Bridge and McChord Field opened in July of 1940, two weeks after five teenagers at Talmud Torah celebrated their confirmation.

Talmud Torah 1940 Confirmation Class
Left to right: Rabbi Treiger, Edith Brodsky, Sylvia Friedman, Beverly Goldfarb, Adelyn Meier and Philip Simon (two days before his bar mitzvah)

In September of 1940 the U.S. began its first peacetime military draft, requiring all men aged twenty-one through forty-five to register for Selective Service. Fort Lewis would again train soldiers, dozens and dozens of them local Jews.

Rabbi Treiger, now well-known in the Puget Sound area, delivered a September New Year radio message over station KVI. Just after the Sukkot shelters came down, so did the new bridge. The Tacoma Narrows Bridge "Galloping

Gertie" collapsed on November 7, 1940, and would not be rebuilt until after the war. Tacoma's mayor Harry P. Cain was among the many dignitaries offering greetings to Rabbi Treiger at his fifth anniversary congregational banquet later in November.

Center Span, Torn by Wind, Falls to Water

Great Narrows Structure, Twisted and Whipped by 40 Mile Gale, Partly Disintegrates; Catastrophe Blamed on Failure of Cables to Move in Unison

Page one Tacoma News Tribune November 8, 1940

During December, as his listeners gave more of their attention to the map of Europe, Rabbi Treiger gave a series of sermons on the cities of Prague, London, Paris, and Salonika. In January of 1941 he discussed Warsaw, the history of the ghetto, and its "recrudescence today." This from a man who didn't graduate from high school until he was 25.

American Way, Topic

Fourth Annual Lecture Series Opens Feb. 10

Tacoma News Tribune January 30, 1941

Talmud Torah's rabbi continued fighting propaganda by his own example as an articulate, educated, and caring Jewish leader. The topic of his fourth annual lecture series was "The American Way in This Troubled World." The *News Tribune* on February 12 noted that "some of the most prominent educational figures in this part of the country have appeared in a series of talks which had been arranged on a non-sectarian basis." The concertmaster of the Tacoma Philharmonic led the musical entertainment in February. One program discussed "hemispheric solidarity," as world events continued to dominate. Admission was offered free to servicemen in uniform.

Rabbi Treiger served as advisor to the members of AZA, who in January of 1941 honored their chapter sweetheart, Miss Josephine Kleiner. They dedicated the proceeds of their spring carnival to sponsoring a Hillel chapter at the University of Washington. In June many of Rabbi Treiger's former students returned for a "reconsecration" service to celebrate his five years as their teacher. (A play on a child's "consecration" on beginning their Hebrew education.)

RECONSECRATION SERVICE FRIDAY

A special reconsecration service conducted by former pupils of the religious and Hebrew schools of Talmud Torah synagogue, South 4th and I streets, will be held Friday at 8:15 p. m. Rabbi B. I. Treiger will welcome the former pupils, many of whom are attending the university. The service, sermonette and chanting of selected portions of the service, will be performed by former pupils.

During the five years of Rabbi Treiger's ministry in Tacoma the following boys and girls have become Bar Mitzvah or been confirmed: Sidney Blechman, Philburn Friedman, Estelle Lamken, Simon Rose, Gerald Meier, Beatrice Sussman, Bernard Friedman, Rhoda Sussman, Melvin Novikoff, Florence Barnett, Roy Slotnick, Jordan Meier, Lorraine Sussman, Walter Etsekson, Jerry Donion, Gerald Goldfarb, Leon Meier, Esther Goldberg, Jerry Spellman, Harold Novikoff, Sylvia Friedman, Adelyn Meier, Edith Brodsky, Beverley Goldfarb, Philip Simon, Myron Donion and Kenneth Lorber who became Bar Mitzvah last week.

Tacoma News Tribune June 6, 1941

Expanding Leadership

Rabbi Treiger was clearly what would today be called a "news junkie." His sermons were often inspired by controversial news articles. During and after services he continued to discuss current events. His congregants learned to look to him to make sense of a world at war.

At Talmud Torah synagogue, South 4th and I streets, Rabbi B. I. Treiger will discuss the modern implications, as well as the traditional interpretation of "The Biblical Story of Creation". Another feature of interest during the synagogue service hour will be a brief resume by the rabbi of Jewish current events and news gleaned from many English, Hebrew and Yiddish periodicals and journals not readily accessible to the general public. Following the services there will be the tea and social hour in the synagogue vestry rooms.

Tacoma News Tribune October 18, 1941

His expanding responsibilities included serving as the local representative of the Jewish Welfare Board. He was also chaplain for all Jewish servicemen in the area. He brought Friday evening speakers from Camp Murray and Fort Lewis. His wife, Lena, served as 1941 president of the Hadassah Joint Council of Tacoma. She was guest of honor at the annual donor luncheon that raised funds for the Youth Aliyah project.

His congregation again supported their men in uniform. Families hosted service members in their homes during High Holy Days. The winter Destiny auxiliary meeting featured a "cigarette shower," collecting packages to distribute at Fort Lewis during the holidays. The event was held on Tuesday evening, December 9, 1941, just as the U.S. declared war on Japan.

Rabbi Treiger's sermon the following week celebrated both the 150th anniversary of the Bill of Rights and the coinciding 2106th anniversary of the Chanukah victory. David Holzman was sworn in as congregational president in December of 1941, with Morris Elyn as vice president, Max Meier treasurer, and Sam Elyn secretary.

On February first of 1942 Rabbi Treiger announced his fifth series of public lectures. The first three programs would look back at the causes of the world crisis. The remaining four optimistically planned for peace and rebuilding Europe after the war.

7 Lectures Announced

Talmud Torah Series to Bring U. of W., C. P. S. Speakers

Announcement is made by Rabbi Baruch I. Treiger of the fifth annual lecture series of Talmud congregation, to begin on Monday evening, Feb. 16 and to continue for seven consecutive Mondays through March 30. These lectures are conducted on a non-sectarian, civic basis. The general theme will be "The World in which We Want to Live."

Tacoma News Tribune February 1, 1942

Over a span of five years Rabbi Treiger organized and directed a total of 38 lectures with sixty four presenters and approximately 350 musicians. Total attendance exceeded 4,000 people, often praised for their high standard of audience participation and interest. The women of the Shul handled ticket sales and distribution.

Mrs. Ben (Freida) Rome was president of the Destiny B'nai B'rith Auxiliary in 1942, with vice president Mrs. Philip (Velma) King. Women of the congregational Auxiliary began knitting and sewing for the Red Cross. Cantor Irving Lindner of New York led the music for several services while he was serving at Fort Lewis as an Army private. Richard Drues and Frank Werbisky both celebrated their bar mitzvahs.

The Tacoma Hadassah Council, with Lena Treiger as president, hosted a Palestine night for the Youth Aliyah project. The guest of honor was Jerusalem native Ittamar Ben Avi. He was noted as the son of Eliezer Ben Yehuda, regarded as the father of the Modern Hebrew language. The same week, Executive Order 9066 called for the relocation and imprisonment of Japanese American citizens, sent locally to Puyallup's mis-named "Camp Harmony."

Purim announcements in 1942 described Haman as the Hitler of ancient Persia. Officers of Talmud Torah distributed Passover supplies and "Matsoth," and families again hosted servicemen. Leon Meier gave the sermon at the May AZA Shabbat, and Mrs. Sam (Goldie) Cone led the congregational Auxiliary mother and daughter Shabbat. At the end of May the newspaper mention of Shavuot services appeared just below a large article about the 50th anniversary of Temple Beth Israel.

On June 19 the students of Talmud Torah's religious school closed their semester by participating in services. At that same service Rabbi Treiger made a crucial announcement.

RABBI TREIGER RESIGNS FROM TALMUD TORAH

Rabbi Baruch I. Treiger announced his resignation as spiritual leader of Talmud Torah congregation at the closing late Sabbath evening services held this weekend. This marks the end of six years of service by Rabbi Treiger.

Tacoma News Tribune June 23, 1942

A Life of Service

The Treigers spent the summer in Orange, New Jersey, near Lena's sister, Ethel (Farber) Slavin. In the fall they took up work in Reno, Nevada. In September of 1943 Reno's Temple Emanu-El celebrated Rabbi Treiger's first anniversary and year of accomplishments. The banquet was strikingly similar to the one held in Tacoma in 1937.

In the fall of 1952 the Treigers moved to Altoona, Pennsylvania, to lead the Agudath Achim Synagogue. Rabbi Treiger died in a New York hospital in 1954 and was buried in Seattle's Bikur Cholim cemetery. His obituary described him as a "pioneer rabbi," known for heading a number of new congregations.

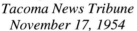

RABBI TREIGER

*Tacoma News Tribune
November 17, 1954*

Lena Farber had been valedictorian of her Stadium High School class. She graduated from the University of Washington and the New York School of Social Work, training in the field of Jewish Social Work. In each city where the Treigers lived Lena served as a staff member of family and child care agencies. In 1955, as Leah Farber Treiger, she was director of field and extension activities for the National Women's League of United Synagogues of America. She remained active in Hadassah, Council of Jewish Women, and B'nai B'rith chapters. Leah married Samuel Schimmel in 1961 and moved to Israel, where she died in 1972.

*Lena Farber c. 1925
Courtesy of the
Farber Family*

Rabbi Treiger's lifelong achievements are even more striking considering his lack of early formal education, as described looking back at this Portland, Oregon, article from 1917.

Lad Who Entered Primary Classes in Portland School Is Forging Ahead.

When three years ago Bert Treiger, then a lad in his teens, came from Russia and knocked at the door of the "Opportunity" room in the Failing school, it was opened to him. Entering, he accepted the spirit of the room, found his seat in the primary class and with the opportunity as incentive completed the grammar grade in two years.

Compelled to Aid Family.

Compelled to give the family assistance, even though a boy, by working in his father's shop in Volenea, Russia, the lad had for his schooling but a few terms in a Hebrew school. With natural aptitude, however, he learned quickly and was able to become a monitor in the instruction of Jewish children in the reading of the scriptures.

Naturally Bert is elated over his advance, but has not allowed his pride to dull his college ambition.

"I am surely going to college," he said. "My only regret is that we didn't come to America sooner, so I could have been farther ahead now. I must work just that much harder to catch up. When I finish high school I mean to work my way through college. I cannot receive assistance from my parents, who are poor, but I know I will succeed. Just now I have some students to teach in Hebrew and that helps, even though I have to give my own study hours in doing it. •

Oregon Daily Journal Sunday March 11, 1917

66

Chapter Nine: Soldiering On

In 1942 President Franklin D. Roosevelt was in the third of his four terms, re-elected by a nation unready to change leaders during a time of crisis. Talmud Torah's next rabbi would lead his congregation through the duration of the war. Almost.

Rabbi Julius DeKoven

Named To Pulpit Here

Rabbi DeKoven Will Fill Post at Talmud Torah

Rabbi Julius L. DeKoven, a graduate of the Hebrew Theological seminary at Chicago, has been called to fill the pulpit of the Talmud Torah congregation, coming here after serving his first pulpit in Cedar Rapids, Iowa.

Tacoma News Tribune September 12, 1942

At first glance Rabbi Julius DeKoven was similar to Rabbi Treiger in several ways. Both were born in Russia and came to the U.S. as young boys. Both were able to attend school, graduate from college, and become ordained as rabbis despite their parents' poverty. Both married intelligent young women who had formal training in social work. And both couples would be childless.

The future rabbi emigrated with his family in 1920 as six-year-old Yossel Duchowna. He grew up in Chicago and graduated from Lewis Institute in 1937 as Julius Lewis DeKoven. He married Miriam Astrachan, daughter of Rabbi Joseph Astrachan, in Chicago in June of 1940. After his seminary graduation Rabbi DeKoven held one-year positions in Cheyenne, Wyoming, and Cedar Rapids, Iowa.

Also like Rabbi Treiger, during his time in Tacoma he was active in the Jewish Welfare Board and was president of the Zionist District of Tacoma. But it would be two decades before another rabbi would capture the hearts of Tacoma's Jewish community as Rabbi Treiger had. Rabbi DeKoven's nearly three years in Tacoma were relatively quiet, with no active public lecture series or engaging youth programs. Then again, the world was still at war.

RABBI JULIUS DEKOVEN

Jewish Transcript September 21, 1942

Rabbi DeKoven next led a congregation in Austin, Texas, for several years, taking the first name Joel. He and Miriam worked in Los Angeles during the Fifties and in Sherman Oaks during the Sixties. In 1966 Rabbi DeKoven formed Temple Beth Daiah, known as the House of Knowledge. He took the unique approach of constructing his own building and charging his members admission, avoiding the frustrations of answering to a full board of directors. His congregation donated a Torah to a kibbutz in Israel in 1973 in memory of murdered Israeli athletes.

He became a passionate yoga instructor and encouraged movement during services. His 1974 book "The Rabbi Stands on His Head" discussed the relationships between yoga and Judaism, calling yoga "a form of prayer wherein man can discover his real self." In 1979 Rabbi DeKoven was murdered in his Sherman Oaks home, less than a year after the death of his wife and shortly before his sixty-fifth birthday.

Wartime Economies

The women of Talmud Torah had consistently supported their community through rummage sales and fundraising events. That only increased during the war. In 1943 the combined B'nai B'rith groups collected furniture and games to furnish a reception room for men at Fort Lewis. As the war continued the Tacoma Council of Jewish Women joined in emergency clothing drives for liberated populations in Europe. Everyone planted Victory gardens.

Greater relief was possible through cash donations from successful businessmen. The vast majority of Tacoma's early Jewish population, especially the extended Friedman family, had operated or worked in clothing stores. Some, like Philip Brodsky, had adapted to the military presence by selling and tailoring uniforms.

As Tacoma's population grew, so did the need for home furnishings. While many firms promoted the name of the proprietor, Tacoma's Jewish-owned furniture stores often had geographic names.

- American Furniture, Louis Lamken
- American Furniture, Samuel Wasserman
- Oregon Furniture, Harry Rotman
- Portland Furniture, David Klegman
- Puget Sound Furniture, Ben Slotnick
- Tacoma Furniture, Thomas Goldfarb
- Washington Furniture, Charles Sussman
- Western Furniture, Samuel Brotman

In the Twenties Henry Winkleman's children had operated a burlap bag factory, making a packaging staple of the time. As technology and machinery evolved, more Jews engaged in manufacturing in Tacoma.

- Ideal Dress Manufacturing, Sam Cone and Jack Karp (clothing)
- Puget Sound Manufacturing, Harris Warnick (plywood and interiors)
- Rome Concrete Products, Ben and Harold Rome (concrete blocks)
- Witenberg Manufacturing, Bernard J. and S.N. Witenberg (work gloves)

However, one of the greatest machinery developments to affect Tacoma's population was the evolution of the automobile. In the Teens "chauffeurs" operated the "machines." In the Twenties individual purchases were proudly noted in the expanding automobile sections of the daily newspapers. In the Thirties families "motored" to vacation destinations. Talmud Torah's change from Orthodox to Conservative meant that families could drive to Shabbat services. Yet in the Forties factories suddenly slowed automobile production, leading to a surge in demand for used cars and auto parts. Many of Tacoma's Jewish merchants were in the thick of the changing markets.

- Herman & Leo Dobry, Standard Auto Parts
- Ben Etsekson, Ben's Auto Wrecking
- Mickey Kaplan, West Coast Investment
- Max LeBid, Tacoma Auto Wrecking
- Ben & Harry Richlen, Richlen Auto Parts

Perhaps even more astonishing was the evolution of the scrap metal industry. "Junk Pickers" transitioned within just one generation to become international metal brokers. During the Forties they donated tons of scrap metal to the war effort.

- Arthur and son Floyd Lamken
- Joseph Simon and sons
- Tacoma Junk, Charles and J.A. Sussman
- Frank Sussman
- Alaska Iron and Metal, Kopel Weinstone and sons

Again Tacoma's wartime economy benefited from the nearby military installations and port activities. Tacoma's Jewish population continued its staunch synagogue support. In 1944 members of Talmud Torah celebrated the burning of a second mortgage, complete with another banquet, and yet another anniversary booklet was indebted to the steadfast Mrs. Harry (Lena) Rotman.

Talmud Torah to Burn Mortgage

Tacoma News Tribune March 11, 1944

Changing Demographics

The Forties also brought changing demographics, as patriarchs passed away and younger generations dispersed. Most Jewish families had only two or three children. Talmud Torah officers in 1943 were Philip Brodsky president, Ben Slotnick vice president, Robert Grenley secretary, and Arthur Meier treasurer. Robert Warnick was president in 1944 when five students were confirmed.

1944 Confirmation Class (Left to right)
Rabbi Julius DeKoven, Richard Drues, Joanne Sussman, David Slotnick, Frank Werbisky, and Alvin Tone
Tacoma Public Library Richards A17644-6

Rabbi DeKoven helped several young men prepare for their bar mitzvahs.
- February 1943, Alvin Tone
- March 1944, Edward Maurice Drues
- March 1944, Alan Warnick
- May 1945, Jack Warnick

The Jewish community also began transitioning from the merchant class to the professional. Graduates of the University of Washington returned to Tacoma to practice law. Talmud Torah welcomed medical doctors Drues, Grenley, and Maier; joining Temple Beth Israel's doctors Hurst and Baskin. These men marked the beginning of decades of Jewish medical practitioners in Tacoma, eventually creating a substantial demographic.

Yet rising antisemitism forced Cecil Friedman to move to Buffalo to find work after earning his Ph.D. in organic chemistry at U.W. Maier Finkelstein applied to medical school as Haskel Maier, Philip Greenberg as Grenley, and Cecil Herskovitz as Hurst. After decades of immigrants changing to American names, American Jews altered their names to mask their Jewish identities. This opportunity often came when moving to a different city. Examples from just one family include:
- Cohen - Cowan
- Goldfarb – Grayson
- Polisky - Pollard
- Wheinstone/Weinstone – Winston

Military Partnerships

Rabbi DeKoven corresponded with the eastern office of the JWB to ensure that Passover supplies were available to Jewish servicemen stationed throughout the Pacific Northwest. During 1943 and 1944 Jewish families again hosted servicemen in their homes during High Holy Days. Talmud Torah participated in multiple War Bond drives, encouraging members to make their purchases through the synagogue.

Most name changes come about because of marriage, and some marriages came about because of the USO-JWB. (United Service Organizations and Jewish Welfare Board.) Some of the most popular activities were likely the monthly USO dances held at Talmud Torah. Those who attended could enjoy food, music and dancing, and enter to win a free telephone call home.

A few of the many local Jewish wartime military marriages were:
Margaret Friedman & Joseph Golden, Feb '42
Rhoda Sussman & Milton Lewis, Aug '43
Fannie Rose & Sam H. Rubin, Nov '43
Toby Sohn & Cpl. Shelton M. Cohn, Feb '44
Lorraine Sussman & Karl Braverman, Aug '44
Ethel Goldberg & Albert Strauss, Nov '44
Favius Witenberg & Lillian Smiley, June '45
Simon Rose & Florence Ostrow, Feb '46

ON THE BEAM

Volume 2, No. 5   Tacoma, Washington

USO—JWB   OCTOBER, 1943   13TH & FAWCETT

WAIT! TAKE A SECOND GLANCE BEFORE YOU THROW THIS AWAY! Now, do you see why we cautioned you? Of course! This is your USO-JWB "ON THE BEAM" coming to you in a slightly different style this month, due to lack of time ('cause of Holidays) and lack of news ('cause so many of our friends are away!) on maneuvers.

First and foremost, *L'Shona Tova Tikosevu* greetings from all of the "On The Beam" staff, as well as your JWB representatives. We certainly hope you all have a most pleasant holiday and we extend to every soldier in the Fort Lewis Area and to his beloved one our best wishes for a New Year of Life, Health and Happiness. Speaking of that subject, reminds me that perhaps you'd like to have a reminder of the schedule of services: So for your convenience, here 'tis!

TACOMA

Talmud Torah Synagogue	ROSH HASHONAH EVE	Sept. 29	7:45 P.M.
(Conservative-Orthodox)	ROSH HASHONAH FIRST DAY	Sept. 30, 8:15 A.M.—8:00 P.M.	
South Fourth and I Streets	ROSH HASHONAH SECOND DAY	Oct. 1 8:15 A.M.—8:00 P.M.	
Rabbi Julius DeKoven	YOM KIPPUR EVE	Oct. 8	7:15 P.M.
	YOM KIPPUR DAY	Oct. 9	8:45 A.M.

Temple Beth Israel	ROSH HASHONAH EVE	Sept. 29	8:00 P.M.
(Reform)	ROSH HASHONAH FIRST DAY	Sept. 30	10:00 A.M
North Fourth and J Streets	YOM KIPPUR EVE	Oct. 8	8:00 P.M.
Rabbi Arthur Zuckerman	YOM KIPPUR DAY	Oct. 9	10:00 A.M.

FORT LEWIS

Main Post Chapel	ROSH HASHONAH EVE	Sept. 29	7:30 P.M.
Chaplain Martin M. Weitz	ROSH HASHONAH FIRST DAY	Sept. 30	10:00 A.M.
	ROSH HASHONAH SECOND DAY	Oct. 1	7:30 P.M.
	YOM KIPPUR EVE	Oct. 8	7:30 P.M.
	YOM KIPPUR DAY	Oct. 9	10:00 A.M.

SUMPIN' SPECIAL aren't they? Those regular evening Socials sponsored by the Tacoma Council of Jewish Women each week at the Temple Beth Israel, No. 4th and J Streets, Tacoma, are rapidly spreading in popularity as the word gets around of the super scrumptious spreads the women have been preparing each week for those buffet suppers. The affair is from 5-8 p. m. with supper served about 6 p.m. And from past indications, it seems wise to get there early—'cause everything is SO-O-O good that seconds and thirds are usually in order and late comers may lose out! Dancing, Shmoosing, just plain fun of the kind you wish completes the order of the day. Our scouts tell us it's a regular affair you can't afford to miss! We take off our hats to the grand job and fine cooperation being shown by this group of women and to the community for making these affairs possible.

UNTIL NEXT MONTH and the return of our regular "ON THE BEAM", we wish you once again a very happy New Year filled with the advent of Victory and Peace and the return to your homes, one and all. May this time next year find each and every one in the midst of family and friends.

See you next month,

ON THE BEAM STAFF

P S.—FLASH—A USO-JWB Dance will be scheduled the latter part of October when the men return from the Oregon Maneuvers. This affair will be held at Talmud Torah with plenty of Seattle girls. We shall get the exact date and other information on this affair to you when plans are completed.

October 1943 newsletter from Jewish Welfare Board correspondence files

The war also brought good music to Tacoma. Unable to perform in Europe, some noted singers toured the U.S. instead. Others made the Pacific Northwest their home. And some sang at Talmud Torah while stationed at Fort Lewis.

Cantor Irving Lindner served in the U.S. Army from May of 1941 to October of 1945. He sang at Talmud Torah services in February of 1942 before going overseas. On his return he sang again in October of 1944.

Radio performer and Russian dramatic tenor "King Niesen" performed coast to coast during the 1940s. Many of his concerts were benefits for Jewish refugee children. Born Max Nissenman in Lublin in 1893, King died in Los Angeles in 1980. Like many performers, his press photo never aged.

Press photo of King Niesen

As a child Maurice Dubin was dubbed the "next Caruso," and the "Young Russian Tenor." After a promising career start in London, Dubin abandoned his wife and two children to come to the U.S. with his accompanist, Rosie. They performed as the Dubin Duo in Pennsylvania in the late '20s, then came to the West Coast. In Portland and Seattle he opened opera schools to search for young talent, then presented recital programs with himself as the star. Dubin led services in Portland's Neveh Zedek in 1936, and his "Opera Company" performed at Talmud Torah in January of 1940. He was a soloist at Yom Kippur in 1943 and performed again in Tacoma in November of 1948 in a recital with his students. He and Rosie lived for a decade in a cottage on the far side of Gig Harbor before their deaths in 1950.

Press photo of Maurice Dubin as Moses Buried in Home of Peace Cemetery, Lakewood

The Bitter End

The war ground toward its bitter end. In December of 1944, as the Allies suffered incredible losses at the Battle of the Bulge, Talmud Torah's children's Chanukah program went on. Their parents must have appreciated being together.

eight days consecutively.
Young people participating in the program include: Clarissa Robinson, vocal soloist; Joanne Sussman, recitation; Beverly and Judy Dobry, Edward and Joanne Drues, Louis Melvin and Phillis Epstein, Charles Goldberg, Stessie and Marcia Rome, Elliott Rosenthal, Norman and Shirley Simon, Billy Tone and Frank Werbisky.

Tacoma News Tribune December 16, 1944

Jack Warnick celebrated his bar mitzvah in May of 1945, just weeks after Hitler's suicide and days after Germany's surrender. The U.S. dropped atom bombs on Japan in August. The war officially ended on September 2, 1945, the same day Talmud Torah announced a change in leadership. Talmud Torah's members would begin the Jewish New Year of 5706 on September eighth by welcoming a new rabbi.

Rabbi Solomon Herbst

NEW RABBI TO OCCUPY PULPIT

Tacoma News Tribune September 8, 1945

Unlike churches that might be assigned clergy by a denominational organization, Jewish congregations hire their own rabbis and staff. Often rabbis start work in September, in keeping with the Hebrew calendar. After the Rosh Hashanah and Yom Kippur sermons, formal installation follows in November. Sometimes an interim rabbi is hired just for High Holy Day services.

In the fall of 1945, as the hearts and minds of Tacoma's Jewish community were turned toward Germany, Talmud Torah welcomed a German refugee to the bima, or pulpit.

DR. SOLOMON HERBST
La Crosse (WI) Tribune May 18, 1941

Rabbi Solomon Herbst fled Germany in 1938, arriving in the U.S. in August. His entry on the ship's passenger list, under the column of Country of Citizenship, was marked *"without."*

He was just 26 and had left his father behind in Düsseldorf. Rabbi Herbst signed his documents for naturalization six days before Kristallnacht. He began his term in Tacoma just one week after the official end of the war. He was likely hired only for the Holy Days, as there were no further public mentions of him in Tacoma.

Understandably, Rabbi Herbst's sermons often struggled with the subject of forgiveness. In 1947 he wrote a Yom Kippur editorial for Milwaukee's "Wisconsin Jewish Chronicle."

> "We had hoped for an open door in Palestine and a destruction of barbed wire fences around a decimated European Jewry... It is not for us to ask for forgiveness... Let the rest of the world take stock of its spiritual failings on these Holy Days - the Jewish world, this year, needs no such catharsis."

Wisconsin Jewish Chronicle, September 12, 1947

Rabbi Herbst would see much of his new homeland, lecturing and presenting radio broadcasts while working in congregations all across the continent.

- 1940 Martinsburg, West Virginia
- 1941 La Crosse, Wisconsin
- 1943 Chicago, Illinois
- 1944 Glendale, California
- 1945 San Bernardino, California (temp)
- 1945 Tacoma, Washington (temp)
- 1946 Wausau, Wisconsin
- 1948 East Liverpool, Ohio
- 1951 Goldsboro, North Carolina
- 1955 Pine Bluff, Arkansas
- 1957 Philadelphia, Pennsylvania
- 1961 Nyack, New York
- 1963 Easton, Maryland
- 1968 Nassau, New York
- 1968 Belleville, New Jersey
- 1969 Saginaw, Michigan
- 1970 Jersey City, New Jersey

At the time of his death in 2007 Rabbi Herbst lived in West Babylon, New York.

Roll of Honor

The following list honors the known veterans from Tacoma's Jewish community who served during the Second World War. It includes many of the veterans buried in Tacoma's Home of Peace Cemetery regardless of temple or synagogue affiliation, a distinction disregarded by war. This list is likely far from complete.

Harold Adler
Lucille (Poole) Aqua
Warren Barde
Herbert Belmonte
Albert Benezra
Kurt Blau
Sidney Blechman
Mike Block
Claire Boonov
Julia Boonov
Jack Brady
Jess Brown
Karl Braverman
Herbert Clayman
Abe Coleman
Samuel Coleman (MIA 1944)
Alex Bernard Cohn
Shelton M. Cohn
Leon S. Diamond
Jerry Donion
Myron L. Donion
Morris Donion (also WWI)
Samuel Elyn
Walter Etsekson
Abraham Allen Farber
Jack Farber
Kenneth Farber
Edward Feldman
Mac Fingeroot
Myron Freyd
Abedeaux Friedman

Bernard Friedman
Charles Friedman Pelin
Edwin J. Friedman
Leonard Friedman
Philburn Friedman
Philip B. Friedman
Siegfried Friedman
Allen Goldberg
Paul Goldfarb
Michael Green (also WWI)
William Green
Arthur Greenblat
Ralph Greenblat
Jay Grenley
Philip Grenley
Arthur H. Hart
Kenneth Heiman
Morris Jaffe
Max Karsh
Herman Kleiner
Norman Kleinman
Kenneth Lorber
Victor Lyon
Gerald Meier
Harry Nemetz
Harold Novikoff
Melvin Novikoff
Edward Olswang
Abram Plotkin
Boris Portnoy
George Posner

Arthur Raphalowitz
Irving Reibman
Phillip Reibman
Walter Remak
Charles Robinson
Samuel Robinson
Simon Rose
Rabbi Bernard Rosenberg
Robert Rozen
Sam H. Rubin
Ben Schwartz
Aben Shallit
Harry Shapeero
Bernice Sigel
David Sigel (also WWI)
Stanley "Buddy" Sigel
Philip Simon
Roy Slotnick
Jack Slotnik
Arthur Sohn
Jerry Spellman
David Spigal
Philip Sussman
Jack Thompson
Edward Turenne (also Korea)
Robert F. Warnick
Wray S. Warnick
Leonard L. Wasserman
Jay Wax
Harry Weston
Favius Witenberg

In Memorium

In 1941 Berdie and John Coleman sent two sons to war. Only one came home.

Samuel Edward Coleman was born in Missouri on May 30, 1916, and grew up in Kansas. He started high school in Wichita, but graduated from Tacoma's Stadium High School. Sam was an outstanding track athlete and in 1932 represented Stadium as the city's mile champion. At the University of Washington he excelled in two-mile events.

Sam enlisted in the Naval Air Corps and took flight training at Pensacola, Florida. He married Sarah Atwood in Wenatchee on August 11, 1942, and the couple had a son, Paul. Sam first saw air combat in the Aleutians, earning a Flying Cross and a Gold Star award. Then he was sent to the Marshall Islands. He was the pilot of a plane with eleven people aboard that did not return from a routine search patrol on January 13, 1944. His wife and parents were informed on February 29, 1944, that he was declared Missing in Action. His body was never found.

(Right) Tacoma News Tribune February 29, 1944

(Below) National Jewish Welfare Board inquiry card

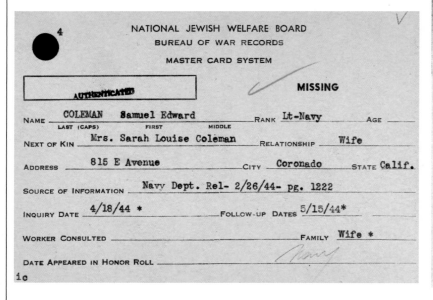

Missing —Lt. Samuel Edward Coleman, U. S. N. R., is missing, following action in the performance of his duty in the service of his country, his parents, Mr. and Mrs. John N. Coleman, 2110 North Steele street, have been notified by Rear Admiral Randall Jacobs. A graduate of Stadium high school, Lt. Coleman attended the University of Washington and joined the navy three years ago. He was awarded the Flying Cross and a gold star for exploits in the air in the Aleutian engagements. Lt. Coleman was prominent in athletics at Stadium and the university, his specialty being the two mile run. His brother, Abe, is in the air force, at present at Fresno, Calif., after serving 30 months in Alaska.

Chapter Ten: Sinai Temple

Prayers for Palestine

Allied forces moved across Europe in the summer of 1945, liberating and rescuing death camp prisoners. Millions of Jews became Displaced Persons. The humanitarian crisis was beyond belief. Jews around the world gathered to pray for a Jewish homeland in Palestine, the name adopted for the region mandated to Great Britain by the League of Nations after the First World War. Yet how that area would be shared or divided among Jews and Arabs is still in contention 75 years later.

Appealing For Jewish Rights

Appeal for full recognition of Jewish rights to Palestine is being made locally Thursday, at 8 p. m., at a meeting at Talmud Torah congregation, when prayers will be said asking for the opening of the gates of Palestine to homeless Jews all over the world. The Jewish people of this city, as well as all over America, recognize that the liberation of Jews from near extinction by Hitler has not solved the problem of where these people can find homes to begin life anew.

Tacoma News Tribune October 5, 1945

Name Change to Sinai Temple

In October of 1945 Tacoma's traditional Jews honored the site of the revelation of the Torah, Mount Sinai, by changing their congregation's name. Three weeks after the Palestine prayer meeting, the newspaper social mention for the Women's Auxiliary said the supper would be at **Sinai Temple**. A year later a High Holy Day article would confirm that Sinai Temple was formerly Talmud Torah. Many later mistakenly used the names Sinai Temple and Temple Sinai interchangeably. Shul members still called it the Shul, or just Sinai.

In February of 1946 Tacoma's annual Hadassah donor luncheon featured Mrs. Gershon Agronsky, wife of the editor of the *Palestine Post*. Mrs. Jay (Bertha) Grenley chaired the event and Mrs. Isadore (Bess) Drues was president of the chapter.

USO efforts turned toward supporting returning servicemen. Among those veterans was Temple Beth Israel's Rabbi Bernard Rosenberg. Purim and Passover programs included dances and meals for military men.

Rabbi Leo Trepp

In the fall of 1946 the members of Sinai Temple again attended Rosh Hashanah services led by a new rabbi. Again they welcomed a German refugee, educated in prominent universities in Germany.

DR. LEO TREPP TAKING OVER SINAI PULPIT

DR. LEO TREPP

Tacoma News Tribune September 26, 1946

Rabbi Leo Trepp was born in Mainz in 1913, earned his doctorate in 1935, and was ordained in 1936. In 1938 he was leading more than a dozen congregations in Oldenburg when he was arrested during Kristallnacht. He later said that his imprisonment in the Sachsenhausen concentration camp deepened his faith and sense of purpose. He also credited his wife, Miriam, with his rescue, secured through the Chief Rabbi of Great Britain. The couple fled to London and after a year were able to come to Boston.

By the time that Rabbi Trepp came to Tacoma he had graduated from Harvard with honors and led a congregation in Greenfield, Massachusetts. Much like Rabbi Treiger, he would build cultural and youth programs and establish a strong relationship with the Tacoma community and press.

Renewed Energy

After Rabbi Trepp addressed 45 members of the Women's Auxiliary group in October, they voted to add a cultural program to their activities and to take an active part in useful community affairs. They officially affiliated with the national Conservative movement, United Synagogues of America, as a Sisterhood.

The men did the same, forming a Brotherhood group. Founding officers were president Leslie Sussman, vice president Philip Brodsky, secretary William Sherman, and treasurer David Klegman. The Brotherhood sponsored guest speakers and offered modern dancing classes on Thursday evenings.

Sinai Temple officers installed in November of 1946 included president Dr. Haskel Maier, first vice president Robert Grenley, second vice president W.D. Meier, Irving Burian secretary, and Ben Slotnick treasurer. Additional board trustees were Philip Brodsky, Bernard Brotman, Herman Dobry, Samuel Fingold, Louis Lamken, and Leslie Sussman.

SINAI TEMPLE ELECTS; GROUP PLANS ACTIVITY

Tacoma News Tribune October 21, 1946

Rabbi Trepp's board announcement to the press noted that the Temple offered Hebrew school on weekdays, Sunday school, and a full program of adult and young adult activities. He also worked to establish a lending library.

Tacoma's chapter of the Council of Jewish Women partnered with the Travelers' Aid Society in meeting incoming refugees dockside. Mrs. Bernard J. (Charlotte) Witenberg joined one group as a translator.

The Tacoma chapter of Hadassah held its first Hadassah Shabbat service at Sinai Temple, with special readings prepared by Rabbi Trepp. Participating officers included chapter president Mrs. Kenneth (Alice) Farber, and Mrs. Lester Baskin, B. Brotman, and H. Mandles.

Rabbi Trepp was an accomplished writer and speaker. He immediately began addressing community organizations, holding his audiences spellbound. He used the opportunities to "urge every individual in the United States to use his full strength, energy and devotion to defeat the legacy of hate that Hitler's regime bequeathed the world."

Nazi Ideas Still Alive

Probably the most amazing chronicle of stark terror the Young Men's Business club has ever heard was delivered at luncheon Friday by Dr. Leo Trepp of Sinai temple in a simply worded address whose every forceful syllable led to the one blunt question: "Has Hitler Won the War?"

Tacoma News Tribune December 16, 1946

The December 1946 dinner honoring Rabbi and Mrs. Trepp included welcoming the *fourteen* new families who had joined in the past two months. Rabbi and Mrs. Trepp held an evening open house at their home on New Year's Day, 1947.

Sisterhood officers elected in the spring of 1947 were Mrs. Sam (Goldie) Cone president, Mrs. Floyd (Rose) Lamken and Mrs. Farber vice presidents, Mrs. Robert (Sarah) Tone treasurer, and Mrs. Ben (Freida) Rome secretary.

Tacoma's B'nai B'rith chapter No. 741 met at Sinai Temple every other Tuesday. Jerome Grenley was elected president in January of 1947. Bernard Brotman was vice president, with Wilbur Meier as second vice president, Herman Kleiner secretary, and Jack Fields treasurer. The group sponsored an ambitious community Brotherhood Rally on March fourth at the Tacoma Armory, in conjunction with the USO and other religious and civic organizations. The free program was reminiscent of the Treiger lectures, with welcomes from college presidents and Mayor Angelo Fawcett, remarks from church leaders, and music by the Lincoln High School choir and band. The main speaker was Orson Welles, who took time from his "busy radio and screen schedule to fly north without pay to take part in the rally."

Orson Welles in Tacoma 1947
Courtesy of Tacoma Public Library HBS-022

In stark contrast to the previous few years, Sinai Temple hosted activities nearly every day of the week. In addition to scheduled services and classes, events on the calendar in the weeks before Passover in 1947 included:

- Tuesday February 25, 1:30 p.m., Hadassah tea and JNF program
- Tuesday, February 25, 1 p.m., funeral of Henry Bell at Chevra Kadisha Cemetery
- Sunday March 2, wedding of Ann Brown and Irving Gussman in the Trepp home
- Tuesday March 4, 8 p.m., Brotherhood Rally at Tacoma Armory
- Wednesday and Thursday March 5 and 6, Purim services at 8 p.m.
- Wednesday March 12, 8 p.m., reactivation meeting of Tacoma Zionist district
- Thursday March 13 8:30 p.m., B'nai B'rith chapter, guests from Bremerton lodge
- Saturday March 15, 9 p.m., Purim dance and cabaret, skit by Men's club

In April Tacoma's Jewish community was shocked to learn of the deaths of Fanny and Irving Burian, drowned when their bus plunged into the Duwamish River. After fleeing Vienna in 1938 they had operated the Marvel Dress shop in Tacoma. At the time of their deaths Irving was secretary of Sinai Temple.

That same month Rabbi Trepp spoke at a conference of the United Synagogues of America, held at Seattle's Herzl congregation.

The "Palestinian Problem" continued to gain headlines, as Great Britain deferred the situation to the United Nations. Rabbi Trepp spent the summer of 1947 on a lecture tour for the Zionist Organization of America. Before he left he officiated at the funeral of Nathan Friedman. On his return in September he did the same for the late Morris J. Friedman.

Rosh Hashanah and Yom Kippur services were enhanced by the singing of a voice teacher and opera singer who performed as Sebastian Burnetti. In Tacoma he was also Samuel Burnett, brother of jewelers Morris and Louis. Morris Burnett's wife was Rebecca Grinspan. Four of the five Grinspan siblings had Burnett spouses.

S. BURNETTI

Tacoma News Tribune September 19, 1947

In October and November Rabbi Trepp publicly supported the majority report of the United Nations' special Palestine committee. He offered to speak to any group on the topic of dividing Palestine. The Hadassah Sabbath welcomed incoming officers Mrs. Bernard (Pearl) Brotman and Mrs. Irving (Ann) Gussman. Newlywed Irving Gussman was president of the Tacoma Zionist district and spoke at a special Thanksgiving service supporting the establishment of a Jewish state. Monday night study courses took place in the comfort of private homes, with a variety of participating hosts.

1948 Birth of Israel

Rabbi Trepp began 1948 by reviewing some of his favorite books of the previous year. He also worked successfully to develop a U.W. summer psychiatric training course for clergy, similar to courses he had taken at Harvard. The following month he lectured at the University of Oregon.

In 1948 the Sinai Sisterhood was led by Goldie Jean Dobry, Edith Jaffe, Mrs. Emanuel Levin, Freida Rome, Julie Posner, and Bea Martin. Youth leaders Beverly Dobry, Lois Sussman, Lewis Epstein and Charles Goldberg participated in "Freedom Train" services.

The annual Hadassah donor luncheon in March took place in the new Wedgewood room of the Winthrop Hotel. Nearly 200 women heard a surprise visitor filling in for his wife. Rabbi David deSola Pool spoke as a frequent traveler to Palestine. The following month the members of Sinai Temple joined Jews around the nation in renewed prayers for Palestine, protesting changing U.S. policy. Three weeks later the Hadassah chapter gathered to mourn the deaths of Hadassah workers and to hear from Seattle's Bailey Neider, recently returned from fighting with the Haganah forces.

TO OFFER PRAYER FOR PALESTINE

Tacoma News Tribune April 8, 1948

The events unfolding in Palestine were again parallel to Jewish activities in Tacoma. The vibrant congregation celebrated its 40th anniversary in May, just as the Tel Aviv proclamation announced the new independent state of Israel, followed by the Arab League's declaration of war. (See following page.) President Harry Truman recognized the new nation just as Tacoma's Hadassah chapter elected new officers and hosted a regional conference. And Leo Dobry took his racing car, "The City of Tacoma," to the Indianapolis 500.

Rabbi Trepp kept congregants informed, delivering sermons on "Fighters in Israel," and "Israel Sings." Beverly Dobry and Lois Gussman were confirmed as Jerusalem was in a state of emergency, rocked by Arab artillery.

1948 Sinai Temple Confirmation
(Left to right) Lois Gussman, Rabbi Leo Trepp,
Beverly Dobry, courtesy of Temple Beth El

Just weeks before the last British soldier left Palestine, Temple Beth Israel's former rabbi, Montague N.A. Cohen, left Tacoma to live in Victoria, British Columbia. He had earlier debated against Rabbi Trepp on the "Palestine Triangle," taking the position that Jews represented a religion, not a race or nation, and could live anywhere peacefully.

Rabbi Trepp's growing recognition as a speaker unfortunately drew him away from Tacoma. He left in September to lead Temple Beth El in Berkeley, California. He continued lecturing on the college level and later led congregations in Napa and Santa Rosa. Miriam taught elementary school for twenty-five years.

Rabbi Trepp devoted the remainder of his life to reconciliation with post-war Germany, often working and speaking there. At the time of his death in 2010 he was the last living pre-Holocaust German rabbi. After his death his second wife, Gunda, compiled his notes and published his autobiography, "The Last Rabbi." He was the subject of a documentary by the same title.

New Nation of Israel Proclaimed

Jews Form National State

British Flag Lowered in Jerusalem After 25 Years; Arabs Declare State of War

By Associated Press
The state of Israel, first Hebrew nation in 2,000 years, was born today in a Jewish declaration of independence asserting the "historic right" of the Jews of Palestine to reconstitute their national home.

Tacoma News Tribune May 15, 1948

Jerusalem Battle At Climax

Decision Due Soon in Fight for City; State of Emergency Declared in Israel

By Associated Press
The battle for Jerusalem roared on today. A Jewish communique said the Arabs were shelling the Hebrew university and the Hadassah hospital, strongpoints held by the army of Israel.

Arabs said they expected a decision today or tomorrow over Jewish fighters, estimated at 8,000 in the violent continuing battle for the Holy City.

The Jewish army said it had captured Mount Zion and broken through the nearby Zion gate and raised the month-long siege of 1,700 Jews in the old walled city.

Tacoma News Tribune May 21, 1948

In November six Jewish organizations in Tacoma united to celebrate the first six months of Israel's accomplishments, through music, dance, and film. The sponsoring organizations included the Council of Jewish Women, Temple Beth Israel Sisterhood, Hadassah, B'nai B'rith, Sinai Temple, and the Tacoma Zionist organization.

Rabbi Trepp's position was not immediately filled. Rabbi Treiger returned for the funeral of his mother-in-law, Goldie Farber. Seattle's Rabbi Horowitz led young Charles Goldberg in his December bar mitzvah.

Passover 1949

As the emerging nation of Israel was fighting on four fronts in 1949, Tacoma's Jewish women were also active on four fronts. The Hadassah chapter's February millinery fashion show was titled "Talking through Your Hat." Tacoma's Council of Jewish Women set up one of many Red Cross donation booths across the city. A Hadassah youth forum included Joanne Sussman, Richard Drues, and Daryl Brotman. Sinai Sisterhood sponsored several square dancing parties.

Tacoma Busy Compiling Its Quake Losses

Lowell Boy Met Death In Line of Duty

Tacoma News Tribune April 15, 1949

Tacoma's 1949 Passover was scarred by the death of young Lowell Elementary student Marvin Klegman, grandson of Sinai Temple's David and Helen Klegman. Marvin was killed by debris falling from the school during the April 13 earthquake.

In contrast to the Tacoma Passover tragedy, a week earlier the nation of Israel had signed an armistice with Trans-Jordan, ending the war for the time being. Jews observed Passover actually in Jerusalem, not just praying for "next year in Jerusalem." That fall Mrs. Kenneth (Alice) Farber led the Hadassah chapter, supported by Mesdames Cohen, Lamken, Goldfarb, and Posner.

1949 Passover to See Jews' Dream Fulfilled

JERUSALEM, April 9.—Æ—For Jews all over the world, passover this year has a special poignant meaning.

For 2,000 years the theme of their passover prayer has been, "Next year in Jerusalem." This has symbolized for centuries the Jewish dream of returning to Palestine.

Now, for the first time, "next year" has become "this year." For passover, 1949, marks the first year since the days of Moses that Jews in large numbers are going to Israel, to their own nation, to be their own masters.

Tacoma News Tribune April 10, 1949

As one war ended, another began. North Korea invaded South Korea in June and the US would provide 90 percent of UN support over the next three years. Several young men from Sinai Temple served, including Alvin Tone and Gabriel "Gabe" Touriel.

1950 brought another Hadassah donor luncheon and more Sisterhood rummage sales. Clothier Hy Mandles and his longtime salesman George Barnett died just one day apart and were buried on the same day.

A new "Sturdy Gertie" Narrows Bridge opened, encouraging development in Tacoma's West end. It was financed partially by a fifty-cent one-way toll per car.

Bridge To Open On Saturday

Tacoma News Tribune October 14, 1950

Chapter Eleven: Fifties

1951 Rabbi George Rosenthal

Sinai Temple secured a new leader early in 1951. Rabbi George Rosenthal's first public event in Tacoma was part of February's Brotherhood Week. He presented a Tuesday evening program for Christians, explaining the symbolism of Jewish ritual items. Rabbi

Rosenthal had just been ordained in Baltimore in 1949 and would be the congregation's only American-born rabbi. His "other Washington" birthplace fit with his given name, George.

Tacoma News Tribune
February 21, 1951

Other than an occasional lengthy letter to the editor, Rabbi George Rosenthal's name was rarely mentioned in Tacoma's newspaper. The women, however, continued to publicize their activities. Mrs. Kenneth (Alice) Farber and Mrs. George (Julie) Posner chaired the annual March Hadassah donor luncheon. In 1951 Sinai Temple's president was Harry Posner, with Abedeaux Friedman as vice president, David Klegman treasurer, and Joseph Rome and George Martin secretaries.

Cantor Isadore Schwartz and the choir provided music for Rosh Hashanah services in 1951. That year's Chanukah celebration included several skits and a gift exchange, evidence of the holiday's growing significance.

Tacoma's Hadassah chapter celebrated the organization's 40th anniversary in 1952. The donor luncheon at the Winthrop Hotel featured a millinery style show, awkwardly described in the press as a parade of Easter hats.

Fall Hadassah officers were Mrs. Jay (Shirley) Wax president, with Mesdames Saul (Ruth) Levy and Abedeaux (Rose) Friedman vice presidents, Alice Farber treasurer, and Bea Martin and Mrs. Jerry (Blossom) Spellman secretaries. Fall 1952 Sisterhood officers were Mrs. Harold (Reta) Rome president, Mesdames Robert (Sarah) Tone vice president, Fav (Lil) Witenberg and Abedeaux Friedman secretaries, and Saul Levy treasurer.

In November of 1952 Tacoma's chapter of the Council of Jewish Women began a focus on work for the blind that would dominate later decades. The same week the downtown Tacoma Public Library opened a major new addition to the historic Carnegie building.

In the spring of 1953 the Hadassah chapter held a dance at the Top of the Ocean Restaurant, built on pilings along Tacoma's Ruston Way. "The Top" was designed to resemble an ocean liner and featured a façade created from World War II surplus shipbuilding materials.

George Martin and Norman Kleinman co-hosted Sinai's 45th anniversary celebration in May of 1953. Also that month the Sisterhood re-elected Mrs. Harold (Reta) Rome as president. Her vice presidents were Mrs. Fav (Lil) Witenberg and Mrs. Norman (Dena) Kleinman, her secretaries Mrs. Simon (Flo) Rose and Mrs. Ben (Freida) Rome, and her treasurer Mrs. Philip (Fanny Sussman) Weinstone.

July of 1953 brought an armistice in the Korean War. Rabbi George Rosenthal left for New York to continue his education. In 1954 he enlisted in the U.S. Army as a chaplain, expecting to go to Korea. Instead he spent two years in Augsburg, Germany. On his return he served for half a century as a Reform rabbi.

At age seventy-five he returned to college to study macro economics. His 2016 obituary noted that his savvy investing had helped him become one of the wealthiest individuals in America.

Hartford Courant March 22, 2016

1953 Rabbi Haskell Wachsmann

September of 1953 brought Rabbi Haskell Armin Wachsmann and his family to Tacoma. He quipped that they nearly made up their own U.N. He was born in Czechoslovakia and went to school in Holland. He had married his German wife, Friedel, in London, where he was ordained in 1947. By the time Israel became an independent nation he was leading a congregation in Regina, Saskatchewan, Canada, birthplace of his son. Rabbi Wachsmann came to Tacoma after brief stints in Sacramento, California; and Council Bluffs, Iowa. Within two years he would return to Regina, tempted by an offer of a lifetime contract.

Tacoma News Tribune November 8, 1953

Rabbi Wachsmann worked part-time in Bremerton and was also chaplain at the state penitentiary on McNeil Island. In December of 1953 he led a Sisterhood-sponsored ministerial conference, teaching other clergy about Jewish concepts, customs, and ceremonies. The event was described in the *Tacoma News Tribune* by young journalist Denny MacGougan.

Rabbi Wachsmann frequently wrote long newspaper editorials. He kept readers informed of his viewpoints on current events in the Middle East and encouraged international statutes on medical ethics, spurred by the exposure of Nazi medical crimes.

In the summer of 1954 Steven Kay Weinstone celebrated his bar mitzvah, the first public mention of such a celebration in years. Sinai Sisterhood elected Mrs. Fav (Lil) Witenberg president, supported by Mesdames Jay Wax, Robert Tone, Abe Farber, George Martin, P.L. Weinstone and Simon J. Rose. The annual dance held after Yom Kippur was called "Club 5715," co-sponsored by B'nai B'rith, Hadassah, and the Council of Jewish Women.

In November of 1954 Rabbi Wachsmann wrote about the American Jewish Tercentenary, 300 years after 23 refugees arrived in New York. That same week Tacoma residents learned of the death of their beloved Rabbi Baruch Treiger in a New York hospital.

Mrs. Floyd (Rose) Lamken coordinated Jewish National Fund contributions through the Tacoma chapter of Hadassah, reminding members to bring their "blue boxes" to meetings.

*Jewish National Fund Donation Box
Wikimedia Commons*

Rabbi Wachsmann represented Sinai Temple at the March 1955 dedication of the new Mary Bridge Children's Hospital. Sinai Sisterhood elected Mrs. Hy (Edith) Nemetz president, along with Mesdames Kenneth Farber, Max Stern, Al Benezra, Louis Sherman, David Spigal, and Simon Rose. Philip Grenley recognized Sunday school teachers Mrs. Fav (Lil) Witenberg, Miss Stella Bass, Miss Marsha Rome, Miss Sharon Rubin, and Norman Kleinman.

Rabbi Wachsmann ended his time in Tacoma by co-officiating at the July wedding of Joanne Sussman and Bernard Arfin. He was identified as having built up the Sunday school from 30 students to 65.

Rabbi Leaves Sinai Temple

Tacoma News Tribune June 23, 1955

Rabbi Wachsmann served in Regina another dozen years, then lived in Jacksonville, Florida; and Chicago, Illinois. He died in Fort Lauderdale, Florida, on November 4, 2001.

Times of Transition

Reform Temple Beth Israel's rabbi also left in the fall of 1955. Rabbi Bernard Rosenberg had led the congregation since 1941 and had served in the military during the war. His leaving left the members in turmoil and his replacement, Rabbi Allan H. Schwartzman, would stay just one year.

Sinai Temple was guided by lay leaders for the next year, relying again on strong support from the women of the congregation.

Tea Will Open Season Of Sinai Sisterhood

Tacoma News Tribune October 4, 1955

Recently widowed Lena Treiger was guest of honor at the October 1955 Sinai Sisterhood dinner. She was noted as the Director of Field Work and Extension Activities of the National Women's League of the Conservative Synagogues of America.

Hadassah Luncheon

Tacoma News Tribune October 9, 1955

Hadassah publicity on October 9 waxed poetic. "A gala membership luncheon is the spark which will unite the flame of endeavor and purpose of the Tacoma Chapter of Hadassah for the 1955-56 year."

Sinai members focused on local events during the spring of 1956. The January Sisterhood luncheon topic was Tacoma's proposed city charter revision. State senator Albert Rosellini spoke at the March B'nai B'rith program.

The scrap metal drives of World War II came full circle in 1956. Leslie Sussman formed a branch of General Metals to salvage and recycle military equipment and supplies abandoned in the Aleutians, including over 25,000 Quonset huts and tons of iron and steel.

In May the women of the Sisterhood held their Strawberry festival in the home of Mrs. Harry Posner. They elected Mrs. Irving (Bess) Farber as Sisterhood president.

Sisterhood Will Install

Mrs. Harry Posner will open her North Tacoma Avenue home to members and friends of the Temple Sinai Sisterhood for the annual Strawberry Festival luncheon Wednesday at 12:30 p.m.

New officers will be installed. Mrs. Max Lederman, president of Herzl Synagogue Sisterhood in Seattle and a past president of the National Women's League of United Synagogues, will be installing officer.

Mrs. Irving Farber will be the new president. Other officers are Mrs. George Martin and Mrs. Bernard Friedman, vice presidents; Mrs Louis Sherman, secretary; Mrs. Kenneth Farber, corresponding secretary; Mrs. David Spigal, treasurer, and Mrs. Mike Block, financial secretary.

Mrs. Hy Nemetz, retiring president, will present her annual report.

Committee members for the event are Mesdames Favius Witenberg, Philip Weinstone, Haskell Maier, Philip Grenley, Morris Jaffe, Joseph Rome, Harry Friedman and Harry Nemetz.

Tacoma News Tribune May 14, 1956

Many students studied with Solomon Epstein in the interim between rabbis. Jerome Rogoway conducted the bar mitzvah service of Jim Farber. Seattle's Rabbi Joseph Wagner officiated at the bar mitzvahs of Herbert Simon and Louis Nemetz. Both congregations hired a new rabbi in the fall. The members of Reform Temple Beth Israel welcomed Rabbi and Mrs. Richard Rosenthal to Tacoma in August of 1956. The same month, Leo and Goldie Jean Dobry hosted a reception at their home to welcome Sinai Temple's new rabbi, Ralph Carmi.

1956 Rabbi Ralph Y. Carmi

Rabbi Carmi had most recently led a congregation in Fond du Lac, Wisconsin, but had lived in the U.S. for less than a decade. He was born Yerachmiel Chorowsky in Volpo, Poland, in 1924. He and his parents later lived in Palestine, often confused as his birthplace. He emigrated to the U.S. from Tel Aviv in October of 1947 and married Rosalie Rein in New York in 1950, the same year as his ordination there.

In Tacoma Rabbi Carmi focused on education. In October Mrs. Fav (Lil) Witenberg led a new PTA association for the Sinai religious school, under the sponsorship of the Sisterhood. Rabbi Carmi taught a renewed education program with the lofty title Adult Institute of Jewish Studies, offering eight weeks of beginning Hebrew and a study of the prayer book.

Jewish teenagers organized a new Sinai Youth club "for cultural, religious, social and athletic purposes." Sharon Rubin, Steven Weinstone, Jules Friedman, and Barry Posner were the first elected officers..

Sinai Teenagers Found New Club

Rabbi Joseph Wagner of Hertzel Temple, Seattle, was guest speaker at a meeting in which Sinai Temple teen-agers organized for cultural, religious, social and athletic purposes, it was announced today.

Tacoma News Tribune October 13, 1956

Also in October the Sisterhood welcomed new members Mesdames Gabe Touriel, Harry Weston, Morris Shapiro, William Klein, Norman Becker, Meyer Herring, John Haas and the second Mrs. Ben Etsekson.

Mrs. Harry (Rose) Posner was elected as chairman of the Tacoma chapter of Hadassah. The group's November event included copper-colored decorations in keeping with the theme "Pennies from Heaven." Just as Israel was invading the Sinai Peninsula, Sinai Temple installed George Martin as president, vice president Albert Benezra, secretary Favius Witenberg, and treasurer Simon Rose.

The Sinai Youth Organization advisors in 1957 were Mrs. Ben (Freida) Rome and Stadium teacher Isadore Epstein. (Isadore was the son of Solomon and Ida (Farber) Epstein, and first cousin of Lena Farber Treiger.) In March the Council of Jewish Women met at Sinai Temple and took a vicarious trip to Hawaii. At Passover Rabbi Carmi noted that the memorial Yizkor service would remember those who had died in the past year and also since the founding of the temple.

Mrs. Carmi led the May installation of Sisterhood officers Mesdames Max Karsh, Jay Wax, Eric Deutsch, Stanley Sigel, David Spigal, and Mike Block. The incoming officers would begin their work in the fall.

Ceremony At Sinai Temple

Sinai Temple presented three young members with Bibles and certificates at Bas-Mitzvas Friday evening at Sinai Temple.

The ceremony conducted by Rabbi Ralph Y. Carmi was followed by a reception for family and other friends in the church vestry.

Tacoma News Tribune June 8, 1957

Rabbi Carmi's last publicized service in Tacoma was the Friday evening June bat mitzvah of three young ladies: Miss Carol Farber, Miss Roberta Martin, and Miss Tobyann Nemetz. Mrs. Karsh presented each with a Bible and Mr. Epstein awarded graduation certificates.

Rabbi Carmi held several posts across the country throughout the remainder of his career and died in Florida in 2018.

Dr. Frank Rosenthal of the U.W. Hillel led Rosh Hashanah services in September of 1957. On the 27th Rabbi and Mrs. Richard Rosenthal held a reception in their home to welcome members of both Temple Beth Israel and Sinai Temple.

The Sinai Temple Sisterhood observed the 50th anniversary of the congregation in November.

> This Sunday the Sinai Temple congregation is celebrating 50 years of achievement in Tacoma with a community dinner at 5:30 p.m. The Sinai Temple Youth Group will entertain members and friends with a program.

Tacoma News Tribune November 17, 1957

By the spring of 1958 the members of Sinai Temple had been without a rabbi for eight months. Rabbi Gamze was the guest speaker at a Sisterhood dinner in February and would return to Tacoma as Sinai Temple's rabbi in time for Passover and Israel's tenth anniversary.

In the interim the congregation mourned the death of Abe Rose and the B'nai B'rith group heard from former NFL football player Ron Paul. Hadassah honored Bernard Witenberg's support of their Youth Aliyah project by naming him Man of the Year, and Mrs. Fav (Lil) Witenberg chaired the Torah Fund campaign of the Women's League for Conservative Judaism.

Will Honor 'Man of Year'

Bernard Witenberg, Hadassah's "Man of the Year," will be honored at a 6:30 p.m. Youth Aliyah supper Sunday in Temple Sinai. He will be feted for his many years of devotion to Youth Aliyah, a child rescue project, as an outstanding donor to child welfare projects in Tacoma, throughout the United States and in Israel.

Tacoma News Tribune February 19, 1958

1958 Rabbi Noah Gamze

Rabbi Gamze was born in 1924 in Lithuania, but grew up in Chicago. There his father, Rabbi Elias Gamze, led the Chicago Loop Synagogue. After Rabbi Noah Gamze's 1951 ordination he led the same congregation for four years. When he arrived in Tacoma Rabbi Gamze was just 33. His first interview was an indicator of his Chicago perspective.

> "Tacoma offers a challenge to any churchman due to its isolation from major cultural centers. I believe it is my duty to stimulate the people of the temple to take a greater degree of personal responsibility in the activities."

Tacoma News Tribune April 5, 1958

In November the Tacoma Section of the National Council of Jewish Women presented a seminar on Community Leadership Training at the Winthrop Hotel, in conjunction with Council's 65th anniversary. The day-long event, an outgrowth of a scholarship won by Mrs. Homer (Leonore) Goldblatt, would later be seen as a pivotal moment in Tacoma's Jewish history. At the time Mrs. Goldblatt was president of the Temple Beth Israel Sisterhood.

Tacoma Group Holds Leadership Seminar

Patterns in community living were reflected yesterday when the Tacoma Section of the National Council of Jewish Women presented a seminar on Community Leadership Training at the Winthrop Hotel.

Tacoma News Tribune November 13, 1958

In December of 1958 Rabbi and Mrs. Gamze observed the ritual of redemption of their first-born son. They were aided by Joseph Rome, former Sinai Temple president and a Cohen descendant.

Tacoma's four Jewish groups joined together in sponsoring a Community Sabbath at Sinai Temple in January of 1959. Members of the Council of Jewish Women, B'nai B'rith, and Sisterhoods of both Temple Beth Israel and Sinai Temple heard a speaker from the Los Angeles Israeli consulate, and participated in religious services led by both Rabbi Richard Rosenthal and Rabbi Gamze.

Two weeks later the United Synagogue Youth of Sinai Temple held an annual carnival and spaghetti dinner, led by Stan Farber, Jim Farber and Harvey Spigal. Hadassah planned a "Break the Bank" dinner at the home of Mrs. Harry Posner and honored Mrs. Joe A. Sussman on her return from her trip to Europe and Israel.

In March Tacoma's same four Jewish groups sponsored an Israeli Festival Banquet as part of an Israel Bond campaign. Yiddish humorist Emil Cohen was the "guest star." These types of events likely did much to build unity across Tacoma's Jewish community.

Sinai Temple Sisterhood held a summer luau in the garden of Mr. and Mrs. Ben Rome. Descriptions of the fall tea included a mention of display of gift shop items. Rabbi and Mrs. Gamze hosted a Jewish New Year's open house to welcome his aunt, Dr. Miriam Weinberger, visiting for the month of October, 1959. It would be one of the last public mentions of Rabbi Gamze in Tacoma.

Rabbi Gamze returned to Chicago. He next worked three years as an assistant librarian and as a Hebrew school teacher. Then he served for nearly forty years as the leader of the Downtown Synagogue in Detroit. He retired in 2001 and joined relatives in Rhode Island, where he died in 2003.

Detroit Free Press April 22, 1963

1959 Opportunity

Rabbi Gamze's departure in 1959 created an opportunity for Tacoma's entire Jewish community. Thirty years later Rabbi Richard Rosenthal described the circumstances in an interview with Isabel Stusser. *(August 24, 1989, Washington State Jewish Archives, Oral History Collection, OHC0172)*

"I think actually what happened was that… Leonore Goldblatt was president of Council of Jewish Women, and she was a really creative person. And she and Council… had a workshop or symposium, a kind of public meeting about Jewish unity in Tacoma. I've forgotten the exact subject matter, but people for the first time had this agenda item in front of them… I'm sure that Leonore wasn't looking for merging the congregations or anything like that. But she was then a mother of young kids, and I think the thing that stared most people in the face was that Jewish kids were growing up in Tacoma in two very separate communities."

"I think it was sort of the inevitable result of the changes that occurred at Temple Beth Israel… That is, that the younger people, many of whom had grown up within the traditional congregation, who had moved to Reform, could see no reason why there should be two congregations in Tacoma. It was aggravated by the fact, I think, just the plain practical fact that at 90-odd families Temple Beth Israel could just barely maintain itself financially and was stuck in an inadequate building."

As for the Sinai Temple congregation, "It was at a borderline of being able to raise enough money to support a rabbi… They just didn't have enough members, the salary wasn't adequate, so young rabbis came here and they lasted a year or two. And they found a pulpit someplace else."

"So as the Fifties wore on… you had a new generation of Jews living in this community, and whatever alleged differences existed before now were wiped away."

An Inheritance

(Continuing excerpts from Rabbi Rosenthal's August 24, 1989 interview.)

"In 1960 the Jews as a whole were as monolithic as they were going to be in their entire history, as it turns out… These were people who were very much alike. They had had the same kind of growing up experiences. They had all of them had the Second World War as part of their background, the rise of Israel. Things that shape people created a generation of people, regardless of how they felt about the - what I call the 'aesthetics of worship' - on almost every other issue were pretty much alike. And I think it was almost inevitable in that sense that the congregations would merge. I mean, after all, at the same moment that this happened in Tacoma, or a year later, the same thing happened in Spokane."

"A lot of things happened in a positive way to say that maybe this is the time to do it. And they did it very cautiously. I think the people who were leaders of the Temple and the Shul were people – well I think that Leon Diamond was president of the Temple – it helped to have a psychiatrist as president! – and Al Benezra was president of the Shul. And they were both reasonable people."

"There was this vast middle ground of people who wanted this thing to work. And they formed a committee, and the committee decided they would go really slowly, and they would work out through a series of sub-committees, all things they thought were issues."

"What in my mind was the important process is that for a long period, for a year almost, people sat down and kept meeting monthly and talking these things out, and eventually arriving at a consensus… They got to know each other a lot better that way from within a Jewish perspective."

"In a sense it's sort of an inheritance we have as a community here."

Rabbi Richard Rosenthal

The Merger Process

On October 18th, 1959, a joint fact-finding committee presented its report at a special Beth Israel congregational meeting. The Reform congregation voted to give the committee "authority to effect a merger of Tacoma's two congregations." The same report would have been presented at Sinai Temple. The committee went forward with the process, breaking into subcommittees and working out language and details.

Meanwhile, Chaplain Weinberg of Fort Lewis participated in a program with the Sinai Sisterhood, an indication that he may have been providing interim leadership. In January of 1960 the members of Tacoma's chapter of B'nai B'rith installed Kurt Blau as president, following outgoing Dr. Leon S. Diamond. The program concluded with a dinner and dance at the popular Top of the Ocean. Leslie Sussman served as program chair for the February Israel Bond event, again sponsored by four Jewish groups.

In early March of 1960 the merger committee presented a draft constitution. Temple Beth Israel's congregation voted on March sixth to accept the constitution and the reports of the Education and Budget and Finance sub-committees.

The following week the four Jewish groups again joined in a Community Sabbath, held at Temple Beth Israel. The 39th such annual event was sponsored by the chapter of National Council of Jewish Women and happened to fall on the eve of Purim in 1960. Two weeks later the combined youth groups of AZA and B'nai B'rith Girls hosted a "South Sea Fantasy" evening at Sinai Temple. Young Jeff Brotman, who would go on to found Costco Wholesale, was one of the candidates for "Beau."

The special congregational meetings continued. On April third the members of Temple Beth Israel approved a shorter constitution to be revised as by-laws, and accepted reports of interim and ritual sub-committees. At the same time the merger committee began soliciting names for the new congregation. Two weeks later the committees proposed a slate of candidates for board members. Throughout the month of May members mailed in cards with their vote for the new temple's name.

Mrs. Richard Rosenthal chaired the National Council of Jewish Women's spring luncheon in May. Lorraine (Sussman) Braverman, daughter of Frank Sussman, was chapter president.

Both temples graduated a confirmation class in 1960. Rabbi Richard Rosenthal guided both events, held a week apart. Temple Beth Israel's group had eight students. Sinai Temple's sole confirmand was Lynnel Kleinman, daughter of Mr. and Mrs. Norman Kleinman. Her grandfather, Portland's Rabbi Philip Kleinman, helped officiate. It would be one of the last events under the name Sinai Temple.

The final vote was on Sunday, June fifth. The new articles of incorporation were signed by former Sinai trustees Albert Benezra, Philip Brodsky, Norman Kleinman, Eric Deutsch, Philip Grenley, and George Martin. Section one of the "Religious Practices" portion of the new constitution stated that "wearing of Yamalka and Tallis shall be optional with the individual member." Section two prohibited serving pork and shellfish products; or meat and dairy at the same time. Section three guaranteed that "The Congregation shall provide facilities for traditional services for those members desiring them." Section four provided that the choir was to be entirely of Jewish members, if feasible.

Temple Beth El

Rabbi Rosenthal was away on vacation during much of June. When he returned in July he wrote in the new *Beth El Bulletin* that he was busy preparing for fall. "Our congregation is now a legal entity, but we need your interest and activity to make it a true holy congregation, a *kehilo k'dosho*. So come let us meet together, let us worship together and let us join hands so that our community will be one truly worthy of the name of Beth El, house of God."

Mr. and Mrs. Frank Sussman celebrated their 50th wedding anniversary in July. Their children donated a silver Torah breastplate in honor of the occasion, held at the newly formed Temple Beth El. The newspaper Society article about their anniversary explained the temple's name change for the wider Tacoma community, noting that the couple had been founders of Talmud Torah and had also witnessed the name change to Sinai Temple.

MR. AND MRS. FRANK SUSSMAN
On Eve of Their Golden Wedding Date

Tacoma News Tribune July 11, 1960

The new congregation elected Dr. Leon S. Diamond as its first president, known to both temples from his B'nai B'rith leadership. Rosh Hashanah services were observed at the newly named North Temple Beth El. Sinai Temple was referred to as the South Temple. Some of those celebrating bar mitzvahs were Mike Wax, Harold Friedman, Stuart Farber, Neal Grenley, and Bruce Witenberg.

Over the next three years members held meetings and Friday evening services at the North Temple, and the South Temple housed temple offices and the religious school. In the spring of 1964 the congregation sold the building on North 4th and J Streets to an Apostolic Faith Church. All temple activities were at South 4th and I Streets until 1968, when the congregation moved into a newly constructed building on South Vassault Street.

Memories

Many men remembered playing golf together, especially the B'nai B'rith tournament honoring the late Dr. Abedeaux Friedman.

Tacoma Lodge B'nai B'rith
Dr. Abedeaux Friedman Memorial
Golf Championship Trophy
Courtesy of the Donion Estate

Stars on the Ceiling

I remember the main classroom, with a plaque dedicating the room to my Aunt, Lena (Farber) Treiger. I remember that when she came for the ceremony she was interviewed at the airport because she had flown a half million miles for her work. I remember the upstairs balcony with folding glass windows that closed in the space for use as an additional classroom. Most of all, I remember trying to count the golden stars on the pale blue ceiling of the main sanctuary.

Steph Farber

I remember trying to count the stars. The ceiling was filled with stars. There were too many stars to count in the entire ceiling; I tried and tried to count the stars in the section just above our pew. It was as futile as trying to count the stars outside. We always sat in the same pew, near the second radiator from the front, adjacent the window. In the evening, the light was not good.

The Shul wasn't separate, it was part of our home, our life. My father, Abedeaux, died when I was six years old, leaving me few memories of him. In one of those, he is sitting on the bimah of the Shul, during the High Holidays, waving me up to sit with him in front of the congregation.

I have other High Holiday memories, too. I remember a young couple sitting behind us during Rosh Hashanah services. The young man was newly stationed at Fort Lewis. The congregation always welcomed strangers, and my mother, Rose, and Grandma invited them to join us for dinner after services. They soon became regulars at our home. I remember congregants from Temple Beth Israel "shul hopping," among them, my uncle Saul Friedman, who would sit near us during musaf services. And I remember that the High Holidays seemed to always coincide with the World Series. I remember during breaks in the services my friends would be on the steps of the Shul, hovering over a new invention, a transistor radio.

Suddenly we were able to learn the World Series score as the game was being played.

My grandma, Lena Rotman, lived with us. She always kvelled when she spoke of the Shul. She told me how her husband, Harry Rotman, my grandfather, had a role in finding the property for the Shul, directly across the street from Wright Park. It was such a beautiful location.

I remember my grandma volunteering for the Shul. Grandma was often in charge of the Talmud Torah and Sinai Temple rummage sales, and I remember our basement full of donated items that would accumulate in our home in advance of the annual sales. Grandma was a tireless solicitor. She took advantage of an age before answering machines. If a merchant didn't respond to her initial solicitation for a donation, she would call and tell the merchant she had just missed the ringing phone – but she was sure it had been him calling with a donation. She got results!

My mother and my grandma would take me to services Friday nights. Services would begin at eight, and sometimes they were very brief. There was no cantor; congregants helped lead the familiar Shabbos melodies. Sometimes we would be home in time to watch 77 Sunset Strip.

On Shabbos morning I would walk to the Shul, arriving just before nine. Everyone always entered on the South 4th Street side, near the alley. The morning minyan was nearing the end. I remember hearing the davening entirely in Hebrew. Soon the men (they were all men) would rush out to go downtown to their businesses. Then it was time for Junior Congregation. We had our own Junior Congregation prayer book. After our service, we had a grape juice Kiddush and the chance to play ping pong.

There were about ten of us in regular attendance, a cohesive group. We saw each other not only at Junior Congregation, but also in Sunday School and cheder, which I remember being after school twice a week. I remember meeting in the classroom near the top of the stairs, to the left, as we entered the building. We had memorable teachers.

I remember many events downstairs in the social hall. There were model Seders and Purim carnivals. There were lunches after bar and bat mitzvahs. I remember seeing something uncommon today, women honored by "pouring tea."

Many of the members of the Shul were immigrants, others were the first generation, their children. Most were from what is now Latvia, but I didn't understand that then. I did understand that my grandma was from the same place.

The Shul was very important to them. I remember them; I remember all of them as part of a wonderful community centered on the Shul.

Harold G. Friedman

Chapter Twelve: The Building

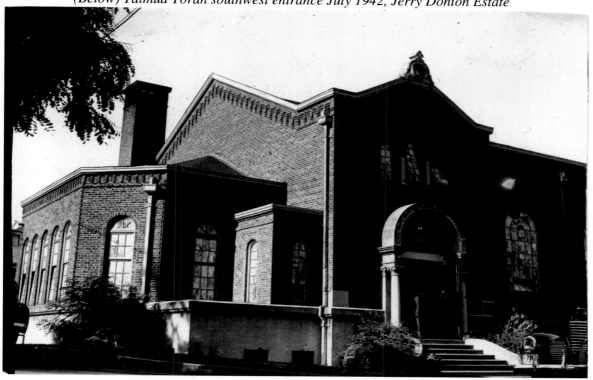

(Above) Talmud Torah exterior 1925, Tacoma Public Library Richards D141770-15
(Below) Talmud Torah southwest entrance July 1942, Jerry Donion Estate

(Above) Wedding of Jerry Donion and Mary Eastern, July 26, 1942, Jerry Donion Estate
(Below) Interior 1964, Tacoma Public Library Richards Studio D141770-2

(Above) Sinai Temple in 1948, Tacoma News Tribune May 12, 1948
(Below) Exterior 1964, Tacoma Public Library Richards Studio D141770-15

Chevra Talmud Torah

Architectural Blueprints

December 1924

Hill and Mock Architects

Selected Excerpts

Courtesy of Tacoma Public Library
Northwest Room/Special Collections

Enhanced by Clif Taylor

Hill and Mock Architects Blueprint Identifier December 8, 1924

East Elevation

South Elevation (left side)

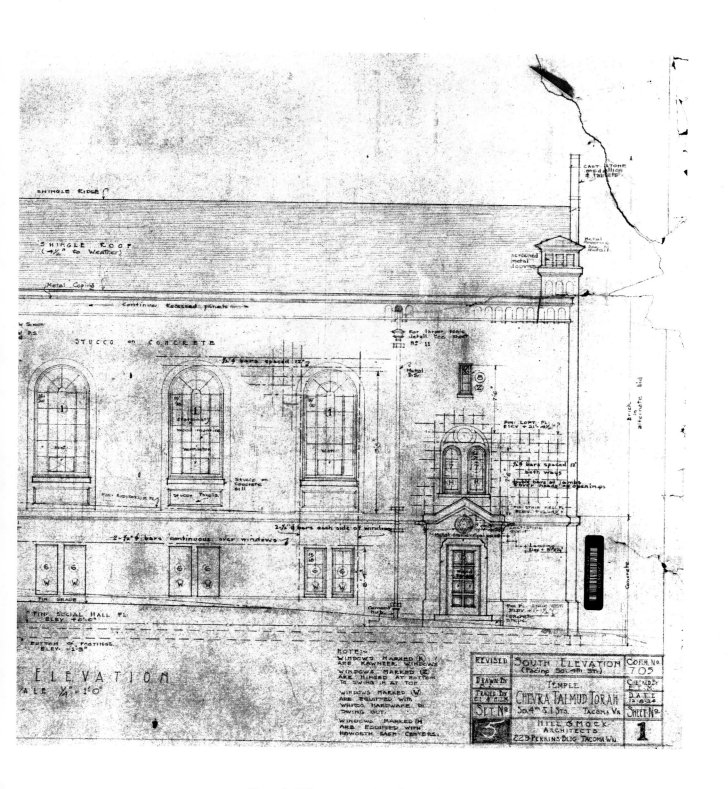

South Elevation (right side)

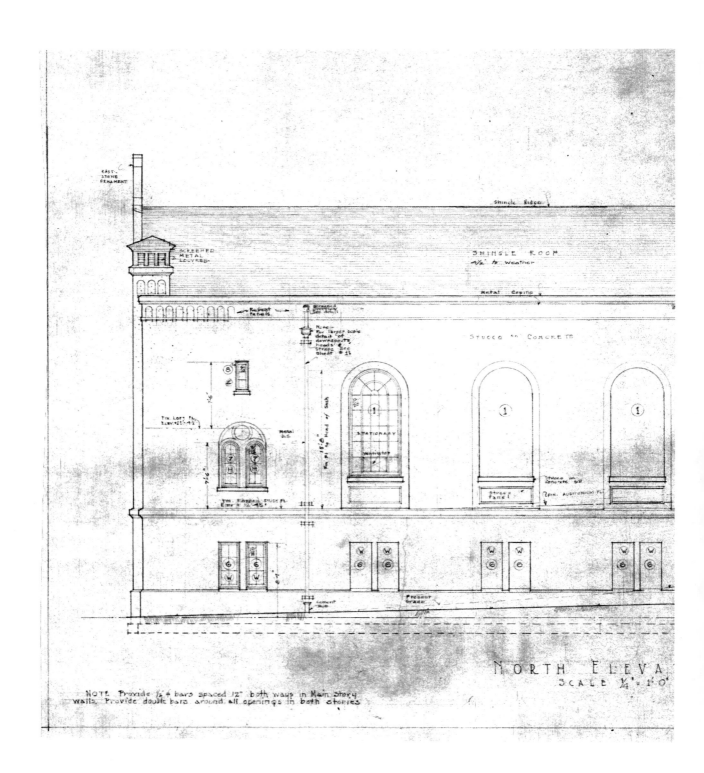

North Elevation (left side)

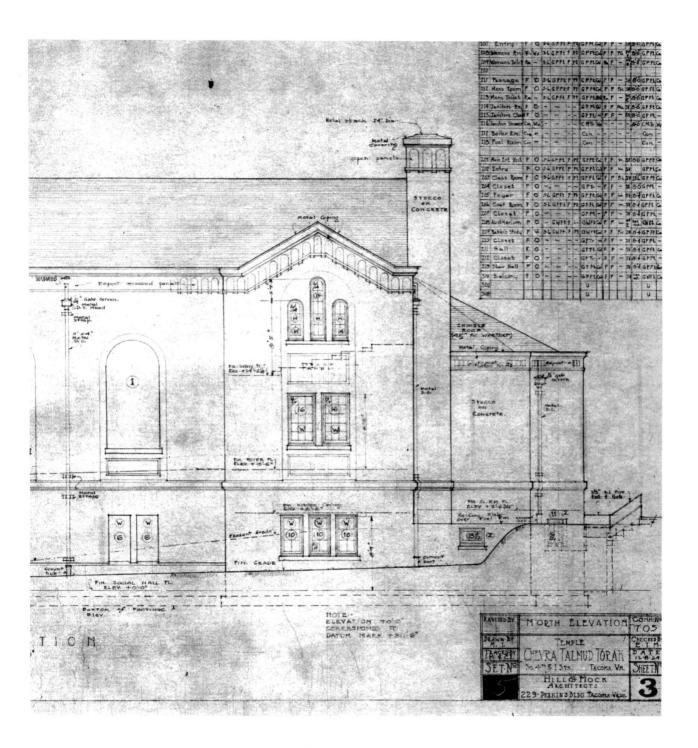

North Elevation (right side)

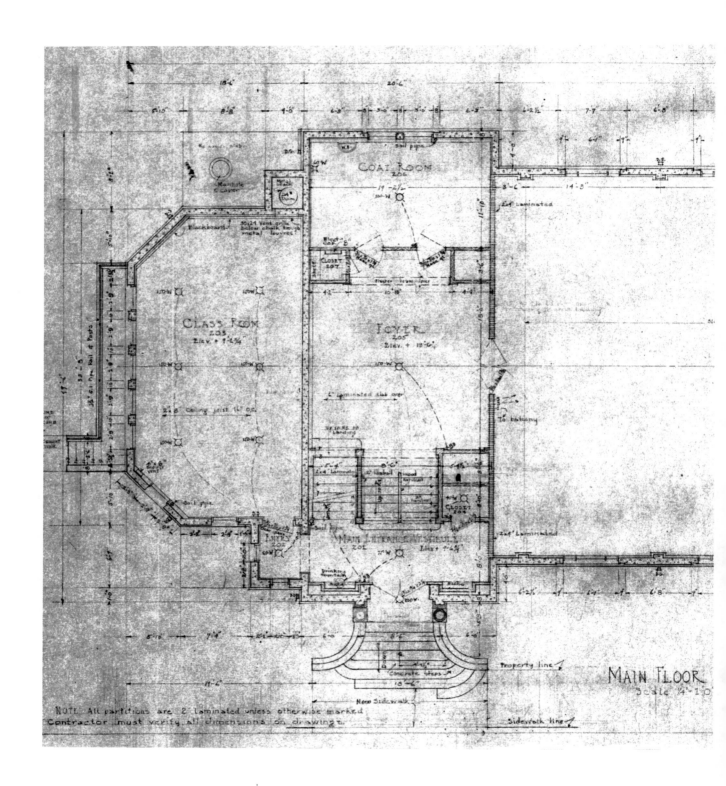

Main Floor (left side)

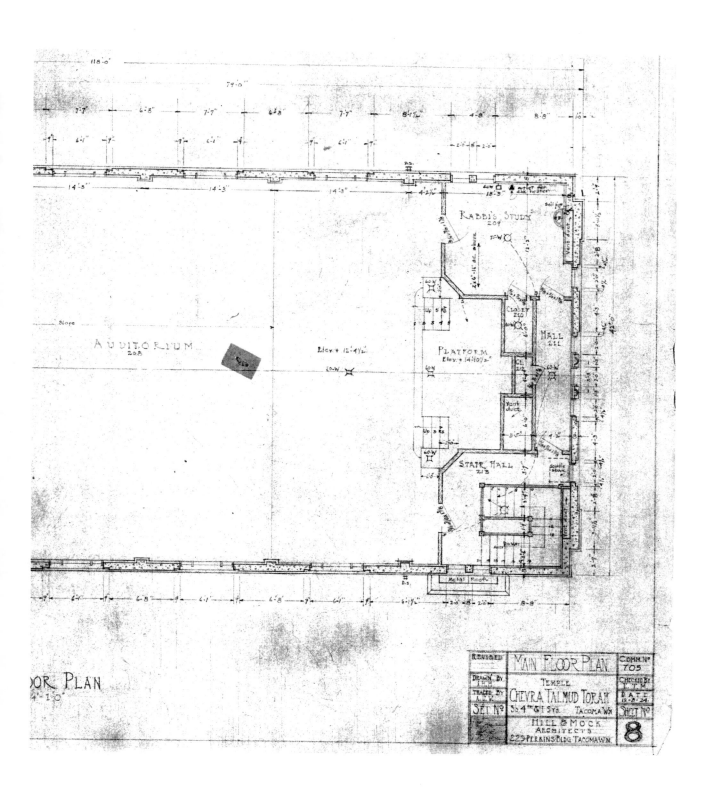

Main Floor (right side)

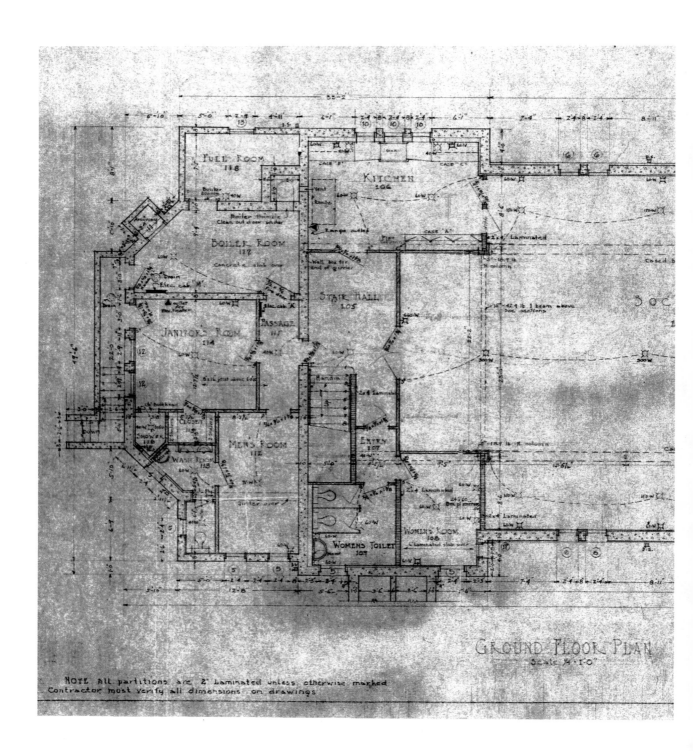

Ground Floor (left side)

102

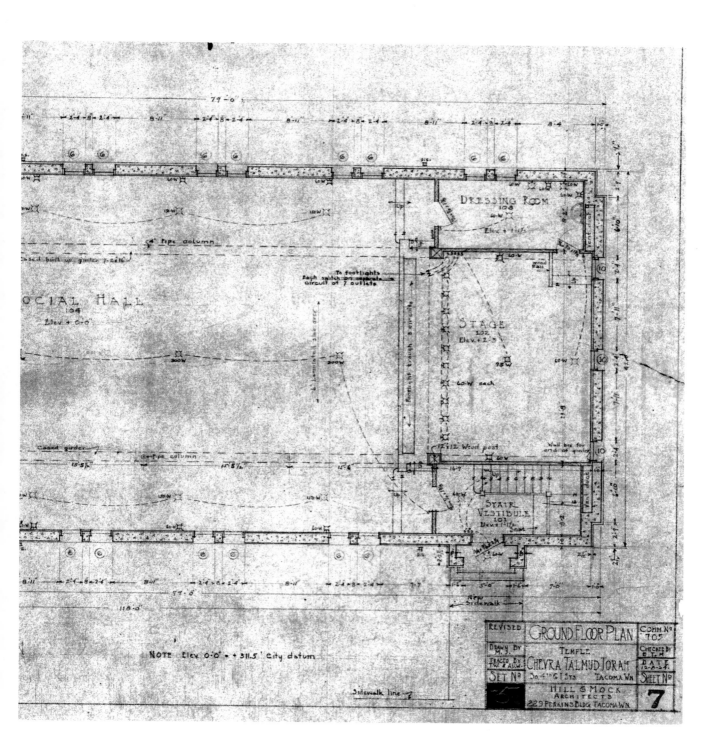

Ground Floor (right side)

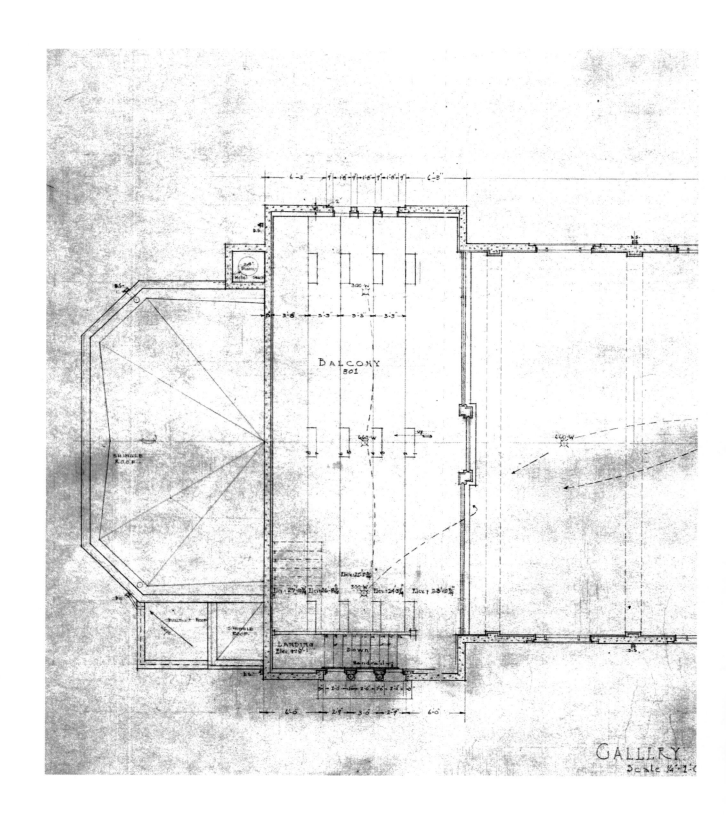

Balcony Gallery

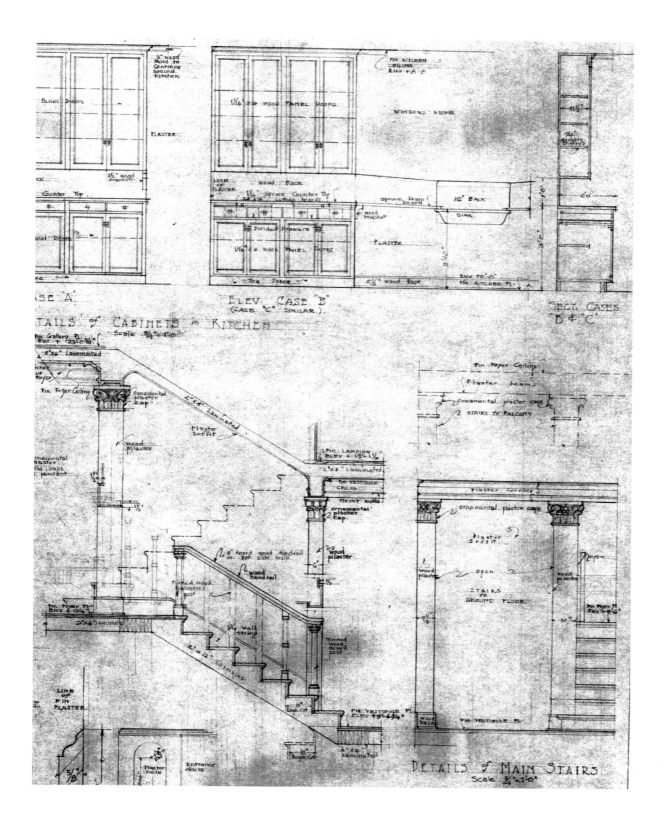

Stair and Cabinetry Detail

West Elevation

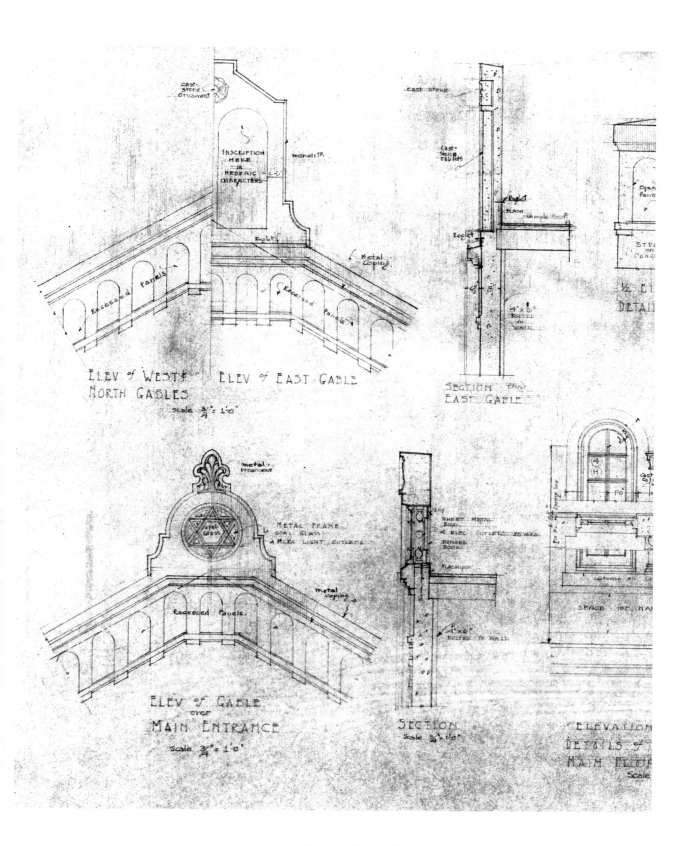

Gable Detail

107

Fragments

In 1968 Tacoma was more focused on urban renewal than historic preservation. The former Sinai Temple building was demolished to create parking for neighboring medical facilities. Rabbi Rosenthal received the copper box found in the cornerstone, and members salvaged several exterior architectural items.

"These lintels representing the Ten Commandments stood over the doorway of Sinai Temple at South 4th and "I" Streets from 1925 until 1968, when the building was razed. The lintels were rescued by Dorothy Grenley and stored for forty years at MacDonald Building Co. They were returned to Temple Beth El in 2006 and installed here through the generosity of an anonymous donor."

Lintel pieces displayed in the courtyard of Temple Beth El

Another representation of the Ten Commandments was removed from atop the gable, but was damaged during demolition. In 2004 the Washington State Historical Society created freestanding frames for the fragments and included them in a Family of Strangers exhibit. The twin tablets are currently in Temple Beth El's conversation nook, displayed near items salvaged from Tacoma's first Temple Beth Israel building.

(Above left) Talmud Torah gable fragments
(Above right) Talmud Torah eternal lamp

The eternal lamp from Sinai Temple hangs above the ark in the Rosenthal Chapel. The large memorial *yarzheit* board honoring the congregation's deceased is on the wall near the entrance to Temple Beth El's main sanctuary.

Rabbi Rosenthal carried a disturbing memory of the building's demolition. After salvage work was completed, the first swing of the wrecking ball caused the building to collapse. Experts told him that the synagogue likely had suffered hidden structural damage during the 1949 Passover earthquake. Barbara Rosenthal remembered that he was still shaken later that evening as he dealt with the realization that the building could have buckled earlier when it was occupied by "my people, my people."

Chronology of Clergy

Chevra Talmud Torah 1907-1924
1907-1912: Rabbi Meier Elyn (1872-1921)
1912-1914: Rabbi Max Samuel Aronin (1877-1955)
January 1921: Rabbi Jacob B. Gordon
1922-1924: Rabbi Leib Slotnik (1874-1966)

Talmud Torah Synagogue 1925-1945
1925-1932: Rabbi Leib Slotnik (1874-1966)
1929: Teacher Ira Funck
1929-1931: Teacher Dr. Ivar Spector (1896-1989)
1932-1933: Teacher Rabbi Gabriel Agouff (1878-1936)
1936-1942: Rabbi Baruch I. Treiger (1895-1954)
1942-1945: Rabbi Julius L. DeKoven (1914-1979)
September 1945: Rabbi Solomon Herbst (1912-2007)

Sinai Temple 1945-1960
1946-1948: Rabbi Leo Trepp (1913-2010)
Feb 1951-July 1953: Rabbi George Rosenthal (1925-2016)
Sept 1953-July 1955: Rabbi Haskell A. Wachsmann (1917-2001)
Aug 1956-Jul 1957: Rabbi Ralph Y. Carmi (1924-2018)
April 1958-Oct 1959: Rabbi Noah M. Gamze (1924-2003)

Temple Beth El
1960-1997: Rabbi Richard Rosenthal (1929-1999)

Temple Beth Israel
1893-1903: None
1903-1904: Rabbi Montague N.A. Cohen
1904-1919: None
1919-1920: Rabbi Raphael Goldstein
1920-1921: Rabbi Samuel Margolis
1921-1924: None
1924-1928: Rabbi Montague N.A. Cohen
1928-1936: None
1936-1941: Rabbi Montague N.A. Cohen
1941-1955: Rabbi Bernard D. Rosenberg
1955-1956: Rabbi Allan H. Schwartzman
1956-1960: Rabbi Richard Rosenthal

Rabbi Richard Rosenthal

Rabbi Richard Rosenthal

Tacoma News Tribune December 14, 1963
It's said that when two Jews come together, they bring three opinions. Yet Tacoma's Jews overwhelmingly agree that the merger of the two congregations was only possible because of the impactful leadership of Rabbi Richard Rosenthal.

Richard Rosenthal was born in Usingen, Germany, on April 14, 1929. At nine, he witnessed the Nazis' first widespread violence against Jews during Kristallnacht, the Night of Broken Glass, on November 9, 1938. His father, Carl Rosenthal, was so badly beaten that young Richard didn't recognize him, but Carl recovered. The next year the family - Carl and Alice (Baum) Rosenthal, Richard, and his younger sister Cecile - emigrated via London and New York. With the assistance of the Jewish Resettlement agency, they reached their final destination, Shreveport, Louisiana, in April of 1940. After graduating from Centenary College in Louisiana in 1949, he was ordained at Hebrew Union College in 1954. He served as Army Chaplain at Fort Leonard Wood, Missouri, for two years. Rabbi Rosenthal married Barbara Miller (1935-2020) in 1955. He came to Tacoma in the summer of 1956 as the new rabbi of Temple Beth Israel. After the historic merger in 1960 Rabbi Rosenthal led Temple Beth El until his retirement in 1997. He served as Rabbi Emeritus until his death on March 3, 1999.

Congregational Presidents

Nochem "Nathan" Anches (1915)
Albert Benezra (1960)
Philip Brodsky (1937, 1943)
Julius Friedman (1924, 1927, 1930)
Morris J. Friedman (1936)
Nathan Friedman (1918)
Philip B. Friedman
Samuel I. Friedman (1938)
David Holzman (1942)
Max Jacobson (1907)
David Klegman (1919, 1920)
Louis Lamken

Haskel Maier, M.D. (1946)
George Martin (1957-1958)
W.D. Meier (1931, 1935)
Harry Posner (1951)
Joseph Rome
Abraham Rose
Hugo Stusser
Frank Sussman (1913)
Joseph A. Sussman (1917)
Robert Tone (1940-1941)
Emanuel Waldocks (third)
Harris Warnick (1928)
Henry Zeidell (1916)

Biographical Sketches

The following pages include biographical and genealogical information on over 200 families who in some way were affiliated with Congregation Talmud Torah and Sinai Temple. Nearly 80 percent were of foreign birth. Many were from unidentified areas of the former Russian empire. At least 20 percent were from what is now Latvia and over 10 percent were from what is now the Ukraine. 56 percent were buried in Tacoma's Home of Peace Cemetery, 12 percent in Seattle's Bikur Cholim, and 14 percent in California. The biographies are organized by the men's names, typical of the era and traditional Judaism. In multiple instances some younger family members later affiliated with Tacoma's Temple Beth Israel. They are included here for completeness and for demonstrating demographic patterns.

A note about birth dates:

In today's world, social security numbers are issued to infants. Exact birth dates are required for medical care and school registration. In the 1800s birth dates were more fluid. A Jewish child might have grown up in Russia knowing only that her birthday fell around Purim. As she aged it was possible for her to adjust the date, especially if she was still unmarried when in her thirties. It was even more common for Jewish men to report varying ages. Emigration offered an opportunity to add or subtract a few beneficial years. Documents such as ship passenger lists, naturalization petitions, and census records might each bear a different birth date for the same person. There was little incentive to provide correct information on draft registration forms. Russia's change from the Julian to Gregorian calendar in 1918 further muddied the waters. For the purposes of consistency in this work we have generally used dates as they appear on gravestones.

(The authors have compiled biographical sketches to the best of their abilities using available sources, often without the assistance or collaboration of relatives. Errors and omissions are probable and corrections are welcomed. We apologize in advance for any families we may have missed. We have carefully tried to respect the privacy of the living.)

Rabbi Gabriel Agouff

Born January 4, 1872, in Kasno Selky, Russia
Married Rachel in Nikolaenko, Russia, in 1900
Parents of Rebecca and Minnie, born in 1904 and 1906
Emigrated in 1907 aboard the *Pomeranian* via Nova Scotia to Montreal
Died September 2, 1936, in San Francisco, California

HELP IS SOUGHT BY EXILED RUSSIAN TO RETURN HOME

Rabbi Gabriel Agouff, Denied Passport, Interests Senator Shafroth.

Gabriel Agouff was a traveler, teaching languages wherever he went. His trail wound through Hartford, Connecticut; and Denver, Colorado; before he failed in his attempt to return to his aging mother in Russia in 1917. More teaching positions followed in Minneapolis, Pittsburgh, Salt Lake, Des Moines, Iowa; Fort Worth, Texas; and Akron, Ohio. He made return trips to Europe in 1923, 1924 and 1930. On his last trip he lived in Riga, which perhaps was his connection to Tacoma. He taught in Tacoma from the spring of 1932 to the fall of 1933.
Denver Post July 15, 1917

Nochem "Nathan" Anches, son of Chaschkl and Bluma Anziss

Born in Russia between 1879 and 1881
Married Lubil "Libby" Elyn (1881-1978) in Russia about 1906
Arrived N.Y. aboard the *Potsdam* December 20, 1907, as Nochem Anziss, with wife and infant daughter
Parents of Rochel Leah Scher (1907-1956) and
    Irving (1909-1983)
Died March 2, 1951, in Seattle; buried Bikur
    Cholim Cemetery, Seattle

*Irving and Leah Anches with cousins
Lena and Irving Farber c 1915
Courtesy of the Farber Family*

Nochem's paper trail indicates five different dates of birth, ranging from October of 1879 to October of 1881. He operated the OK secondhand store in Tacoma in 1910, selling everything from knives and watches to clothes and suitcases. He served as vice president of Chevra Talmud Torah in 1913, and in 1914 was a trustee of the Chevra Kadisha Cemetery. In the fall Nochem was secretary of a joint corporation of over 100 downtown merchants that offered five floors of holiday shopping in one downtown location. In 1915 he was president of Chevra Talmud Torah and led Passover services in April. That same year he became a U.S. citizen, took the name Nathan, and operated the OK Loan.

Nathan partnered with Harry Simon in running several firms in Seattle after the First World War, including an army and navy surplus and supply, and The Fair department store. In the Thirties he began developing real estate and operating apartments and hotels. Nathan was treasurer of the Seattle Hebrew School in 1934 and an officer of Bikur Cholim in the 1940s. Throughout his life he and his wife were active in many Jewish welfare organizations. His wife, Libby, who died in Seattle in the spring of 1978, was a sister of Rabbi Meier Elyn and Mrs. Solomon J. (Goldie Elyn) Farber.

Rabbi Max Samuel Aronin, son of Samuel and Fannie Aronin
Born May 20, 1877, in Borisoff, Russia (now Barysaw, Belarus)
Married Jennie Klebanow/Kleban (1879-1946) on August 15, 1904 in Borisoff
Arrived N.Y. aboard the *Barbarossa* on June 6, 1906, as Mendel and Gutte, with infant Schule
Parents of Schule (1905-?), Sarah (1907-1989), Anne (1908-1954), Dorothy (1910-1920), and
     Rebecca Clark (1912-1991)
Died January 8, 1955, in Seattle; buried Bikur Cholim Cemetery, Seattle

(Below) 1914 Tacoma city directory listing

Max Aronin lived in Seattle when his three middle daughters were born. He taught Hebrew school at Tacoma's Talmud Torah from 1912 to 1914, and he and his family lived in the

> Aronin Max Rev (Jennie) pastor Hebrew Synagogue h rear 1529 S Tacoma av

rear of the synagogue building. Max then moved back to Seattle, where he worked as a junk peddler. He later operated the Workingmen's Clothing Store. His wife, Jennie, lived for a time on a farm in Lakebay, near the anarchist colony of Home. Max filed for citizenship at least three times, each time declaring that he was not an anarchist. In 1938 he published a newspaper notice that he was not responsible for the debts of his wife. His Hebrew name was Menachem Mendel b' r' Shmuel ha Cohen. (Not the same Mendel Aronin who died in 1942.) Two of his daughters died in childhood, two did not marry, and the fifth married in a church; and the Cohen line ended.

Warren Irwin Barde, son of Ben L. and Rebecca (Barrell) Barde/Bardechefsky
Born February 27, 1922, in Portland, Oregon
Married Adelyn "Addie" Estelle Meier (1926-2013) in Tacoma on November 30, 1946
Parents of Wendy, Glen, and Ross
Died December 13, 2017, in Tacoma; buried Home of Peace Cemetery

(Right) Tacoma News Tribune October 25, 1981
(Below) Tacoma News Tribune September 11, 1969

"RANDY" BARDE TONIGHT ON TACOMA CHANNEL 62

Coin collecting as a hobby will be explained, illustrated . . . and perhaps encouraged . . . by Warren "Randy" Barde. Then stay tuned for the other provocative features:

7:30 BARDE ON COIN COLLECTING
8:00 MASS MEDIA, LIBERATING OR PERVERTING?
9:00 JAZZ ALLEY: "DOC" EVANS
9:30 BOOK BEAT: THE THROWAWAY CHILDREN.

TONIGHT KTPS CH. 62 Tune Channel 62 as follows: Attach the UHF loop antenna to the UHF terminals in back of set. Turn the dial marked 2-13 to its "U" position. Then turn dial marked 14-83 to 62.

Warren grew up in Seattle and served in the Navy during World War II. After his military service he attended the University of Washington, where he met his future bride, Addie. Her father, William D. Meier, took him into the family jewelry and loan business, renamed Randy's Loans. Decades later Warren would take his own son, Ross, into the same firm. Addie was active in Hadassah and Sinai Temple. Warren served as president of the Tacoma Coin Club in the Sixties and as "Sir Boss" of the Daffodilians in the Eighties. Addie and Warren supported educational programs across the city, especially later at Temple Beth El, where their descendants are still active members.

George Barnett
Born November 5, 1881 or 1882, in Russia or Lithuania
Married Ruby Toub (1879-1968) on January 1, 1901, (1/1/1) in St. Joseph, Missouri
Parents of Edward Valentine Barnett (1903-1983) born in Centerville, Iowa
Died in Tacoma on September 30, 1950; buried Home of Peace Cemetery

George Barnett worked briefly in Denver, Colorado, in 1910 as an optician. He spent the rest of his career selling clothes for Hy Mandles. (Hy was also in Denver in 1910 and in Iowa in 1903.) George worked for decades for Hy in Chehalis, Washington, before moving to Tacoma around 1936. Both men retired in 1945, and died one day apart in 1950.

George and Ruby's only son, **Edward Barnett**, married in 1923 to Anna P. Friedman (1903-1982), daughter of Abraham M. Friedman. At the time she had just returned from visiting relatives in England, Ireland, and Chicago. Edward and Anna lived in Chehalis and Bremerton in the Twenties and in Tacoma in the Thirties. Their children, Florence (1924-1995) and Howard (1928-2004), taught in the Talmud Torah religious school. Florence was confirmed in 1937. Edward worked as an optometrist for Tacoma's Peoples Store before opening his own practice. The family later lived in Spokane and retired in Reno, Nevada.

Miss Anna Friedman, Tacoma Daily Ledger September 24, 1922

—Photo by Hartsook Studio.
Miss Anna Friedman, young Tacoma girl, who has just returned from a six months' tour of Great Britain.

Henry Bell, born October 1, 1874, in Riga, Russia (now Latvia)
Married Sarah Ethel Janovsky before 1903
Immigrated about 1906
Parents of Samuel (1903-1979), Phillip (1905-1971), David (1911-1993), Frances Oransky (1913-2002),
    and Eva Piearson/Blas (1916-1995)
Died February 22, 1947; buried Chevra Kadisha Cemetery, Home of Peace Cemetery

Henry's first two children were born in Riga. Three more were born in California. Henry worked in San Francisco as a shoemaker from about 1907 until his divorce in the late Twenties. He operated a secondhand clothing and shoe store in Tacoma during the Thirties. In November of 1937 Henry donated a Torah scroll to the Talmud Torah congregation in memory of his father.

Henry Bell, 1937 Torah donation ceremony
Courtesy of the Farber Family

John Robert "Jack" Bender, son of Heiman and Rachael (Friedman) Binder
Born March 20, 1892/4, in Kekava, Russia (now Latvia)
Arrived New York July 5, 1907, aboard the *Andalusia* as Jacob Binder
Married Florence Kubey (1900-1927) in Seattle on October 4, 1923
Parents of Henrienne (1926-1986)
Married second to Alice Carrick (1905-1992) in Seattle on March 20, 1932
Died in Tacoma on October 25, 1982; buried Home of Peace Cemetery

As a teenager Jack lived with Julius Friedman in Tacoma, working as a clerk for Julius while attending business school. He worked nearly a decade in Alaska, applying for naturalization from Wrangell in 1917. Jack lived in Seattle in the early Twenties and after his first wife's death returned to Tacoma. Along with his second wife, Alice, he was active in Talmud Torah, serving as vice president of the congregation in 1937. Jack's brother, Morris, occasionally filled the role of Cantor. Jack worked in retail ready-to-wear from 1932 to 1945, and in 1950 opened a store called Bender's. His daughter, Henrienne, attended Seattle's Ryther School and did not marry. His wife, Alice Carrick Bender, was the daughter of David and Jennie Carrick and sister of Minnie (Carrick) Weinstone. She was president of Tacoma's Council of Jewish Women in 1942. Alice had a career in nursing and at the time of her death was surgical supervisor at Tacoma General Hospital.

Jack Bender, courtesy of Jay Schupack

Albert "Al" Leon Benezra, son of Leon Jack/Jouda and Pearl (Franco) Benezra/Benestra
Born June 4, 1915, in Seattle, Washington; twin of Jack
Married Annabelle Becker (1923-1997) in Seattle on August 2, 1945
Parents of Saralyn, Janet Lee, and Elaine
Died November 29, 1990 in Tacoma; buried Home of Peace Cemetery

Tacoma News Tribune August 31, 1958

Although Albert and Annabelle were both born and raised in Seattle, they came from very different backgrounds. Albert's parents were Sephardic, born in Istanbul and the Isle of Rhodes. Annabelle's parents, Josephine Eichenwald and Solomon Becker, were part of the Courland, Latvia, cluster of families. Two of Anabelle's siblings married Friedmans. Albert and Annabelle's 1945 marriage was remembered as one of the early "inter-marriages" in Seattle.

Annabelle was active in the Sinai Temple Sisterhood in the 1950s and also in Hadassah. Albert was a B'nai B'rith trustee and president of Sinai Temple in 1960 at the time of the merger. He operated the Pacific Loan and Jewelry pawn shop for decades. Shared ads from 1958 indicate a close relationship among the proprietors of the neighboring loan shops.

- Western Loan – Leo & Morris Plotkin
- London Loan – William Sherman
- Pacific Loan – A.L. Benezra
- Century Loan – Allen I. Kosin

Mendel "Max" Baer Berlin, son of David and Ella (Zineet) Berlin
Born May 20, 1884, or March 4, 1888; in Sebezh, Russia
Arrived in Detroit, Michigan, January 12, 1906, going to Chicago
Married Ida E. Miller in Seattle on July 10, 1909
Parents of Louis (1910 - 2001)
Died in Los Angeles on December 9, 1964; buried Mount
Sinai, Los Angeles, California

Tacoma Daily Ledger October 17, 1926

Max and Ida lived in Seattle when their son was born. During World War I Max and Ida lived in the Home Colony in Lakebay, raising chickens for breeders. They moved to Tacoma about 1922 and operated Art Tailors. Their son, Louis, was a member of Talmud Torah's Young Hebrew Moderates club in 1925 and celebrated his bar mitzvah there. Max and Ida moved to Los Angeles about 1929 and during World War II Max operated a men's clothing and uniform business in Long Beach. He had applied for citizenship in 1921 from Lakebay as Max, and applied again in 1943 from Los Angeles as Mendel. Their son, Louis, married first to Grace Bowman in Tacoma in 1929. He worked as a cabinet maker and in 1931 operated Berlin Manufacturing, making refrigerators. Louis married second to Zepha McClurg and died in Riverside, California.

Jacob Blechman, son of Solomon Blechmann
Born July 4, 1894; in Libau, Russia (now Liepaja, Latvia)
Arrived in New York aboard the *United States* on November 9, 1915
Married first to Anna Tone (1902-1956) in 1922, daughter of Abraham and Jennie (Friedman) Tone
Parents of Sidney Blechman (1923-2008)
Married second to Lois Oakley (1902-1960) on September 18, 1943, in Pierce County, Washington
Died February 4, 1973 in Tacoma; buried Home of Peace Cemetery

Jacob spent his entire career as a fine tailor. He stated in newspaper interviews that he worked in Russia, Germany, Denmark and Sweden. When still a teenager he made an evening wrap for the Queen of Sweden. In the U.S. he worked first in Duluth and then Spokane. Jacob came to Tacoma when he was drafted in 1918, but was rejected due to his short stature. He briefly joined Temple Beth Israel in 1919. His marriage to Anna ended in divorce and he raised their son, Sidney, on his own. Sidney was confirmed in Talmud Torah in 1937. Jacob remarried to Lois Oakley in 1943 and she died in 1960. Jacob then lived in a downtown hotel near his store and often worked on clothing late into the night. His son, Sidney, served in the Army Air Corps in World War II and later lived in Baltimore, Maryland.

Tacoma News Tribune September 23, 1951

Myer "Mike" Block, son of Ben and Rose (Adrem/Adirim) Block
Born January 11, 1918, in Bellingham, Washington
Married Rebecca "Beck" Lillian Gordon (1922-1995) on December 20, 1941, in Bellingham
Parents of David and Michael Block
Died January 10, 1997, in Sarasota, Florida; buried Home of Peace Cemetery

Mike enlisted in the U.S. Army on September 12, 1942, while still a newlywed. His wife, Rebecca, was born in Montreal and raised in Vancouver, daughter of Charles and Fanny (Clauson) Gordon. She worked with Mike in their furniture store in Olympia in the Forties, and then for decades in Tacoma. In the Fifties she was active in the Sinai Temple Sisterhood and was elected president in 1959. Mike served on the board of the Bank of Tacoma and the Tacoma Tigers.

Block's Furniture, 8205 South Tacoma Way, February 1959
Tacoma Public Library Richards A119719-4

David Boonov, son of Shimon and Judith (Pastevaski) Boonov
Born January 1, 1889, in Kherson, Nikolaiev, Russia (now Ukraine)
Arrived in Minnesota by rail in 1915 from Winnipeg, Canada
Married Rose Lichterman (1894-1975) on December 24, 1916, in Minneapolis, Minnesota
Parents of Irving (1917-1947), Florence Romey (1920-1994), Julia Madsen (1923-1977), and
     Claire Litchman (1925-2017)
Died June 21, 1945, in San Francisco, California; buried Eternal Home Cemetery, Colma, California

David and Rose lived in Minneapolis in 1917 when their son was born. They moved to Tacoma in September of 1918 and had three daughters. David operated his own sheet metal working business in downtown Tacoma. The couple performed several Russian duets during a Russian literature program led by Dr. Spector in 1930. Two of their children were in a Talmud Torah play in 1932. The family moved to Seattle about 1937, and David and Rose divorced in 1940. Their only son, Irving, lived at Western State Hospital in Steilacoom from 1942 until his death in 1947 from Hodgkin's disease. His two younger sisters both studied nursing at Seattle's Providence Hospital and served in the Cadet Nursing Corps in World War II. His widow, Rose, lived the remainder of her life in Seattle and was buried in the Seattle Sephardic Cemetery.

Claire and Irving Boonov, Tacoma Daily Ledger March 20, 1932

Pincus Philip "Phil" Brodsky, son of Chaim and Cerna Dora (Schwartzman) Brodsky
Born June 16, 1894, in Kishenev, Russia (Later Romania, now Chisinau, Moldova)
Arrived in N.Y. January 23, 1914, aboard the *Carpathia,* via Trieste, Austria, as Pincus Brodski
Married Anne Plotkin (1898-1979) in Seattle on June 26, 1916, daughter of Sam and Mary
Parents of Dorothy Maier (1917-1997), Gladys Skorman (1921-2010), and Edith Jaffe (1926-2017)
Died in Pierce County on September 26, 1975; buried Home of Peace Cemetery

Pincus emigrated with his sister, Chane (Anna) in 1914. She married barber Samuel Moises in Seattle in 1915. Pincus worked in a Seattle bakery and lived with his sister until his own marriage the next year. His mother and younger sister joined them in 1920. By then Pincus, now Phil, was operating Victory Tailors at Camp Lewis. His brother-in-law, Abram Plotkin, worked with him and lived with the family in an area of DuPont then known as Greene Park. Phil and his wife Anne moved into Tacoma in the fall of 1928. Anne was active in the Women's Auxiliary of Talmud Torah in the Thirties and was vice president in 1939. Phil was president of Talmud Torah in 1937 and 1943.

Increased mobilization at Fort Lewis in 1940 forced the uniform tailoring business off-post and into a store on South Tacoma Way. Three years later Phil bought a downtown building on the corner of South 13th and Pacific. His son-in-law, recent veteran Morris Jaffe, joined him in managing the store. After Phil's death the store name was changed to Brodsky's Men's Wear and Uniforms. The extended family operated Brodsky's for many more decades.

5433 South Tacoma Way in 1940
Tacoma Public Library Richards A9839-3

Samuel "Sam" Brotman, son of Edel and Leah (Katz) Brotman
Born September 20, 1873, in Montreal, Canada
Married Fanny Pelenovsky (1880-1977) in 1898 in Wapella, Saskatchewan, Canada
Six children born in Saskatchewan, Canada, between 1900 and 1915
Arrived in Washington November 8, 1923, via Vancouver, British Columbia
Died December 29, 1962, in Tacoma; buried Home of Peace Cemetery

Sam and Fanny married in the Jewish farming community of Wapella on December 25, 1898, in a ceremony performed by Sam's father. They later lived in the town of Balgoni, just east of Regina. After the deaths of Sam's parents the couple moved to Tacoma. They immediately bought a home on North 29th Street, just as they celebrated their twenty-fifth wedding anniversary. (They would celebrate their sixtieth anniversary from the same home.) The Brotman family was initially active in Talmud Torah. Three of their boys were members of the Young Hebrew Moderates in 1925. Sam worked first as an auctioneer, then operated Western Furniture and Hardware. During the Twenties and Thirties he sold secondhand goods from a variety of locations on Commerce Street. Tacoma's flourishing economy in the Forties encouraged Sam to open his own menswear store, as did his sons.

Sam and Fanny's eldest son, Manuel, (1900-1979) stayed in Vancouver, B.C. Their eldest daughter, Rose, (1902-1996) married David Sanford in 1926 and moved east. Morley (1910-1980) partnered with his brothers in selling clothing, operated a photo studio, and then promoted major events and advocated for construction of the Tacoma Dome. Bernie (1912-1996) worked with his brothers and later had several clothing stores in Seattle. By 1942 both Morley and Bernie were members of Temple Beth Israel. Sam and Fanny's youngest daughter, Meta, (1915-2008) married Carl Williams and lived in Olympia.

Sam and Fanny's son **Harold "Hal" Brotman** (1906-1982) was president of Talmud Torah's Young Hebrew Moderates group in 1925. Hal married Phyllis Lamken (1914-2004) in Tacoma on March 25, 1939. She would be a mainstay of Hadassah events for decades. They had three children: Pamela, Arlen, and Paul. Hal chaired the Sinai Temple's 40th anniversary dinner in 1948, but in 1957 served on the board of Temple Beth Israel. Just before his marriage Hal started the Stevens-Brotman Toggery, then partnered in Brotman Brothers. Located at 9th and Commerce, the store was advertised as the "Doorway to a Man's World." In 1947 their second location, on Broadway, was home to the "Three Busy Bees." By 1955 Hal owned Brotman's independently. He and his brothers often sponsored local recreational teams.

Tacoma News Tribune August 16, 1947

Jess J. Brown, son of William I. and Rose (Sentner) Brenan/Brown
Born October 22, 1920, in Seattle, Washington
Married Sylvia Schwartz (1925-2020) in Seattle on March 28, 1948
Died February 4, 1994, in Seattle; buried Sunset Hills Memorial, Bellevue

Jess was born and raised in Seattle, the youngest of five siblings. He served in the military from 1942 to 1946. After his marriage he moved to Tacoma and operated Brown's Shop-N-Save Pharmacy in South Tacoma. In the late Fifties he ran a pharmacy in Fircrest. His wife, Sylvia, was born in Tacoma, daughter of Mosbs and Julia Schwartz. Sylvia participated in Sinai Temple Sisterhood events, along with Jess's sister, Ann (second wife of Irving Gussman and Ben Etsekson). Jess and Sylvia returned to Seattle around 1960.

Joseph J. Buckner, son of Philip and Lena Buchner
Born November 11, 1888, in Lomza, Russia (now Poland)
Arrived N.Y. September 5, 1905, aboard the *Potsdam* as Yudel with his sister Yides
Married Fannie J. Marylander (1895-1987) in Tacoma on July 2, 1916
Parents of Dawne Carrol (1917-1998), Harriette Kolker/Coret (1919-2015), and Fillmore Buckner
Died October 2, 1944, in Tacoma; buried Home of Peace Cemetery

1920 Tacoma city Polk directory ad

JOE'S RELIABLE LOAN OFFICE, (Jos Buchner) New and Second Hand Goods, Buy and Sell everything of Value, 1145 Commerce

Joseph began his American career peddling vegetables from a wagon in Babylon, New York. He came to Tacoma in the spring of 1912 and immediately filed his petition for naturalization. Like many others from Tacoma's Jewish community Joseph brought Julius Friedman to court with him to testify as his witness. And like many others, he operated a secondhand clothing business that gradually evolved into a loan and pawn company. For many years his firm was at 1145 Commerce. In 1919 it was called Joe's Reliable Loan. That year Joseph bought a bungalow-style home on North Lawrence for $5500. Fannie's sister and husband, Eva and Adolph Miller, lived with the couple. Fannie was active in Hadassah and in 1931 served as recording secretary of Talmud Torah's women's Auxiliary. That same year Joseph served on the Workmen's Circle convention committee. The family spelled its surname Buchner until the 1930s, then transitioned to the phonetic Buckner. After Joseph's death Fannie moved to Seattle. Their daughter, Harriette Coret, later wrote several manuscripts and stories about growing up in Tacoma.

Irving/Irwin Izaak Burian, son of Salmon and Laura (Piapis) Burian
Born May 11, 1884, in Lemburg, Poland
Married about 1920 to Fanny Gittel Silver (1896-1947) daughter of David and Zlata (Bohrer) Silver
Arrived N.Y. October 8, 1938, aboard the *Pilsudski,* continuing to Seattle
Both died April 7, 1947 in a Seattle bus crash; buried Herzl Cemetery, Seattle

Izaak Burian served in the Austrian army during World War I. During the war he was captured by the Russian army and held as a prisoner of war until he escaped and made his way back to Austria. He and his wife made yet another escape, fleeing from Vienna in September of 1938, but leaving his brother Moritz behind. Together they operated the Marvel Dress Shop in Tacoma for nearly a decade, specializing in large dress sizes. In 1947 they did not escape from their bus that collided with an oil tanker and fell into the Duwamish River, killing nine of the twenty-seven occupants. At the time of his death Irving was secretary of Sinai Temple. Fannie was survived by her brother, Henry Silver of Seattle, and a nephew of Portland, likely Michael Green.

Tacoma News Tribune October 22, 1944

Rabbi Ralph Y. Carmi, son of Shabatai and Faiga Tzipora (Abramitsky) Chorowsky
Born May 15, 1924 in Volpo, Grodno, Poland (now Belarus) as Yerachmiel Chorowsky
Arrived N.Y. October 29, 1947, from Haifa, Israel, aboard the *Marine Jumper*
Married Rosalie Rein (1924-2020) in Brooklyn, New York, on August 8, 1950
Parents of five daughters
Died May of 2018 in Deerfield Beach, Florida

Yerachmiel Chorowosky lived with his parents in Jerusalem in the 1930s when his younger sisters were born. He studied at the Yeshiva Petach Tikvah and emigrated to the U.S. in 1947 from Tel Aviv. Yerachmiel attended Yeshiva College in New York and was ordained as a rabbi at the Isaac Elchanan Theological Seminary in July of 1950. A month later he married Rosalie Rein. The couple lived in Fond du Lac, Wisconsin, in 1955, still as Chorowosky. There he led the K'hilath Jacob Synagogue. As Ralph Carmi he served as rabbi of Sinai Temple in Tacoma from August of 1956 through July of 1957. He later held positions in New Brunswick, Canada; Fitchburg, Massachusetts; and in several locations in Florida. In 1990 he celebrated the 40th anniversary of his ordination and his marriage, and the 25th anniversary of his congregation, Temple Beth Raphael in Miami Beach, Florida.

Miami (Florida) Herald September 24, 1992

David Carrick, son of Alexander and Esther (Chamilansky) Kurcik
Born November 26, 1880/1882, in Mogilev, Russia (now Mahilyow, Belarus)
Emigrated to Glasgow, Scotland, about 1890 with his parents and family
Married Jennie Galon (1887-1983) in Glasgow, daughter of Jacob Galon
Parents of Alice Bender (1905-1992) and Minnie Weinstone (1908-1973), both born in Glasgow
Arrived Tacoma July 11, 1909, at the invitation of the Warnick and Polisky families
Died December 14, 1963 in Tacoma; buried Home of Peace Cemetery

David's first position in Tacoma was working as a cabinetmaker for Harris Warnick at the Wheeler-Osgood Company. In 1914 he opened a grocery store at 1934 South E Street (later Fawcett Avenue) in the heart of the Orthodox Jewish community. He ran the same grocery for forty years, selling a steady stream of daily newspapers from the front displays. In January of 1921 he purchased a home at 1906 North Junett for $5,000. David withdrew his savings from Tacoma's Scandinavian-Bank to make the cash purchase just one day before the bank closed in failure. His wife, Jennie, was a life member of Hadassah and the girls both attended Talmud Torah activities. In 1926 Minnie performed in a small orchestra with her Rabstoff cousins as part of the Young Hebrew Moderates. Jennie joined the B'nai B'rith Destiny women's auxiliary in 1936, after both of her daughters had married.

(Right) Tacoma News Tribune October 22, 1954

David's oldest brother, Myer, and his wife, Sarah Polisky, immigrated to Montreal from Glasgow around 1910. They moved to Detroit in 1923. The rest of the Carrick family followed David to Washington. All but his mother were buried in the New Tacoma Cemetery.

- Mother Esther (1846-1933) died in Tacoma; buried Cheva Kadisha Cemetery, Home of Peace
- Sister Gertrude (1883-1955) married Nathan Rabstoff (1885-1961)
- Brother Harry (1889-1968) worked as a barber in Montesano, Washington
- Sister Anna (1893-1966) married barber Alexander Davis (1889-1964)

Leon Judas Charney, M.D., son of Samuel J. and Rebecca (Goldberg) Tschernawsky
Born December 5, 1899, in Chernigov, Russia (now Chernihiv, Ukraine)
Married Rose Irene Magidson (1903-1984)
Parents of Millicent, Nancy (1931-1997), and Sanford (1940-2009)
Died December 29, 1972, in Denver, Colorado

Leon Charney and his family lived in Tacoma briefly during his military service in World War II. His eldest daughter, Millicent, participated in Talmud Torah services for the B'nai B'rith Girls' Sabbath in 1942 and sang in the choir. She graduated from Clover Park High School in 1943. Her younger sister, Nancy, also participated in Talmud Torah school activities. The family later lived several years in Albuquerque before returning to Denver, Colorado, where Leon had grown up.

Samuel Clayman, son of Max Simon and Dora (Goldberg) Claymann
Born May 2, 1879-1881, in Pilwiszki, Marjampol, Russia (now Pilviskiai, Lithuania)
Arrived N.Y. June 27, 1891, aboard the *Normannia* as Shmuel, aged 7, with his family
Married Lena Eichenwald (1881-1951) on October 5, 1911, in Missouri
Parents of Belle Ruth Witkin (1917-1998) and Herbert (1919-1984)
Died April 27, 1943, in Tacoma; buried Bikur Cholim Cemetery, Seattle

Sam and Lena (Eichenwald) Clayman, courtesy of Jay Schupack

Samuel grew up in a large family in Des Moines, Iowa. He worked for three decades for the Milwaukee and St. Paul Railroad. Samuel was a resident of Seattle when he married into the Eichenwald family in 1911. He moved to Tacoma about 1924 and worked as a life insurance representative. His wife and children took leadership roles in Tacoma's Jewish community in the Thirties. Lena was involved in the Women's Auxiliary in 1930. Their son, Herbert, was in a play at Talmud Torah in 1932 but was confirmed at Temple Beth Israel in 1933. In 1937 their daughter, Belle Ruth, performed Kol Nidre on KMO radio as part of Talmud Torah's Yom Kippur programming. For the next two years she led Talmud Torah's choir. After Samuel's death in 1943, Lena moved back to Seattle, where both of her children married.

Herbert earned an engineering degree from the University of Washington and spent his entire career with the Boeing Company. He served in England during World War II with the rank of major. Belle Ruth was valedictorian of her Stadium High School class. She earned her bachelor's degree in English literature in 1939 and taught briefly at the Gig Harbor High School. In 1941 Belle Ruth suffered major injuries in an automobile crash and spent the summer convalescing. After her 1944 marriage she traveled with her military husband, returning to Seattle to earn a master's degree in speech pathology and a doctorate in speech science. In the Fifties she was on the speech faculty at U.W., and in the Sixties and Seventies led an educational creativity program in California.

Lena Clayman with Joe, Belle Ruth and Cheryl Witkin, courtesy of Jay Schupack

Jacob Cohen/Jack Cowan, son of Joseph and Rachel (Apalca) Cohen
Born about 1888 in Glasgow, Scotland
Married Rebecca "Ruby" Weinstone (1890-1942) in Glasgow
Parents of Woolfe Cohen/Will Cowan (1911-1994)
Arrived N.Y. May 25, 1921, aboard the *Cameronia*, passage paid by wife
Died as Jack Cowan in Los Angeles on October 22, 1939, buried in Forest Lawn, Los Angeles

Rebecca (Weinstone) Cohen came to Tacoma with her son, Woolfe, in 1919, just in time to contribute to the War Relief campaign. She joined her parents, Froem and Bertha (Kurash) Weinstone, four months before her mother's death. Rebecca's husband, Jacob, joined her in 1921. In 1923 the family moved to Los Angeles, adopting the names Jack, Ruby, and Will Cowan. Jack worked as a tailor and a salesman. His son, Will, worked in Hollywood in the Forties and Fifties and produced over 200 short films.

Jacob Solomon Cohen, son of Israel Abram and Anna (Lindenbaum) Kahn
Born about August 1863 in Suwalki, Russia (now Poland)
Married Sarah Phildofsky/Phillips (1864-1944) about 1883
Died February 22, 1922, in Los Angeles; buried Beth Israel Cemetery, Los Angeles

Sarah and Jacob had nearly one dozen children in New York, Saint Louis, New Orleans, San Francisco, and Indianapolis. After a decade in Indianapolis they moved to Vancouver, British Columbia; about 1910. Sarah opened a branch store in Tacoma in 1918, the Liberty Clothing store at 1318 Pacific Avenue. After Jacob's death Sarah developed several properties in Tacoma's Sixth Avenue district and built a home on Junett Street. At the time the Sixth Avenue merchants were actively working together to secure funding for the first Tacoma Narrows Bridge. In 1939 Sarah served on the Talmud Torah Purim banquet committee. Her obituary noted that she had been present for the synagogue cornerstone ceremony. A plaque bearing her name was taken from the 1968 demolition site.

Sarah and Jacob's children lived in Los Angeles and in Vancouver, British Columbia. Their son, Samuel (1897-1966), developed a prominent Canadian chain of Army and Navy Stores. Their daughter, Bessie (1894-1978), performed as an actress in Shanghai under the name Carmen Carlyle and married financier Arthur Julius Israel. Their daughter, Anna (1901-1985), married Joseph Robinson and stayed in Tacoma and Seattle.

Abe Cohn, son of Isaac Leponsky (per death certificate)
Born April 15, 1880, in Maxtovia (now Yanova, Russia)
Arrived N.Y. September 12, 1900 aboard the *Barbarossa* from Bremen, Germany
Married Rose Gordon (1878-1933) and Dora Miller (1891-1947) in 1944
Parents of Philip Colin (1902-1989) and Alex Cohn (1906-1986)
Died February 5, 1953, in Steilacoom; buried Home of Peace Cemetery
(Below) Tacoma News Tribune July 25, 1924

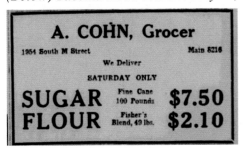

A. COHN, Grocer
1954 South M Street   Main 8216
We Deliver
SATURDAY ONLY
SUGAR Fine Cane 100 Pounds $7.50
FLOUR Fisher's Blend, 49 lbs. $2.10

Abe and Rose likely married around 1900. Their first son, Philip, was born in Baltimore in 1902. They next lived in Chicago, where their son, Alex, was born in 1906. By 1910 Abe worked as a tailor in the Pierce County community of Lakebay, although his sons graduated from high school in Tacoma. Alex was vice president of the Young Moderates in 1925. For decades Abe ran a grocery store at 1954 South M and lived nearby at 1930 South M Street. Both buildings still stand and the storefront is now a church.

Abe and Rose were active members of Workmen's Circle. In 1931 the regional convention was held in Talmud Torah. Abe served on the local committee and was elected treasurer. Rose was district recorder in 1933 and Abe was president in 1939. Rose died late in 1933 and Abe remarried in 1944. At the time of his second marriage his son, Alex, had just been promoted to staff sergeant. Alex served in the U.S. Army from 1942 until 1945, then returned to continue his father's grocery store. He never married.

Abe and Rose's eldest son, Philip, was a brilliant scholar who earned a doctorate and became a research chemist. He took the surname Colin and worked in research and development for Tidewater Associated Oil. In 1941 Philip became head of chemical engineering research for Merck. During his career he helped develop processes for synthetic vitamins, penicillin, cortisone, and other drugs. At the end of his career in the Sixties he was vice president of Merck International, living in the Bahamas.

John N. Coleman, born July 24, 1884, in Leipzig, Germany
Married Bertha "Berdie" Harris (1887-1970) in August of 1915 in Hannibal, Missouri
Parents of Samuel (1916-1944), Abe (1921-2015), and Goldie Siron/Robinson (1922-2014)
Died January 9, 1951, in Tacoma; buried Home of Peace Cemetery

John and Berdie lived in Missouri when their first child was born. They were in Kansas for the births of the next two. John worked as a furniture merchant in both places. They moved to Tacoma about 1931. Their eldest son, Samuel, was an outstanding track athlete at Stadium High School and at U.W. He married Sarah Atwood in 1942, but was lost in action in the Marshall Islands in 1944. Their second son, Abe, also served in the military. After the war he married Naomi Hasson Vangler, niece of Joseph Rome. A decade later Abe married Anna Schaffner Ball. John and Berdie's only daughter, Goldie, participated in Junior League and BBG events at Talmud Torah in 1938 and 1940. She married first to George Siron and second to Clarence Robinson. Berdie's nephew was the noted designer, A. Lester Gaba, son of her sister, Mamie (Harris) Gaba.

Samuel "Sam" Cone, son of Jacob
Born Solomon Chon on June 2, 1879 in Pietro, Romania
Arrived in Washington on October 11, 1901, via Victoria, British Columbia
Married Goldie Rickles (1885-1971) on March 14, 1905, in Seattle
Parents of Rosalie Karp (1906-2006), Gerald (1915-2017), and Julian "Morton" (1917-1997)
Died November 24, 1957, in Tacoma; buried Bikur Cholim Cemetery, Seattle

Goldie Rickles moved to Seattle with her parents, George and Lena Rose (Tomashin) Rickles, shortly after the 1889 downtown fire. Her younger brother Pincus, known as Pinky, was active in the regional B'nai B'rith. Sam and Goldie married in Seattle in 1905, where all three of their children were born. From 1926 to 1933 Sam operated the Home Furniture store in Port Angeles. The family then moved to Tacoma. They ran three related businesses: Ideal Dress Manufacturing, the Betty Lou Dress Shop, and the Remnant Shop. Sam was elected treasurer of Talmud Torah in 1938. The next year Goldie was elected president of Talmud Torah's Women's Auxiliary, and her daughter, Rosalie, (Mrs. Jack Karp) served as treasurer. Their son, Gerald, married Tacoma's Molly Lamken (1918-2016) in September of 1939. In 1940 Sam and his son-in-law, Jack Karp, agreed to comply with the new minimum wage hour law that required salaries of thirty cents per hour. Sam and Goldie celebrated their 50th wedding anniversary in 1955 at Tacoma's Top of the Ocean restaurant. Sinai Temple paid tribute to the couple by creating a children's library fund in their honor.

Tacoma News Tribune August 26, 1938

123

Boris Herman Dannenhirsch, son of Herman and Cecelia (Boruchowitsch/Brooks) Dannenhirsch
Born May 5, 1888, in Riga, Russia (now Latvia)
Arrived N.Y. June 4, 1904, aboard the *Island* via Copenhagen, Denmark
Married Annabelle Levitt (1896-1967) on February 15, 1921, in Portland, Oregon
Parents of Harold H. Dannenhirsch/Dannen (1927-1988)
Died September 22, 1948, in Alameda, California; buried Golden Gate National Cemetery, San Bruno

Boris emigrated with his father as a teen, a year after his mother and five other siblings. He lived with his family in Seattle for nearly ten years before moving to Tacoma. Boris worked as a clerk for several Jewish clothing merchants, including David Shafer, Morris Cheim, Sam Sondheim and Nathan Bloom. In 1919 he donated to the war relief fund as a member of Talmud Torah. Boris served in the U.S. Naval Reserve Forces from March of 1918 until September of 1921. His wife, Annabelle, had previously married Abraham Domb and had a son Leonard in 1918. After his marriage Boris operated his own clothing store at 1348 Pacific Avenue. In 1926 he briefly partnered with Arthur Meier in the firm of Danno and Meier, and joined Temple Beth Israel. He later worked as a department manager for the Hub Clothiers, around the time of his 1931 divorce. Boris moved to San Francisco in the mid-Thirties, worked in wholesale men's clothing, and was an officer in the B'nai B'rith there. At the time of his death his son, Harold Dannen, was serving in the U.S. Navy. His stepson, Leonard, died in a prisoner of war camp in Germany in 1945 while serving in the U.S. Army.

Tacoma News Tribune June 17, 1926

Rabbi Julius Louis DeKoven, son of Louis/Lieb Yehuda and Sarah/Sura (Corn) Duchowna/Duchovna
Born July 12 or 18, 1914, in Kazatin, Kiev, Russia (now Kozyatin, Ukraine)
Arrived N.Y. October 12, 1920, with his family aboard the *New Amsterdam*, as Yossel Duchowna
Married Miriam Astrachan (1915-1978) on June 21, 1940, in Chicago, Illinois
Killed May 12, 1979, in Sherman Oaks, California; buried Young Israel Cemetery, Norwalk, California

Julius grew up in Chicago. There he attended the Lewis Institute and graduated from the University of Chicago. Shortly after his marriage he worked in Cheyenne, Wyoming, for a year, then led Beth Jacob Synagogue in Cedar Rapids, Iowa, for another year. He and Miriam lived in Tacoma for nearly three years, then moved to Austin, Texas, in the fall of 1946. In Austin he took the given name Joel. The couple moved to California about 1948, where they lived and worked for the remainder of their lives. Rabbi DeKoven started his own synagogue as a business, Temple Beth Daiah, in 1966. He was murdered in his Sherman Oaks home in 1979, shortly after he sold his synagogue.

(Above right) 1941 Jewish Welfare Board correspondence signature
(Right) Los Angeles Times ad August 25, 1975

Eric Raphael Deutsch, son of Max Wilhelm and Hannah (Pfifferling) Deutschlaender
Born June 7, 1908, in Hamburg, Germany as Erich Raphael Deutschlaender
Married Hanni Kessel (1914-1999) in Hamburg, Germany
Arrived N.Y. April 27, 1939, aboard *Manhattan,* from Hamburg, Germany
Parents of Harvey Deutsch, born in St. Louis, Missouri
Died December 27, 1994, in Santa Barbara, California

Eric's younger brother, Alfred, left Germany first. He arrived in New York in 1937, joining his aunt, Freida Rosenstein, in St. Louis. His mother, Hannah, came next, in March of 1939. Eric and his wife, Hanni, followed a month later. Eric immediately applied to become a U.S. citizen and in October of 1940 registered for the draft from St. Louis as a hat salesman. His father, Max, joined the family from Shanghai in the fall of 1946. By that time Eric and Hanni had a son, Harvey. Eric and Hanni lived in Oakland, California, and them moved to Tacoma around 1954. Both worked for the Karl's Shoe Store chain. Hanni was corresponding secretary of the Sinai Sisterhood in 1957 and was still active as a hostess in 1964. Eric was elected to the first board of Temple Beth El in 1960. The couple moved to Santa Barbara and both managed the Karl's Shoe store there for another decade.
Tacoma News Tribune July 13, 1961

Leon Hillel Diamond, son of Harry and Ida (Goodman) Diamond
Born March 1, 1909, in Roanoake, Virginia
Married Estelle "Stella" Bulos (1908-1991) in Seattle on June 16, 1931
Parents of Irene, Martin, and Nancy
Died April 29, 1957, in Redwood City, San Mateo, California; buried Sacramento, California

Leon was born and raised in Roanoke, Virginia. In the early Twenties he moved to Tacoma with his parents, who operated a grocery store. While still a student at Stadium he worked as a jewelry clerk. In 1925 Leon was a charter member of the Young Hebrew Moderates. He moved to Seattle, where he married in 1931. His mother died in 1934 and he and his father moved to San Francisco in 1939. Leon continued selling jewelry throughout his career.

(Not the Dr. Leon S. Diamond [1915-1995] son of Charles and Lena [Greenberg] Diamond, who served as the first president of Temple Beth El in 1960.)

Herman Moses Dobry

Born May 10, 1876/8, in Tomsk, Siberia, Russia, as Michayeel Dobrovolsky
Married Rose Pologeya LeBid (1883-1960) on March 20, 1901, in Tomsk (Sister of Max LeBid)
Parents of Leoinditis "Leo" Dobrovolsky born in Tomsk
Arrived in Tacoma on March 21, 1913, on the *Chicago Maru* from Japan
Died June 17, 1958, in Tacoma; buried Home of Peace Cemetery

AUTOMOBILE TRADING CO., M. Dobry, Mgr., 1348 Commerce. Main 4215. Automobile accessories and repairing.

Tacoma News Tribune June 3, 1920

Moses and Rose Dobry purchased twenty acres of land in Pierce County near Lakebay in 1914 and 1915 through loans from the Jewish Agricultural and Industrial Aid Society. The property was foreclosed in the summer of 1917. By then the couple was living in Tacoma, where Moses sold junk and later worked in auto wrecking. In the Twenties he operated the Automobile Trading Company, including auto accessories and repairing. The couple invited 200 guests to their 25th wedding anniversary party in 1925. Moses officially changed his name to Herman as part of his 1926 naturalization. In the Twenties and Thirties Rose occasionally assisted in Talmud Torah Auxiliary activities and was a member of the Council of Jewish Women. Rose's brother, Max LeBid, moved to Tacoma in 1928 and operated Tacoma Auto Wrecking and later Top Auto.

Herman and Rose's son **Leo Dobry** (1902-1980) opened the Credit Auto Repair in 1926. He offered batteries and tires, a body repair shop, and a used car department. Together Herman and Leo operated the Standard Used Car Market that later became Standard Auto Parts. Leo married Goldie Jean Samuelson (1910-1989) on June 5, 1932. She was active in the Temple Beth El Sisterhood, then was an officer in the Talmud Torah Auxiliary in 1939. They were the parents of Beverly Petal and Judy Goldfine Brooks. Beverly was confirmed in 1948. Leo's business grew, supplying truck and auto parts over several states. In 1948 he was able to purchase and build a custom racing car that finished sixth in the Indianapolis 500. The car was named the "City of Tacoma," and later won first place in the 1952 Pikes Peak Climb. Leo moved to Mercer Island around 1970 and died in June of 1980. In 2006 he was posthumously inducted into the Tacoma-Pierce County Sports Hall of Fame.

Dobry Enters Tacoma Car In 500-Mile Race

Tacoma will be represented in the Memorial day racing classic at the Indianapolis speedway this year, it was revealed Tuesday, by Leo Dobry, local auto parts dealer and sportsman.

Dobry announced that the "City of Tacoma,' a racing car which is being built to his specifications in Los Angeles, would be completed in ample time to be entered in the 500-mile competition.

Tacoma News Tribune March 17, 1948

"City of Tacoma" racing car in custom trailer

*Tacoma Public Library
Richards D33-68-4*

Morris H. Donion, son of Eugene and Dora Danzker/Donion
Born May 10, 1896/1902, in Uman, Kiev, Russia (now Ukraine)
Married Rebecca "Betty" Friedman (1900-1974) on June 21, 1921, in Tacoma
Parents of Jerome (1922-2009), Myron (1924-1994), and Adele Goldman (1928-2019)
Rebecca married second to Otto Miller on June 18, 1938, in Tacoma
Morris married second to Rea Cremer (1908-1995) on January 5, 1954, in San Francisco, California
Died March 24, 1976, in Watsonville, California; buried Shaarie Torah Cemetery, Portland, Oregon

Morris' first home in the U.S. was in Portland, Oregon, with his parents and siblings. He worked as a jitney driver until he was drafted in 1918. He filed his Petition for Naturalization from Camp Lewis. After his marriage to Rebecca the couple lived in Tacoma, Everett, Aberdeen, and Portland. Morris operated a grocery and worked in a variety of clerking positions. Around 1933 Rebecca returned to the Tacoma home of her parents, Julius and Augusta (Stusser) Friedman, where the children were active in Talmud Torah. Rebecca remarried and Morris re-enlisted in the Army in 1942. Both of their sons served in the Navy.

Jerome "Jerry" Donion spent nearly all of his life in Tacoma. He celebrated his bar mitzvah in 1935 and was confirmed at Talmud Torah in 1937. He was an athlete at Stadium High School and played sports throughout his life. Jerry married Mary Eastern (1921-1993) in Tacoma on July 26, 1942, as he was heading off to the South Pacific. Mary worked 25 years as an educational secretary and Jerry retired from North Pacific Plywood. He earned the B'nai B'rith Akiba Award, and received a Community Service Award from the City of Tacoma for his volunteer work. He twice won the B'nai B'rith "Dr. Abedeaux Friedman Memorial" golf championship trophy. Jerry died in 2009 and was buried in the Home of Peace Cemetery.

Jerry Donion

Myron Donion, both courtesy of the Jerry Donion Estate

Myron Donion celebrated his bar mitzvah at Talmud Torah in 1937 under Rabbi Treiger. He married Lois Birkenstock (1924-2012) and spent much of his career as a real estate agent for the Harold Allen Company. Myron often played golf and was active in the B'nai B'rith league. He died in 1994 and was buried at Mountain View Cemetery in Lakewood, Washington.

Jack W. Drickey, son of Philip E. and Laverne (Larson) Drickey
Born December 24, 1922, in Spencer, Nebraska
Married Dorothy Quint (1914-1980) daughter of Joseph and Minnie (Farber) Quint
Parents of Michael, Judith, and Adele
Died June 19, 1999 in Tucson, Arizona; buried Evergreen Memorial, Tucson

Jack and Dorothy lived in the Tacoma area in the Fifties during Jack's 39-year military career. Dorothy was also a veteran of World War II and had served overseas for most of her three-year enlistment. While in Tacoma she participated in Sisterhood programs and was active in the VFW auxiliary. Jack later served in both the Korean and the Viet Nam Wars. The couple retired to Arizona in 1973.

Isadore Abraham Drues, M.D., son of William and Jennie (Wilner) Drues
Born August 22, 1898, in Meishagola, Vilna, Russia (now Maisiagala, Lithuania)
Married Bess Diane Weisbrod (1899-1978) daughter of Rubin and Rosa (Hecken) Weisbrod
Parents of Richard (1929-1982), Edward (1931-2005), and Joan (1934-1997)
Died July 16, 1959, in Tacoma; buried Home of Peace Cemetery

Isadore Drues came to Chicago with his family as a toddler. In 1917 he worked as a clerk for the Chicago Public Library, then served in the military in World War I. He graduated from the Illinois Medical School in 1923 and did his residency at Chicago's Cook County Hospital. After working as a physician in Elgin, Illinois, Isadore married Bess and moved to Washington in 1928. He practiced medicine in Tacoma for nearly thirty years. Toward the end of his career he had an Eye, Ear, Nose and Throat practice in the Medical Arts Building. As their children started school Bess was active in women's groups at Talmud Torah and served as Sisterhood president in 1947. Both of their sons celebrated their bar mitzvahs at Talmud Torah. Isadore and Bess were avid ski enthusiasts and mountaineers, and he helped train climbing rescue teams.

> **ANNOUNCE BAR MITZVAH**
> Dr. and Mrs. I. A. Drues of North Ainsworth avenue announce the Bar Mitzvah of their son, Edward Maurice Drues, which will be held Friday at 9:30 at the Talmud Torah synagogue, with Rabbi Julius L. DeKoven officiating.
> No invitations have been issued, but all friends will be welcomed at the reception in the vestry rooms which will follow the ceremony.

Tacoma News Tribune March 1, 1944

Rabbi Meier Elyn, son of Isaac and Lena/Leah (Sokolsky) Elyn
Born December 15, 1872/4, in Russia
Brother of Libby Elyn (Mrs. Nochem "Nathan" Anches) and Goldie Elyn (Mrs. Solomon Farber)
Married Rebecca Tropp (1868-1949) about 1895
Arrived N.Y. September 15, 1904, aboard the *Saxonia* from Grodno (now Hrodna, Belarus)
Parents of Isaac (1896-1983), Aaron (1899-1932), Samuel (1902-1991), and Morris (1909-1982)
Died April 27, 1921, in Tacoma; buried Home of Peace Cemetery

1910 Tacoma city directory

> Elyn Mayer Rabbi Russion Orthodox Hebrew Church ctr Bay City Market tchr Talmud Torah Sch h 1009½ So G

Rabbi Elyn declared his intent to become a citizen in Tacoma in May of 1907. His wife, Rebecca, and three sons joined him in November. A fourth son, Morris, was born in Tacoma in 1909. Rabbi Elyn served as a teacher and ritual butcher for Tacoma's Jewish community, and led the Passover Seder in 1913. Of their four sons, only their eldest married. Isaac married Goldie Steinberg (1902-1962) in Seattle in 1923 and had three children there. Meier and Rebecca's second son, Aaron, died in his thirties. Their younger sons, Samuel and Morris were both active in Talmud Torah. Samuel served on the board just before his Army enlistment. Morris was a member of the Young Moderates in 1926 and served as Talmud Torah vice president in 1941.

B'nai B'rith formal installation January 18, 1938
(Left to right) Lester Seinfeld, Ben Schwartz, Morris Elyn
Courtesy of Tacoma Public Library Richards Studio A7027-1

Solomon Epstein, son of Louis/Leizer and Minnie/Michle Epstein
Born June 1, 1889, in Grodno, Russia (now Hrodna, Belarus)
Married about 1907 in Grodno to Ida/Chaie Farber (1886-1964) daughter of Isadore and Anna Farber
Parents of Isadore (1908-1992), Morris (1911-1997), and Henry (1915-1980)
Solomon arrived N.Y. September 5, 1911, aboard the *Kronprinz Wilhelm* from Bremen, Germany
Ida arrived N.Y. January 2, 1913, aboard the *Kroonland* from Antwerp, with their two sons and
      Solomon's mother, Minnie, and sister, Elka
Solomon died January 17, 1969, in Tacoma; buried Home of Peace Cemetery

After emigrating Solomon and Ida lived briefly in New York with his parents and siblings. The men all worked as paperhangers. Solomon declared his intention to become a citizen in 1914, and their third son was born there the following year. The couple moved to Tacoma about 1916. Solomon Farber and Ben Rashbam served as his witnesses for his 1918 naturalization. They also partnered with him in operating the Independent Junk Company in 1920. Then Solomon ran the OK Junk Company, which became OK Furniture, selling secondhand items.

JUNK DEALERS

City Junk Co 2403 Pacific av
O K Junk Co 2422 Pacific av
Polisky Abraham 1524 Commerce
Sussman Frank & Co 1730 Pacific av
TACOMA JUNK CO, 2128 Pacific Av
Weinstone Kopel 1526 Commerce

1925 Tacoma city directory

Their eldest son, **Isadore Epstein**, traveled to Vancouver, British Columbia, in 1936 to marry his first cousin, Dorothy Rashbam. Both were educators. Dorothy was first a social worker and then taught German at Wilson High School for nearly twenty years. Isadore taught for Tacoma Public Schools for 43 years, the last 35 at Stadium High School. He was active in teachers' associations and was a bridge champion. They were the parents of Elizabeth and Allan.

Solomon and Ida's middle son, **Morris Epstein**, was an amateur featherweight boxer in the late Twenties. He also played basketball on the Young Moderates' team in Tacoma's Church League. Morris married Libby Arine in 1933. They were the parents of Lewis, Melvin, Jack, and Phyllis. Libby was active in Talmud Torah and Hadassah events. Morris operated Jack's Loan Office on Pacific Avenue for decades.

Henry Epstein worked for his father and did not marry.

Tacoma Public Library Richards Studio D-59390-1
Epstein family June 3, 1951 *(Likely Melvin's bar mitzvah)*
(Top row standing left to right) Solomon, Morris, Melvin, Lewis, and Phyllis Epstein
(Seated left to right) Ida Farber Epstein, Jack, Libby Arine Epstein, and her mother Esther Pearl Arine

Rabbi Richard Rosenthal remembered that the Epstein and Farber families formed the core of the Saturday morning minyans in the late Fifties. As Solomon's health failed, Rabbi Rosenthal took a Torah to the Epstein home for the minyan services. The Farber family and later the Epsteins lived for many years at 1724 Fawcett Avenue. As of 2021 it was one of the last houses standing in what was once a vibrant Jewish neighborhood, slated for development by the University of Washington Tacoma.

129

Farber/Epstein Home
(Left) 1724 Fawcett Avenue in 1979, Tacoma Public Library BU-1934
(Right) 1724 Fawcett Avenue, current street view

Ben Etsekson, born April 20, 1894, in Mareensk, Siberia, Russia, as Boruh Boris Isaacson
Married first to Sora Riva, who stayed in Russia with their two children
Ben arrived in Seattle on January 7, 1917, on the *Asaka* from Kobe, Japan
Married second in Seattle on August 4, 1923, to Frances Casserd (1900-1954)
Parents of Walter (1924-1996) and Leonard (1928-1992)
Married third in Seattle on June 12, 1956, to Ann Brown (1909-2000)
Died December 20, 1963, in Tacoma; buried Home of Peace Cemetery

Ben lived in Tacoma and worked in the junk business when he registered for the draft in 1917, claiming two dependent children. Two years later he declared his intent to become a citizen, partnering with Herman Dobry in the Auto Trading Company. Ben continued selling used cars in the early Twenties. By 1925 he was the proprietor of Ben's Auto Wrecking at 2302 Pacific Avenue. He spent the rest of his career dealing in auto wrecking and truck parts. For many years his business was located at 2622 South Tacoma Way. At the time of Ben's death in 1963 he was a member of the Tacoma Yacht Club and of Seattle's Glendale Golf and Country Club.

BEN'S AUTO WRECKING CO (Ben Etsekson) Parts for all makes of cars; Automobile Accessories a Specialty 2302 Pacific av cor 23d, Tel Main 858

Ben had briefly belonged to Temple Beth Israel in the Twenties. His second wife, Frances, participated in activities with Hadassah, Council of Jewish Women, and the Sinai Sisterhood. Their son, Walter, was confirmed in 1937 and was involved with AZA in 1940. He served in the U.S. Army from March of 1943 to December of 1945. Walter married Joan Sussman (1934-1982) in Olympia on November 17, 1954. The couple had two sons, Donald and Paul, before divorcing in 1970. Ben's younger son, Leonard, did not marry.

(Above right) 1925 Tacoma city directory ad
(Right) Half-track truck at Ben's Truck Parts, June 8, 1954
1622 South Tacoma Way
Courtesy of Tacoma Public Library Richards Studio D91232-3
(Richards Photography panel truck in background)

Farber Family

Isadore and Chane/Anna (Yudelman/Udmanova) Farber had seven children in Grodno, Russia, now Hrodna, Belarus. Chane died in Seattle on September 26, 1913, and was buried in Bikur Cholim Cemetery, Seattle. They were the parents of:

1. Efroim "Frank" (1878-1910) married Fanny Poupkin about 1904
2. Samuel David (1882-1941) married Bella Zalkind in 1911
3. Solomon J. (1883-1946) married Goldie Elyn about 1903
4. Ida (1886-1964) married Solomon Epstein about 1907
5. Sadie (1890-1974) married Benjamin Rashbam in 1911
6. Leon (1894-1959) married Anna Rashbam in 1919
7. Joseph (1898-1975) married Rose August/Augustower in 1921

Joseph Farber, born July 11, 1898, in Grodno, youngest son of Isadore and Chane
Arrived N.Y. July 25, 1912 aboard the *Prinz Wilhelm*, with his mother Chane
Married first to Rose August/Augustower (1900-1986) in Seattle on March 20, 1921
Parents of Annie Ziegman (1922-2007) and Jack (1924-2012)
Married second to Anna Rose Cohen in Vancouver, Washington, on February 14, 1946
Died July 13, 1975, in Seattle; buried Herzl Cemetery, Seattle

Joseph and his mother came directly to Tacoma in 1912, joining Solomon and Goldie. Julius Friedman gave Joseph a job, witnessed his naturalization in 1919, and witnessed his wedding in 1921. The wedding was performed by Rabbi Jacob B. Gordon during the short time he was at Talmud Torah. In 1932 Rose was president of the Talmud Torah Women's Auxiliary. Joseph briefly operated his own men's furnishings store in Tacoma in the Thirties, then moved to Seattle. There he worked as a junk dealer. Joseph and Rose divorced in 1942. Their son, Jack, served in World War II and was active in the Herzl Congregation. Joseph remarried in 1946.

Leon "Leo" Farber, born July 26, 1894, in Grodno, fourth son of Isadore and Chane
Arrived N.Y. September 3, 1910, aboard the *George Washington*
Married Anna Rashbam (1890-1934) in Tacoma on June 1, 1919
Parents of Abraham (1920-1988)
Died January 22, 1959, in Tacoma; buried Chevra Kadisha Cemetery, Home of Peace

Leo Farber, courtesy of the Farber Family

Leon lived with his brother, Solomon, in Tacoma until he was drafted in 1918. After serving in the Army Leon operated a pawn shop. He later ran Farber and Rabstoff, tailoring clothes with Nathan Rabstoff. For many years Leon operated his own tailoring business at 1313 Commerce, perhaps the source of his badly stooped back. His son, Abe, worked with him. (Farber The Tailor later became Franco The Tailor.)

Abraham Allen Farber was born in Tacoma on March 7, 1920. He served in the U.S. Army from September of 1941 until October of 1945. After his discharge Abe married Estelle Lamken (1924-2021), youngest daughter of Arthur and Fanny (Sussman) Lamken. They had three children: Nancy (1948-1951), Richard, and Linda. Abe died on February 23, 1988, and was buried in the Home of Peace Cemetery.

Shalom "Samuel" David Farber, born March 16, 1882, in Grodno, second son of Isadore and Chane
Arrived in Sumas, Washington, on January 21, 1903, by railway from Quebec
Married Bella Zalkind (1887-1950) in Pierce County in October of 1911
Died August 8, 1941, in Seattle; buried Bikur Cholim Cemetery, Seattle

After their marriage Shalom and Bella lived briefly in Ohio in 1913. They returned to Seattle in time for their second daughter's birth in 1914, then joined the other Farber siblings in Tacoma. Shalom worked first in the Independent Hardware and Junk Company with Ben Rashbam and Solomon Epstein. As Samuel Farber he continued in the secondhand business, operating his own store in the Thirties. Around 1938 he and Bella again returned to Seattle, where he sold secondhand furniture.

Samuel and Bella had five children:

1. Eva (1913-1968) married Charles Sanford in 1942; buried Arlington National Cemetery.
2. Anna (1914-2005) married Stephen Maskule, Harry Dubonsky, Joseph Shussin, and Bernard Greenberg; buried Bikur Cholim Cemetery, Seattle.
3. Irving Isadore (1917-2010) married Bess Kosher in 1940, buried Bikur Cholim Cemetery, Seattle. Bess was Sinai Sisterhood president in 1956. Children Stan and Carol born in Tacoma. Stan (1941-2005) served as Sinai youth president in 1959 and later worked as a sports journalist in Tacoma; buried Home of Peace Cemetery.
4. Bertha Bernice (1919-1995) married Leon Mendelsohn in 1939 and Lewis Friedman in 1970; buried in Beth Israel Cemetery in Bellingham, Washington.
5. Dorothy Louise (1921-1995) married Arthur Johnson in 1950, buried in Beth Israel Cemetery in Bellingham, Washington.

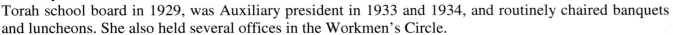

Solomon J. and Goldie (Elyn) Farber and children, Lena and Irving, 1909
Courtesy of the Farber Family

Solomon J. Farber, born March 7, 1883, in Grodno, third son of
     Isadore and Chane
Arrived in N.Y. July 23, 1904, aboard the *Rotterdam* from Holland
Married Goldie M. Elyn (1885-1948) in 1904
Died December 16, 1946, in Tacoma; buried Home of Peace Cemetery

Solomon and Goldie's first child was born in Woodbine, New Jersey, in 1906. The couple lived in Seattle in 1909 when their second was born. Their last two children were born in Tacoma. Solomon operated the OK Loan Office throughout his career in Tacoma. He also served as secretary of Talmud Torah in 1937 and 1938. Goldie served on the Talmud Torah school board in 1929, was Auxiliary president in 1933 and 1934, and routinely chaired banquets and luncheons. She also held several offices in the Workmen's Circle.

Solomon and Goldie had four children:

1. Lena/Leah (1906-1972) married Rabbi Baruch Treiger in 1928. Lena and Baruch lived in Tacoma from 1936 to 1942.
2. Irving (1909-1965) founded LeRoy Jewelers with Jack Slotnik. Irving married Hazel Zweibel (1919-2009) in New Jersey in 1942. They had two sons, Jim and Steph Farber.
3. Ethel Marilyn (1911-2001) buried Bikur Cholim Cemetery, Seattle. Ethel married Sam Slavin in 1939 and Jack Slotnik in 1946. She was the mother of Michael Slavin and Gary and Lynn Slotnik.
4. Kenneth (1914-1980) married Alice Raphalowitz (1916-2004) in 1941. They had three children: Stuart (1947-2015), Gail and Steven. After Kenneth's death Alice married Harmon Matin (1917-1998).

Schloime "Sam" Samuel Feldman, son of Shmuel and Molly (Israelson) Feldmann
Born January 27, 1890/93, in Goldingen, Courland, Russia (now Kuldiga, Latvia)
Arrived N.Y. August 23, 1911, aboard the *President Grant* from Hamburg
Married Alice L. Shaffer (1898-1975) in Tacoma on March 10, 1919
Parents of Edward (1919-2007) and Robert (1925-2001)
Died March 29, 1970, in Seattle; buried Bikur Cholim Cemetery, Seattle

Sam Feldman's 1928 business was first called the Liberal Junk Company, then carried his own name. In the Thirties Sam briefly worked as a bottler. His son, Edward, was vice president of the Junior League in 1937 and served in the U.S. Army during World War II. The family moved to Seattle in 1947. Sam continued his junk business there, then worked for Boeing until his retirement about 1958. Sam's wife, Alice Shaffer, was a sister of Sarah Shaffer, wife of Joseph Friedman.

Mendel "Max" Finegold, born July 18, 1873/4 in Gomel, Russia (now Homyel, Belarus)
Married Anna Herman (1874-1948) in January of 1897 in Russia
Emigrated either 1904 or 1906
Married second to Edith Rose Herman Perlin (1874-1951) on October 26, 1948
Died May 2, 1962 in Seattle; buried Bikur Cholim Cemetery, Seattle

Children:
1. Lillian (1898-1930) married Abraham Greenblat in Montana in 1921, buried Home of Peace.
2. Abe Ruben (1900-1976) married Ida Liebes in Tacoma in 1925, furniture dealer in Centralia.
3. Cyrus Fingold (1901/3/4-1989) married Adeline Hermes, managed Alaska Steel in Spokane.
4. Sybil (1906-1999) married Ruben Katz in Tacoma in 1927, lived in Seattle.
5. Bernard (1908-1996) married Esther Kosokoff in 1936, managed Alaska Steel in Spokane.
6. Morris (1908-2003) married Betty Bloch in 1934, machinist in Seattle.
7. Samuel Fingold (1909-1995) married Marion Meyers (1911-1976) in 1934. (See below.)
8. Ethelyn (1912-2012) married Moe Michelson in 1936, lived in Everett.
9. Fannie (1914-1999) married Nathan Feinberg in 1935.

(Below) Max and Anna Finegold with grandsons Ralph and Arthur Greenblat, courtesy of Arthur Greenblat

Max and Anna's first four children were born in Russia. They had twin sons in Saskatchewan in January of 1908, then moved to Williston, North Dakota, where three more children were born. They lived a few years in Glasgow, Montana, before moving to Tacoma about 1922. The family lived in Tacoma's South End, where Max operated a grocery and sold fruit. Their children, Morris and Sybil, belonged to the Young Hebrew Moderates of Talmud Torah in 1925. Both Abe and Sybil were married by Rabbi Slotnik. Max and Anna's eldest daughter, Lillian (Finegold) Greenblat, died in Tacoma in 1930. Max and Anna lived in Tacoma another decade, then joined their married children in Seattle.

Their son, **Samuel Fingold,** lived nearly his entire adult life in Tacoma. He worked for Frank Sussman, then attended Knapp business school. Around 1931 he took the surname Fingold. Samuel spent his career managing service stations in Tacoma, including Johnson's and the New Deal. At one time he was the

133

service manager for the short-lived Isetta import. In 1934 he married Marion Meyers, daughter of Louis and Rose Meyrowitz. They had two daughters, Sandra and Jeraldine. Marion was active in Hadassah, Camp Fire, and Little Theater. Samuel was a member of Temple Beth Israel in 1942, but served as a Sinai Temple trustee in 1946 and was a lay leader of services in 1948. He was president of the local B'nai B'rith in 1953 and led an Israel bonds banquet in 1959. Marion died in Portland, Oregon; and Samuel died in Denver, Colorado.

Wolf "William" Forman, son of Michael and Anna (Painter) Forman
Born January 24, 1891, in New York
Married Jennie Friedman (1891-1949) daughter of Philip and Rose (Landsman) Friedman
Parents of Nathan "Nat" Julius Forman (1914-1994) and Philip Byron Forman
Died in Brooklyn, New York, on September 20, 1963

Jennie and William first married in Tacoma on April 13, 1913. Their son, Nathan, was born in Tacoma the following year. The couple divorced in 1916 after William returned to New York and Jennie stayed in Tacoma. He served in the military from September of 1918 until January of 1919. Then he came back to Tacoma and married Jennie again on July 26, 1920. This time she went to New York with him, where their son Philip was born in 1921. The couple again divorced in 1926, drawing much attention from the press, as William was by then a prosperous hardware merchant.

Solomon "Sol" Freyd, son of Israel and Bertha (Levenson) Freyd
Born December 23, 1878, in Simno, Russia (now Simnas, Lithuania)
Married Lena Cohen (1886-1936) daughter of Max and Elizabeth (Kaplan) Cohen
Parents of Myron Hershell Freyd (1917-1990)
Died September 18, 1943, in Seattle; buried Bikur Cholim Cemetery, Seattle

Sol's older brother, Benjamin, lived first in Tacoma, in the difficult financial days of the late 1890s. Two of Ben's daughters were born in Tacoma in 1898 and 1901, before the family moved to Seattle. Another brother, Harris, also lived in Seattle.

Sol became a citizen in Seattle in 1906, and worked as a clerk there for a decade. Then he moved to Anchorage, Alaska, where he married Lena Cohen in 1916. She returned to her parents in Tacoma in the fall of 1917 for the birth of their son. Sol then partnered in Tacoma with his brother-in-law, Sol Cohen, but their business failed in 1921. Over the next few years Sol operated several clothing stores in Tacoma. The couple lived several years in Petersburg, Alaska; then settled in Bremerton about 1929. Their son, Myron, lived with his Cohen grandparents in Tacoma while he was studying for his 1930 bar mitzvah at Talmud Torah. The family moved to Seattle a few years later, where Myron attended the University of Washington. Myron served in the military in 1942 and later returned to Bremerton. He was elected Kitsap County prosecuting attorney in 1966 and served on the school board.

Happy Wedding of Couple Proves a Social Event

COHEN-FREYD.

An Anchorage romance culminated yesterday afternoon at the home of Mr. and Mrs. N. N. Jaffe, when their niece, Miss Lena Cohen, of Tacoma, Washington, was united in marriage to Mr. Sol Freyd, a prominent merchant of this city. The house was decorated as a green wood, and at 4:30 p. m. the ceremony was performed by Judge Leopold David, which made the happy couple one. The Hebrew ceremony was read by Mr. I. Bayles.

Anchorage Daily Times August 21, 1916

Abedeaux Friedman, D.D.S., son of Julius and Augusta (Stusser) Friedman
Born April 18, 1905, in Tacoma as Abraham; brother of Rebecca, Saul, and Siegfried
Married Rose Goldie Rotman (1910-1993) in Tacoma on August 5, 1934
Parents of Jules (1939-2012) and Harold
Died April 8, 1954, in Tacoma; buried Home of Peace Cemetery

Abedeaux Friedman graduated from Stadium High School, then the Chicago College of Dental Surgery, and first established his practice in Bremerton. He married Rose Rotman, daughter of Harry and Lena Rotman, at Tacoma's Winthrop Hotel. Abedeaux enlisted in the U.S. Army in February 1943 and was discharged in July 1946 as a captain. He first reestablished practice in downtown Tacoma's Provident Building, and then practiced in the Washington Building. Both were close to Friedman's Clothes Shop, operated by his brothers, Saul and Siegfried. He was active in Talmud Torah, and a vice president of Sinai Temple and of B'nai B'rith. After his early death the B'nai B'rith Golf Championship was named the "Dr. Abedeaux Friedman Memorial." His widow, Rose, raised their two sons and continued her involvement in Jewish community events. She was active in Talmud Torah and Sinai Temple, Destiny auxiliary of B'nai B'rith, Council of Jewish Women, Hadassah, and the United Jewish Appeal.

HEBREW RITES HELD

Notable Wedding Calls Many Score to Hotel Winthrop Sunday Evening

A Lovely Bride

The bride was lovely in a graceful wedding gown of gleaming white satin, modeled on the simplest lines with a semi-court train and long wedding veil of tulle which fell in sweeping folds from a Juliet cap bound in orange blossoms. Her slippers were white satin and she, carried for her bridal bouquet a shower of fragile lilies of the valley held with loops of tulle and maidenhair.

(Left) Abedeaux and Rose Friedman in 1934, courtesy of Harold Friedman
(Right) Tacoma News Tribune and Tacoma Daily Ledger August 6, 1934

Abraham M. Pilin Friedman, son of Joseph/Yossel and Anna Pilin
Born September 10, 1855, or June 15, 1856, in Riga, Russia (now Latvia)
Married Gertrude/Gittel Shapiro/Schapsy (1870-1914) about 1897
Died January 10, 1930, in Seattle; buried Home of Peace Cemetery

Passenger list of the SS Kursk, arriving N.Y. November 21, 1911

When Abraham Friedman declared his intention to become a citizen he said he had immigrated via Liverpool on the *SS Canada* in October of 1907, entering the U.S. by rail at Detroit. When his wife and six children followed him in 1911 they traveled under his original surname, Pelin/Pilin. In Tacoma Abraham operated a secondhand store in the 1300 block of South Commerce Street for nearly twenty years. His wife, Gittel, died in childbirth in 1914 and was buried with her infant son in her arms. Abraham's children remembered that their sister Anna, still a child herself, stepped in to care for her siblings. The younger children were involved in the Jewish Juniors in the Twenties. Several later lived in Bremerton and this line became known as the "Bremerton Friedmans." Abraham moved to Bremerton about 1928.

Children of Abraham and Gittel Friedman:

1. Joseph Samuel (1899-1971) married Sarah Loschbin in Seattle in 1922. Their daughter Marian Friedman married Robert Block, and their son Paul married Marlene Soriano.
2. Julius Lee (1901-1964) married Edith Dunn in Seattle in 1922. Their daughter Jacqueline married Charles Betts.
3. Anna (1903-1982) married Edward Barnett in Missouri in 1923. (See Barnett biographical sketch.)
4. Helen (1905-1996) married Harry Fischer/Turk in Los Angeles in 1934. They were the parents of Avrum Marco and Rose Marie.
5. Mildred (1906-1990) married Julian Chapman in Los Angeles in 1942.
6. Charles (1909-2007) served in the U.S. Navy during World War II and resumed the family's original surname of Pelin. He did not marry.
7. Isaac (1914-1914)

Adolph Friedman, son of Jehuda, brother of Solomon Friedman and Mollie (Friedman) Stusser
Born between 1821 and 1838 in Bauske, Courland, Russia (now Bauska, Latvia)
Married Mascha Stusser (1865-1950) about 1895 in Victoria, British Columbia
Died March 2, 1911, in Tacoma; buried Home of Peace Cemetery
(Additional information on page 12)

Adolph Friedman lived in Dutch Flat, in Placer County, California, in 1860. That same year he became a naturalized citizen in Nevada County. He spent the next several years following the Comstock Lode, operating temporary stores in Virginia City, Nevada, and other mining towns. He found time to continue his education, enough to serve as postmaster in Meadow Lake in 1867. Two years later Adolph found Meadow Lake abandoned and the cabins crushed in by snow. He and the miners had moved on.

(Above) Adolph Friedman, BC Royal Museum Archives

After his 1884 arrival in Tacoma, Adolph operated a dry goods and grocery store. Then he joined in the late 1880s real estate boom. He partnered in developing American Lake Park, on the western shore of American Lake, just south of the present Veterans' Hospital. At the time the area was easily accessible from Tacoma by rail and was a popular summer destination. Rapid sales of lots likely served as impetus for Julius Friedman and other relatives to make Tacoma their home. As the market peaked in the spring of 1893 Adolph served as deputy county assessor. After the economy collapsed he operated a pawnshop and a secondhand store. With his wife, Mascha, Adolph sold trunks and valises. After his 1911 death Mascha remarried to Joseph Miller and moved to Seattle, and then California.

Adolph Friedman's nieces, nephews, great-nephews, and extended relatives helped form the nucleus of Tacoma's Orthodox Jewish community.

American Lake Park

The Plat of this Tract was filed for record in the County Auditor's office July 31, 1889.
Acre lots overlooking the Lake and situated in beautiful groves.
Water front lots of 50 feet front running to the Lake.

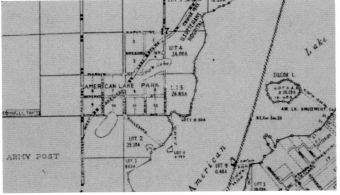

(Above left) Tacoma Daily News August 1, 1889
(Left) American Lake Park, White's Atlas 1928

Bernard Adolph Friedman, son of Samuel I. and Mary L. (Friedman) Friedman
Born April 25, 1924, in Tacoma; youngest brother of Leonard, Stanley, and Phyllis
Married Beatrice R. Sussman (1924-1977) on November 10, 1946, in Tacoma
Parents of Joel and Laurie
Died March 10, 1977, in Tacoma; buried Home of Peace Cemetery

    Bernard and Beatrice grew up together at Talmud Torah. She was a daughter of Joseph A. and Minnie (Benson) Sussman. Both were active in youth organizations, and both attended the University of Washington. Bernard served one term as president of his Sigma Alpha Mu fraternity before joining the service. He spent three years in the U.S. Navy during World War II, mostly aboard destroyer escorts with Halsey's Third fleet in the Pacific. On his return he married Beatrice in a large wedding at the Winthrop Hotel.
(Right) Tacoma News Tribune November 12, 1946

450 See Wedding Of Beatrice Sussman

*(Below left) Sketch of 10015 Gravelly Lake Drive
Tacoma News Tribune June 23, 1974*

Nieman's Hub Clothiers coming to Lakewood
Friedman to open in Lakewood

"Bernie and Beadie" continued to be active in Sinai Temple as adults. He served three terms on the board of trustees and two years as president. In addition he held board positions with Charles Wright Academy and the Oakbrook Golf and Country Club. Bernard was vice president of his brother's Western Clothiers until 1969. In 1974 Bernard started Neiman's Hub Clothiers on Gravelly Lake Drive in Lakewood, as homage to his father's pioneer downtown Hub Clothiers. Bernie created the Nieman name from combining the last syllables of his first and last name. Bernard and Beatrice both died in their early fifties.

Hirsch "Harry" Friedman, son of Philip B. and Rose E. (Landsman) Friedman
Born March 15, 1886, in Bauske, Courland, Russia (now Latvia)
Arrived N.Y. December 19, 1905, aboard the *SS Finland* from Antwerp as Hirsch
Married Dorothy Eichenwald (1890-1959) in Seattle on September 1, 1918
Parents of Annette Trubowitsch (1919-2003), Philburn (1921-1988), and Sylvia Miller/Juvik
    (1925-2010)
Died June 24, 1958, in Tacoma; buried Home of Peace Cemetery

    Harry came to the U.S. with two of his younger sisters, joining their older brother, Morris, in New York. The family was still there in 1910, but by 1911 had moved to Tacoma. Harry first lived with his brother, Nathan, and ran a secondhand store. Two years later he operated a jewelry store on Pacific Avenue. After his marriage in 1918 Harry called the store Eagle Loan and Jewelry. He would run the business for the rest of his life, another four decades.

    Dorothy was active in the Women's Auxiliary at Talmud Torah, serving as secretary in 1929 and treasurer in 1939. The couple often entertained family at their home. Their son, Philburn, celebrated his bar mitzvah in 1934. He was active in theater in Tacoma, and went on to become a stage manager for more than 85 Broadway productions. His sister, Annette, wrote a book about his accomplishments.
Philburn Friedman

Yankel "Jacob" Friedman, son of Solomon, brother of Philip and Selig
Born 1834 in Russia (now Latvia)
Married first to Rebecca Rolov (1834-1880) on March 15, 1863 in
     Aizpute, Russia (now Latvia)
Married second to Liebe Michele Schneider (1848-1910) about 1881
Arrived N.Y. December 29, 1905, aboard the *Graf Waldersee* from Dover with Liebe
Died January 11, 1917, in Tacoma; buried Home of Peace Cemetery

Jacob Friedman courtesy of Jay Schupack

    Jacob had at least seven children with his first wife and five more with his second.

Rebecca
Jennie (Abraham Tone)
Rachel (Chaim Bender)
Julius (Augusta Stusser)
Sarah (Nathan Blasberg)

Olga/Golda (Morris Wowa)
Anna (Louis Levinthal)
Jennie (Morris Levinson)

Liebe
Infants Isaac and Zalman
Philip Bernard (Rose Schneider)
Samuel I. (Mary Friedman)
Rose (Bernard Rackmil)

(Additional information on page 18)

When Jacob emigrated at the age of 70 his occupation was listed as blacksmith. He went first to his son, Philip, in New Jersey, and then lived in Tacoma by 1908. His second wife died in 1910 and was buried at Bikur Cholim Cemetery in Seattle. At the time of her death the family lived at 509 South 15th, on a hill overlooking downtown Tacoma. Jacob lived until 1917.

Current view of 509 South 15th Street, 1910 home of Jacob Friedman

Joseph "Joe" Friedman, son of Philip B. and Rose E. (Landsman) Friedman
Born February 18, 1882 in Bauske, Courland, Russia (now Latvia)
Arrived N.Y. September 16, 1902, aboard the *Moltka* from Hamburg
Married Sarah Shaffer (1880-1964) in New York on April 2, 1905
Parents of Lillian (1906-1953), Edwin J. Julius (1909-1981), and Philip B. (1919-1964)
Died May 29, 1945, in Seattle; buried Bikur Cholim Cemetery, Seattle

    Joe married Sarah Shaffer in New York, and their daughter Lillian was born there the following year. The young family came to Tacoma about 1907. Joe first partnered with his brother Samuel, selling secondhand goods from several locations on Commerce Street. In 1910 he operated his own clothing store at 711 Pacific, with Sam and Morris next door at 713 Pacific. He worked for much of the next two decades as a shoe merchant on Commerce and Pacific. In 1919 Sarah hosted several events in honor of her sister Alice's wedding to Sam Feldman, just months before the birth of her third child. The family moved to Seattle in 1933.

    Their daughter, Lillian, was active in Talmud Torah activities, serving as an officer in the Jewish Juniors and leading Purim events. She died unmarried in 1953. Their son Edwin worked as a lawyer after serving three years in the Army during World War II. He married Julia Hanan and died in 1981. Joe and Sarah's younger son, Philip, worked for several jewelry firms in Seattle. He founded Phil's Jewelry Store in Ballard in 1953, and died in August of 1964, just one month before his mother's death.

Julius Friedman, son of Jacob and Rebecca (Rolov) Friedman
Born December 15, 1872, Bauske, Courland, Russia (now Bauska, Latvia)
Married Augusta Stusser (1880-1942) in Tacoma on December 3, 1899
Parents of Rebecca Donion Miller (1900-1974), Saul (1902-1976), Abedeaux (1905-1954), and
    Siegfried (1910-2011)
Died February 25, 1937 in Tacoma; buried Home of Peace Cemetery

Julius was the only son of Jacob Friedman and his first wife, Rebecca. He emigrated around his 18th birthday intending to come to Tacoma, but erroneously went to Washington, D.C. He worked there as a farrier, shoeing horses to earn funds to come to the West Coast. Although his name didn't appear in the Tacoma city directory until several years later, his store letterhead proclaimed "Established in 1892." Over the next decade Julius would be joined by his six sisters, four half-siblings, his father and stepmother Liebe, and many aunts, uncles and cousins. In 1899 his younger sister, Sarah, married Nathan Blasberg. Five months later Julius also took the matrimonial leap, marrying his second cousin, Augusta Stusser. (See Hugo Stusser biographical sketch.) Their children would remember theirs as a true love match.

Julius briefly operated a clothing store with Isaac Moses at 1528 Pacific. He then managed on his own, initially selling mostly secondhand items. Julius moved his business up Pacific Avenue several times over the next forty years until he reached his final location at 1124 Pacific Avenue. As he moved up, the quality of his merchandise improved as well. He maintained an unusual closeness with his many relatives who operated nearby clothing stores, sharing morning and evening prayers and New York Yiddish newspapers.

Julius' first investment in real property was an 1894 purchase of half a dozen American Lake lots from his great uncle, Adolph Friedman. In 1906 Julius sold his lot in the Flatiron Block on Fifteenth and Pacific for a significant profit, enabling him to purchase a home and continue bringing relatives to Tacoma. He reinvested in additional real estate, including partnering with his brother-in-law, Nathan Blasberg.

Julius was a founder of Tacoma's Orthodox congregation Chevra Talmud Torah. He served at least three times as president and had a major role in the construction of the Shul at South 4th and I Street. Julius was a charter member of B'nai B'rith #741, serving as its second president. He was active in numerous Jewish relief efforts during World War I. He also supported other Jewish benevolent causes and general community charitable activities. He provided jobs and housing for new arrivals. His name was listed as a character witness on dozens of naturalization documents for Jewish immigrants to Tacoma.

Julius was remembered by one of his clothing vendors as the "Father of Pacific Avenue ... his heart was good, his business policy was good. He was good to all."

Augusta Friedman was similarly prominent in Jewish and general community activities. She chaired numerous Women's Auxiliary activities benefitting Chevra Talmud Torah. She was active in Hadassah, Council of Jewish Women, and Destiny auxiliary, B'nai B'rith. She contributed to relief efforts during World War I. She was also a member of the Order of the Eastern Star, Amaranth, the Tacoma Clubhouse Association, and supported the Tacoma Day Nursery.

(Left) Julius Friedman, (right) Augusta (Stusser) Friedman, courtesy of Harold Friedman

Morris Jacob Friedman, son of Philip B. and Rose E. (Landsman) Friedman
Born December 10, 1883, in Bauske, Russia (now Latvia)
Arrived Philadelphia March 4, 1904, aboard the *Merrian* from Bremen, Germany
Married Rose Belle Carp (1895-1967) in Spokane on April 5, 1914
Parents of Frances Ethel/Etta (1915-1989) and Philip Byron Friedman (1917-1996)
Died September 2, 1947, Tacoma; buried Home of Peace Cemetery

The birth of Mozes Yankel, son of Feivish, was recorded in Bauske on November 22, 1882. Morris gave the birth date of October 1, 1883, on his WWI draft registration; and December 15, 1883, on his naturalization application. He declared his intention to become a citizen in New York in 1906, and joined his relatives in Tacoma a few years later. In 1914 he led Talmud Torah's Rosh Hashanah services. In 1919 he briefly joined Temple Beth Israel. Morris spent his entire career selling clothing with his cousin, Sam Friedman. The firm was first called the S and M Clothing Company, and in the Twenties debuted as Hub Clothing. The Hub was still operating on Pacific Avenue when Morris died.

Morris married Rose Carp in 1914, daughter of Sam and Ida Carp. During their marriage Rose frequently traveled to visit her family in Spokane, Milwaukee, and Los Angeles. She led the Ida Straus Hadassah Chapter in 1926. Rose was active in the Destiny auxiliary of B'nai B'rith in the Twenties, served as Sisterhood president in 1931, and was still helping with Sinai Temple dinners in 1958. Their son Philip Byron celebrated his bar mitzvah at Talmud Torah in 1930, the same year Morris chaired the re-dedication committee. Morris was president of Talmud Torah when Rabbi Treiger was installed in 1936. Their son became an optometrist and lived most of his life in Walla Walla. According to her death certificate, their daughter Frances never married.

Rose Carp Friedman, Tacoma News Tribune November 6, 1926

Nathan Friedman, son of Philip B. and Rose (Landsman) Friedman
Born February 28, 1880, in Bauske, Courland, Russia (now Latvia)
Arrived N.Y. April 15, 1903, aboard the *Germania* from London
Married Betty Yudelson (1891-1978) in Tacoma on June 7, 1909
Parents of Cecil (1910-1994), Margaret Golden (1914-2006), and
   Philip Bernard (1918-1987)
Died June 7, 1947, in Tacoma; buried Home of Peace Cemetery

1120 Pacific in 1938, Tacoma Public Library Richards A7475-1

Like his brothers, Nathan lived briefly in London and New York before making Tacoma his permanent home. He was one of the original incorporators of Talmud Torah in 1908 and served as president in 1918. Nathan first operated the Maze Loan Company with his cousin Philip. After his marriage he became the proprietor of his own clothing store, side-by-side with his cousin Sam and his brother Morris. During the Twenties his self-named store, Nathan's, was on Pacific Avenue. He closed the store briefly during World War II due to merchandise shortages, and reopened in the spring of 1947. A week before his death he learned of the birth of twin grandchildren, Linda and Jim, in Buffalo. As an adult Jim would return to Tacoma to take an active leadership role in Temple Beth El.

Nathan's wife, Betty, was one of five daughters of P.J. and Bluma (Stusser) Yudelson. Betty served as president of Talmud Torah's Women's Auxiliary in 1927 and again in 1936. Her eldest son, Cecil (1910-1994) moved to Buffalo to work in organic chemistry. Her daughter, Margaret (1914-2006) married Oscar Joseph Golden in Tacoma in 1943 and eventually moved to Tucson, Arizona.

Nathan and Betty's youngest son, yet another **Philip Bernard Friedman**, (1918-1987) stayed in Tacoma. He worked with his father and later operated Phil's Style Shop. Phil served in the U.S. Army from 1941 to 1945, and married Evelyn Becker in 1946. Her father, Solomon Becker, was from Latvia; and her mother, Josephine Eichenwald, was from Kansas City. Evelyn's sister Annabelle married Albert Benezra, and her brother Jerome married Dorothy Friedman. Another sibling, Rolfe Becker, married Sylvia Schwarz. Phil and Evelyn were the parents of Joyce, Nicholas, and Dennis.

Philip "Feive" Barrish Friedman, son of Solomon, brother of
Jacob and Selig Friedman
Born 1847 in Bauske, Courland, Russia (now Bauska, Latvia)
Married Roche/Rose Elka/Ella Landsman (1854-1939) about 1874
Arrived N.Y. June 26, 1906, aboard the *Nieuw Amsterdam* from Rotterdam
Died August 23, 1917, in Tacoma; buried Home of Peace Cemetery

Rose (Landsman) and Feive Friedman c 1880s, courtesy of Dennis Friedman

Like his brother Jacob, "Feive" and his wife, Rose, had at least twelve children. The eldest and youngest died in infancy. The oldest surviving son, Israel, stayed in Europe, where he died around 1905. Their middle daughter, Celia (1891-1971) stayed in New York and married Abe Lichtenstein. The remaining eight siblings all made Tacoma their home.

Nathan (1880-1947) married Betty Yudelson
Joseph (1882-1945) married Sarah Shaffer
Morris J. (1883-1947) married Rose Carp
Harry (1886-1958) married Dorothy Eichenwald
Bessie (1890-1952) married Samuel Reibman

Jennie (1891-1949) married William Forman
Celia (1891-1971) married Abr. Lichtenstein
Mary (1893-1986) married Samuel I. Friedman
Annette (1896-1968) m. Chernis and Levinson
(Additional information on page 18)

Also like his brother, Feive worked as a blacksmith. He emigrated when he was almost sixty years old. He lived in New York for nearly a decade, then joined his sons in Tacoma for the last few years of his life. His wife Rose, known by her Yiddish name of Roche Elka, was the daughter of Hirsh Vesterman, anglicized to Harry Landsman. Typical of the era, remaining portraits include just the four surviving male siblings.

(Right) Four sons of Philip B. and Rose E. (Landsman) Friedman

(Standing, left to right) Morris, Harry, and Joe Friedman
(Seated) Nathan Friedman

Courtesy of Jim Friedman, from the late Lorraine (Sussman) Braverman

Philip Bernard Friedman, son of Jacob and Liebe (Schneider) Friedman
Born January 5 or 12, 1884, in Bauske, Courland, Russia (now Bauska, Latvia)
Arrived N.Y. September 30, 1901
Married Rose Schneider Thorne (1878-1924) on July 21, 1907, in Vancouver, British Columbia
Parents of Madele Ulrich (1911-1999) and Bernece Hertzka (1913-2003)
Killed May 17, 1920, in Tacoma; buried Home of Peace Cemetery

Maze Loan Office

P. B. FRIEDMAN, Prop.   We sell Unredeemed Diamonds, Watches, Jewelry, Suit Cases,
Leather Goods, Etc.

MONEY LOANED on DIAMONDS, WATCHES, JEWELRY, Etc.

813 PACIFIC AVE.

1910 Tacoma city directory ad

Like his siblings and cousins, Philip lived briefly in New York, then came to Tacoma in January of 1907. He first partnered in the Maze Loan Company with his cousin Nathan, then operated his own loan and jewelry firm, most recently at 942 Pacific. Shortly after his arrival in Tacoma Philip traveled to Vancouver, British Columbia, to marry Rose Schneider Thorne. (An indication that she was likely his mother's relative.) She had also recently come from New York and had three young sons, Robert, Aaron, and Samuel. All three boys used the Friedman surname. Philip and Rose then had two daughters of their own. Philip served on the board of trustees of Temple Beth Israel in 1919.

Rose's eldest son, Robert, enlisted in the U.S. Army while still a senior at the University of Washington. He was discharged in March of 1919 and came home to work in his step-father's jewelry store. In May of 1920 the family was quarantined in their home because the young girls had scarlet fever. Robert and Philip had an argument over Philip's treatment of Rose. The argument escalated into a scuffle and Philip was killed. Robert was initially charged with murder. The prosecutor dismissed the case on grounds of self-defense, causing a further stir in the Jewish community. After their mother's death in 1924 the boys dedicated a large stained glass window at Temple Beth Israel in her memory. All three eventually resumed the Thorne surname, and all three had prosperous careers in the watch and jewelry industry.

Page One Tacoma Daily Ledger May 19, 1920

MURDER IS CHARGED TO YOUTH

First Degree Action Placed Against Robert B. Friedman by Prosecutor, Based on the Killing of His Stepfather

RELEASED ON $15,000 BAIL

Coroner's Examination Shows Dead Man's Skull Fractured 4 Times; Shot 3 Times

A charge of first degree murder was placed against Robert B. Friedman yesterday by Deputy Prosecuting Attorney James M. Selden, based upon the killing of Phillip B. Friedman, the young man's stepfather, in their home at 3118 North 20th street, Monday night. The charge was filed in Justice John W. Linck's court, where a bond of $15,000 was filed immediately for Robert Friedman's release from jail.

The determination of Deputy Prosecutor Selden to place a first degree murder charge against the stepson of the dead jeweler followed an investigation made by him and Coroner G. D. Shaver of the circumstances of the fatal shooting. The scene of the tragedy was inspected, the nature of the wounds which appear on the elder Friedman's body examined, and Sam Friedman, 17-year-old brother of the accused, who witnessed the shooting, was interrogated.

Samuel "Sam" Isadore Friedman, son of Jacob and Liebe (Schneider) Friedman
Born January 15, 1886, in Bauske, Courland, Russia (now Bauska, Latvia)
Arrived N.Y. August 15, 1902 aboard the *Albana*
Married Mary Leona Friedman (1893-1986) on June 17, 1913, in Victoria, British Columbia
Parents of Leonard (1914-2004), Stanley (1915-1996), Phyllis Belmonte (1918-1971), and
      Bernard A. (1924-1977)
Died November 7, 1969, in Tacoma; buried Home of Peace Cemetery

Sam's birth was recorded on October 13, 1885, in Bauske as Itzak Shimon. Family members related that as a young boy Sam was present when his grandfather suffered a fatal heart attack. Like his siblings he emigrated as a teen and lived briefly in New York before coming to Tacoma in 1904. Sam was secretary of Talmud Torah in 1907 and an incorporator in 1909. He lived with Julius and clerked for him, and then opened a clothing store with his cousin Morris. They worked together for nearly four decades. After Morris died Sam continued to operate the Hub until urban renewal took the downtown site in 1966.

MRS. FRIEDMAN
Married June 17, 1913

MR. FRIEDMAN
Native of Latvia

In 1913 Sam traveled to British Columbia to marry his cousin, and his partner's sister, Mary Friedman. Their four children were raised attending Talmud Torah, where Sam was president in 1925 and Leonard had his bar mitzvah in 1927. The couple bought a large home on Borough Road in 1925 and celebrated many happy events there, including their silver wedding anniversary in 1938. That same year Sam served as president of Talmud Torah. In 1942 Sam was also a member of Temple Beth Israel. In 1963 Sam and Mary were fortunate to celebrate their 50th anniversary with nearly all of their family members present. When Sam died in 1969 he was recognized as the last surviving founder of the B'nai B'rith organization, and of the Congregation Talmud Torah.

Sam and Mary Friedman's 50th wedding anniversary, Tacoma News Tribune June 9, 1963

Sam and Mary's eldest son, Leonard, received his law degree from the University of Washington. He married Joan Lipman (1916-2006) in 1941. After his discharge from the Army he accepted a state position in Sacramento. Leonard went on to serve eighteen years as a judge, respected for his manner and abilities. He and Joan had three daughters; Elena, and twins Lauren (1948-2004) and Marcia.

Sam and Mary's second son Stanley "Stack" I. Friedman, married Lucille Wendrow (1918-2017) on July 6, 1941. They had four children: Robert (1943-2022), Paul (1944-1951), Steven and Patricia. Stanley assisted in running Hub Clothiers before moving to Seattle in 1946. There he operated several businesses, including Northern Tailors and then Stack's Store for Men. In 1958 he opened the first Valu-Mart men's and boys' clothing store, then formed Western Clothiers, Inc. to manage that business. Western Clothiers expanded to have 21 Valu-Marts in four states.

Sam and Mary's daughter, Phyllis, was active in Jewish Juniors in the Thirties and sang in the Talmud Torah choir. She was elected secretary of the Young People's League in 1938. In 1942 she worked as secretary at the USO Center. Phyllis married Herbert Belmonte (1916-2014) in 1946. He was a German refugee and a U.S. Army veteran. Herb worked first as an accountant for Hub Clothiers, then continued the firm as Belman's Hub Clothiers through 1966. He then worked with Stanley's Valu-Mart. Phyllis was a mainstay of Hadassah events in the Forties. They had one daughter, Michele.

Sam and Mary's youngest son, Bernard, is the subject of his own biographical sketch.

Saul Friedman, son of Julius and Augusta (Stusser) Friedman
Born March 20, 1902, in Tacoma, brother of Rebecca, Abedeaux, and Siegfried
Married Ida Sylvia Saul (1901-1987) in Seattle on April 16, 1924
Parents of Merilyn "Lynn" Silver (1927-2012)
Died September 28, 1976, in Seattle; buried Home of Peace Cemetery

Saul started his career in his father's clothing shop, and continued as manager. After his father's death Saul partnered with his brother, Siegfried, in operating Friedman's Clothes Shop, still at 1124 Pacific. In 1940 they opened a second store together, Jason's, at 1110 Pacific. Saul's wife, Ida, was active in Sisterhood activities at Temple Beth Israel in the Thirties. Saul served on their membership committee in 1940. They were members of Temple Beth Israel in 1942, but Saul often visited Talmud Torah during High Holidays. Their daughter married Robert Silver.

Tacoma News Tribune September 14, 1940

Siegfried "Sig" Friedman, son of Julius and Augusta (Stusser) Friedman
Born September 20, 1910, in Tacoma, brother of Rebecca, Saul, and Abedeaux
Died July 21, 2011, in Tacoma; buried Home of Peace Cemetery

Siegfried was active in sports throughout his life, from winning tennis championships as a teenager, to participating in B'nai B'rith golf tournaments as an adult. He worked in his father's clothing store and partnered with his brother, Saul, for decades. Siegfried was a 2nd Lieutenant in the U.S. Army during World War II, serving in the medical administrative corps. Although he never married he lived a full 100 years, supporting his community, the Elks, and Temple Beth El.

Siegfried Friedman c. 1935, courtesy of Harold Friedman

Rabbi Noah Mendel Gamze, son of Rabbi Elias and Hannah (Levin) Gamze
Born May 24, 1924, in Kovno, Russia (now Kaunas, Lithuania)
Arrived U.S. June 24, 1929, entering Texas from Mexico, en route to Chicago, Illinois
Married Annette R. Sherman (1927-2006) in Chicago on February 15, 1957
Parents of Eli and Lori
Died January 20, 2003, in Warwick, Rhode Island; buried Adat Shalom Cemetery, Livonia, Michigan

Noah Gamze grew up in Chicago, where his father, Rabbi Elias Gamze, led the Chicago Loop Synagogue. After Rabbi Noah Gamze's 1951 ordination he led his father's congregation for four years. Then he served Tacoma's Sinai Temple from April of 1958 until October of 1959. He returned to Chicago and worked as a Hebrew school teacher for several years. Rabbi Gamze then led Detroit's Downtown Synagogue for nearly four decades. After his 2001 retirement he moved to Rhode Island, where he continued working as a part-time hospital chaplain.

Detroit Free Press January 22, 2003 **Noah Gamze**

Joseph Peter Gevurtz, son of Jacob and Feiga Puchla Geverc
Born August of 1880 or 1882 or 1885 in Lubartow, Lublin, Russia (now Poland)
Arrived Detroit July 5, 1909, by rail as Perec Geverc
Died March 7, 1960, in Tacoma; buried Home of Peace Cemetery

Joseph came to Tacoma before 1914, joining his married sister, Helen (Gevurtz) Klegman. He worked for nearly forty years as a furniture salesman for Harry Rotman and for David Klegman.

I, __Perec Geverc, known as Peter Geverts or Joe Gevurts__
now residing at __1429 No. Prospect St., Tacoma, Pierce County, Wash.__
occupation __Salesman__, aged __48__ years, do declare on oath that my personal description is:
Sex __male__, color __white__, complexion __medium__, color of eyes __blue__
color of hair __dk. brown__, height __5__ feet __4½__ inches; weight __170__ pounds; visible distinctive marks __eyes slightly crossed__
race __Hebrew__; nationality __Polish__
I was born in __Lubartow, Poland__, on __Aug. 29, 1882__
I am __not__ married. The name of my wife or husband is

1930 Declaration of Intention of Perec Geverc, known as Peter or Joe Gevurtz

Max Goldberg, son of Aaron and Bertha Goldberg
Born April 2, 1871, in Russia
Married Molly Diamond (1875-1964), daughter of Jacob and Sheyna Diamond
Parents of Bertha Koppel (1899-1967)
Died November 30, 1943, in Seattle; buried Bikur Cholim Cemetery, Seattle

Max immigrated about 1885 and lived in Maryland in 1899 when his daughter was born. In the early 1900s he worked as a buyer for Tacoma Junk. Max briefly operated the Newport Hotel and was a member of Talmud Torah during the 1919 relief campaign. In 1926 his daughter was married at the historic Tacoma Hotel. Max operated a clothing store and a fruit company before moving to Seattle about 1938. There he sold secondhand goods.

Robert N. Goldberg, son of Samuel and Lena (Reback) Goldberg
Born March 21, 1896, in New York, New York
Married Eva Elizabeth King (1900-1995)
Parents of Allen (1919-1969), Jules (1921-1934), Ethel Esther Strauss Walker (1922-2015), and
    Charles (1935-1991)
Died August 14, 1961, in Tacoma; buried Home of Peace Cemetery

Robert served two years in the Army during World War I and lived in Nebraska, Wyoming, and Oklahoma before coming to Washington in the Twenties. He worked on the state level for the Maccabees program of fraternal life insurance. In 1934 his son, Jules, was killed in an accident. His eldest son, Allen, served in the Marines from 1938 to 1947. His youngest son, Charles, was active in Talmud Torah youth activities in the Forties and celebrated his bar mitzvah in December of 1948.

Jules Goldberg, 13 year old son of Mr. and Mrs. Robert Goldberg, 1018 South Sprague avenue, succumbed Sunday to head injuries. He was hurt Thursday afternoon when he walked into the front fender of an automobile driven by Mrs. Emma Samuelson, living on route 6, Tacoma. The mishap occurred at South 11th and Sprague street.

Tacoma News Tribune September 3, 1934

Thomas Goldfarb, son of Joseph and Pauline (Shneider) Goldfarb
Born March 26, 1893, in Keidan, Russia (now Kedainiai, Lithuania)
Arrived N.Y. January 1908 aboard the *Muskova* from Rotterdam
Married Anna Weinstone (1895-1982) in Tacoma on November 26, 1919
Parents of Paul (1920-2006), Gerald (1922-1972), Beverly Hillman
      (1926-2010), and Charlene
Died January 3, 1963, in Santa Clara, California, as Thomas Grayson
(Right) Beverly and Charlene Goldfarb, courtesy of Jack Warnick
(Below left) Tacoma Daily Ledger ad June 3, 1920

TACOMA HARDWARE & JUNK STORE. Good & Goldfarb, Props.; 1314 Commerce. Main 2394. Junk, Machinery, Pipe, Sacks and Furniture Bought and Sold.

Thomas lived with his uncle, Harry Goldfarb, in 1910 in Connecticut, and later joined the Army. He applied for citizenship in 1918 from Camp Lewis. After his marriage to Froem Weinstone's youngest daughter, Thomas operated the Tacoma Furniture and Hardware Company with Anna's brother-in-law, David Good. Later Thomas and David sold secondhand furniture at 1318 Commerce. Thomas and Anna's sons Paul and Gerald celebrated their bar mitzvahs at Talmud Torah in 1933 and 1935, and Anna often assisted with Auxiliary programs. Their son, Paul, married Tacoma's Bea Novikoff in 1941 and served in the U.S. Army during World War II. Thomas and Anna joined their married children in California about 1950 and later took the surname Grayson.

David Guy Good, son of Barry/Berl and Frances (Ingerman) Good/Gegusinsky
Born August 10, 1888, in Russia
Sister Rose born Rasche Gegusinsky in Sumelishki, Vilna, Russia (now Semeliskes, Lithuania)
Married Mildred Weinstone (1892-1973) November 17, 1918, daughter of Froem and Bertha Weinstone
Parents of Bruce Gerald and Lawrence Emanuel Good
Died June 9, 1972, in Oakland, California; buried Home of Eternity Cemetery, Oakland
(Right) Tacoma Daily Ledger March 16, 1928
(Below left) Bruce and Lawrence Good, courtesty of Jack Warnick

Auction Sale
STAR FURNITURE & HARDWARE CO.
1148 Commerce St.

David's sister, Rose, married Joseph Willner in Seattle in 1913. Five years later David came to Tacoma from Chicago and married Mildred Weinstone. In the early Twenties he operated the Tacoma Hardware and Junk store with his brother-in-law, Thomas Goldfarb. In 1927 David ran the Star Furniture and Hardware Company. That same year Mildred participated in Council of Jewish Women activities and was elected president of the Destiny lodge of the B'nai B'rith auxiliary. Around 1929 David and Mildred moved to Oakland, California, joining several of Mildred's siblings. Her father, Froem, lived with them until his death in 1933. David continued in the junk and iron business, and during World War II worked in a shipyard. Their son, Lawrence, enlisted in the military in 1943.

Michael Green, son of Moses Aaron and Sarah (Schreiber) Greenbaum (later Morris Green)
Born November 25, 1891, in Russia (Stated New York)
Married Esther Gittelsohn (1894-1952) in Seattle on April 3, 1923
Parents of William Leon Green (1927-2006)
Married second to Esther's sister, Gertrude Gittelsohn (1896-1958)
Died September 21, 1972, in Seattle; buried Bikur Cholim, Seattle

Michael's decade in Tacoma was a byway in a life of many twists and turns. He was likely born near Warsaw and emigrated with his parents as a toddler. The family lived a few years in New York, then settled in Chicago. There Michael worked as a newsboy, and later noted that he had helped to organize the *Chicago Daily* newsboys' band, playing trumpet. From there Michael's story jumps to Brownsville, Texas, where he spent eight months as a second lieutenant with "Pancho" Francisco Villa before switching sides and joining the First Illinois Cavalry. His job as bugler, and his height of 5'2", earned him the nickname "Squeak." On his return to Chicago he enlisted in the Field Artillery in 1917, which took him to the battlefields of France. After the war Michael moved with his family to Seattle, where the family took the shortened surname Green.

The Spud House

FOLKS!—

Come down and get acquainted. Meet "Bill, the Potato Chip," and see the boy's smile. A fellow that doesn't smile can't work for me. Service—all you want.

"SPUD" GREEN.

Yakima Spuds, small, medium, sack..	$1.65
Yakima Spuds, large size, sack......	$2.35
Local Spuds, large, per sack........	$2.45
Grapefruit, 64-size, 5 for...........	35c
Winesap Apples, wrapped, per box......	$1.50
Oranges, 150-size, dozen.............	40c
Yakima Jonathan Apples, box	$1.45
Onions, 11 pounds for...............	25c
Carrots, 11 pounds for	25c

Seed Spuds of All Kinds

FREE DELIVERY
AT OUR CONVENIENCE
901 Center St.   1123-25 Market
Main 3942   Main 2916

Michael married Gertrude Gittelsohn, daughter of Snohomish pioneers Wolf and Etta (Pearl) Gittelsohn. The young couple took up residence in Tacoma, where their son, William, was born in 1927. That year Esther was active in Hadassah activities, and in the Thirties she helped with several Auxiliary events. For the next five years Michael operated a fruit and potato stand called The Spud House and went by yet another nickname, "Spud." He eventually had multiple locations, at 901 Center, at 1125 Market, and a drive-in store at 1605 South Tacoma Way. In February of 1930 he incorporated the company and invited customers to come meet his smiling son Bill, dubbed "The Potato Chip." A few years later he ran as a candidate for precinct committeeman and then park commissioner. His involvement with the local Democratic Club and his veteran status earned him an appointment as a deputy U.S. marshal, taking him back to Seattle.

When World War II broke out Michael re-enlisted in the Army and his son joined the Navy. After the war they both continued in the produce business. Michael was active in multiple veterans' groups, and as Capt. Green was elected post commander of the Seattle chapter of Jewish War Veterans in 1956. After the death of his wife Michael followed the Jewish custom of marrying her sister, Gertrude.

Tacoma News Tribune February 14, 1930

Hyman "Hy" Greenberg, born August 10, 1879, in Chizew, Russia (now Czycew, Poland)
Married Molla Appel near Warsaw in September of 1897
Arrived St. John's, New Brunswick, on December 2, 1901
Parents of Ben (1898-1965), Esther Lampart (1901-1986), and Martha Weisler (1906-1974)
Died April 15, 1966, in Los Angeles; buried Hillside Memorial Cemetery, Culver City

Hyman and Molla's first two children were born in Mazowieckie, Russia, now Poland. Their third child was born in Seattle in 1906. The family next lived in Olympia for several years before settling in Tacoma. Like several others, Hyman sold secondhand merchandise from a variety of locations on Commerce Street. In 1913 Ben and Molla were among a cluster of close friends who attended the Shapiro wedding anniversary party. That September Hyman was one of the trustees of the incorporation of Chevrah Ahavas Israel, and in 1914 he helped purchase land for the Chevra Kadisha Cemetery. Their daughter, Esther, married landsman Pincos Lampart (1892-1962) in 1920, and the family business expanded to include gents' clothing. Esther's siblings would each marry in Los Angeles. Ben married Mirrela Abraham (1901-1984) in 1930, and Martha married David Weisler (1908-1969) in 1935. When Hyman died there in 1966 he was buried in the same cemetery where the unrelated baseball legend Hank Greenberg would be laid to rest twenty years later.

Abraham "Abe" Greenblat, son of Elia and Esther (Moszkowicz) Grünblat
Born July 2, 1888, in Kaleczew, Russia (now Poland)
Arrived N.Y. October 12, 1909 from Antwerp aboard the *Vaderland*
Married Lillian Finegold (1898-1930) on December 25, 1921, in Wolf Point, Montana
Parents of Ralph (1923-1967) and Arthur Greenblat
Married second to Frances Levinson (1896-1977) in Tacoma on June 14, 1938
Died April 2, 1980, in Seattle; buried Home of Peace Cemetery

Abe's 1909 passenger record mentioned that he was blind in his left eye. He lived first with his married brother, Joseph, in Spokane, working as a farm laborer and for the Great Northern Railway. After Abe's marriage he moved with the Finegold family to Tacoma, living near the railroad shops in South Tacoma. Both of his sons were active in AZA sports as teenagers, and both served in World War II. Abe worked as a junk buyer, sold gas and oil, and operated the secondhand Square Deal Trading Post. He later operated Standard Plumbing Supply with his younger son, Arthur.

(Left) Abe and Lillian (Finegold) Greenblat c. 1925
Courtesy of Arthur and Mark Greenblat

Robert Grenley, son of Isaac and Esther (Spiegler) Greenberg
Born Rubin Greenberg on October 10, 1887/1889, in Jossey (now Iasi) Moldavia, Romania
Married Sarah Schrader (1889-1968) on January 9, 1912, in Manhattan, New York
Parents of Philip (1912-1994), Jay (1914-1993), and Jerome "Jerry" (1921-2004)
Died June 15, 1952, in Tacoma; buried Home of Peace Cemetery

Robert Grenley grew up in Manhattan as Rubin "Ruby" Greenberg, the eldest of at least seven siblings. He married Sarah in January of 1912, and their first son was born in Seattle in December. The family lived in Brooklyn during the Twenties and Thirties, then came to Tacoma about 1940 as Grenley. Robert served as secretary of the Talmud Torah board in 1943. Throughout his career he worked as a clothing salesman. He ran his son's store during World War II while Jay served in the armed forces. Later Robert operated Victor's Men's Shop.

Robert and Sarah's eldest son, **Philip Grenley** M.D., married Dorothy Sarney (1916-2000) in New York in 1938. They were the parents of Laurie, Neal, Jane and Robert. He was already a practicing physician when he enlisted in the Army medical corps. After his discharge he joined his parents in Tacoma, where he worked for many decades as a urologist. The Mary Bridge Children's Hospital established the Philip Grenley Orthopedic Guild in his honor.

Jay Grenley's career with Hughes women's wear brought him from Chicago to New York, and to Tacoma. After his service in World War II he married Bertha Klorfein (1921-2005) in Portland in 1944. He operated Oakes Apparel and was active in the downtown retail merchants' organizations.

Robert and Sarah's youngest son, Jerry Grenley, was born and raised in New York. After the family's move to Tacoma he was active in the B'nai B'rith, serving on the 1947 committee that brought Orson Welles to the Armory. In 1949 he traveled to Portland, Oregon, to marry Suzanne Tonkin. He worked as a buyer for the Bon Marche, which took the couple to Spokane. They later lived in Oakland, California.

Sarah's widowed sister, Gussie (Schrader) Goldstein Kellen Wolf (1892-1960) moved to Tacoma from Portland in 1954 and was a member of Sinai Temple's Sisterhood.

Irving Gussman, son of Jack and Etta (Lewin) Gussman
Born October 2, 1902/1904, in Chasnik, Vitebsk, Russia
Married Ann Brown (1909-2000) January 10, 1947, in Tacoma
Died May 28, 1955, in Tacoma; buried Bikur Cholim Cemetery, Seattle

(Right) Tacoma News Tribune April 16, 1950

Irving was born in Russia and later lived with his siblings in Montreal, Canada. He entered the U.S. in 1923 and worked in Seattle before coming to Tacoma in 1941. In both cities he sold men's furnishings. His brother-in-law, Harry Wiseblatt, came from Montreal to work with him. Irving first operated Irving's Clothes Shop on Pacific Avenue, then moved to 11th and Commerce for nearly a decade. In 1949 he signed a ten-year lease at 919 Market Street. Two years earlier he had married Ann Brown at the home of Rabbi Leo Trepp. She was the daughter of Seattle's Rose and Isadore Brenan/Brown and had previously married Harry Cohen. Her daughter, Lois, was confirmed at Sinai Temple in 1948. Together Ann and Irving took leadership roles in Zionist groups in Tacoma. Ann was Hadassah vice president in 1947 and was active in the regional conference the following year. She frequently participated in Hadassah donor events over the next decade. Irving was identified as the district president responsible for re-organizing the Tacoma Zionist group in 1947. After his death, Ann married again to Ben Etsekson, also widowed.

Joseph Barnett Gyle, born May 27, 1860, in Germany
Naturalized 1879 in Tehama, California
Married Cora (Pope) Cates (1870-1913) on March 13, 1913, in Tacoma
Died April 9, 1925, in Tacoma; buried Tacoma Mausoleum

Joseph lived in California and Arizona in the 1880s and 1890s. He then lived another decade in Eastern Washington. He opened a jewelry store in Tacoma about 1910 with Herman Wolff of Seattle. Joseph married Cora in March of 1913, but she died just five months later. That year Joseph was one of the incorporators of Chevrah Ahavas Israel. His store at 1336 Pacific was next to that of David Shafer, another incorporator. Both stores were damaged by fire in April of 1914. Over the next ten years Joseph was active in the leadership of Tacoma's Moose lodge. He belonged to Temple Beth Israel from 1920 to 1922.

John Ivan Haas, son of Samuel and Selma (Sinasohn) Haasz
Born July 9, 1911, in Berlin, Germany
Married Gerda Buchheim (1914-2012) in Berlin in December of 1935
Parents of Henry
Arrived U.S. April 7, 1947, aboard the *SS Marine Lynx* from Shanghai, China
Died November 16, 1993, in Seattle; buried Home of Peace Cemetery, Tacoma

John and Gerda escaped Germany in 1938 and lived nearly a decade as refugees in Shanghai, China. In the U.S. John operated the Centralia Outdoor Store before moving to Tacoma. There he ran the Bargain Mart at multiple locations. Gerda joined the Sinai Temple Sisterhood in 1956, and John sang at the installation of Rabbi Carmi. John's love of soccer led him to co-found Pierce County's junior soccer movement and to sponsor many adult soccer teams. John and Gerda openly shared their Holocaust experiences and were committed in supporting Jewish social service agencies. Their son, Henry, continues their work.

(Left) John Haas and his son, Henry
(Center) Tacoma News Tribune ad May 6, 1960
(Right) Gerda (Buchheim) Haas and her son, Henry, courtesy of Henry and Kate Haas

Arthur Henry Hart, son of John Henry and Myrtle Ethel (Nixon) Hart
Born December 12, 1914, in Vancouver, British Columbia
Married Celia Jaffe (1915-1992) in Seattle on October 23, 1938
Parents of Deane and Susan
Died October 9, 1983, in Seattle; cremated

Arthur's wife, Celia, was the daughter of Seattle's Samuel Aaron and Tillie (Leshkovitch) Jaffe. At the time that Arthur enlisted in the Army he was working in Seattle for his brother-in-law, Harry Pinch, first husband of his wife's sister, Sonya Jaffe. After his military service Arthur moved to Tacoma and worked for Sonya's second husband, Morris Plotkin, managing the Diamond Shop. Celia attended Hadassah events with her sister and participated in Talmud Torah Sisterhood programs in the late Forties. The couple moved back to Seattle in the Fifties and divorced. Celia worked in clothing sales for her brothers, Irving and George Jaffe. Arthur continued selling jewelry.

Tacoma News Tribune April 21, 1948

Meyer Herring, son of Pesach and Chaia Sara Hering
Born April 12, 1903/5, in Nemokshty, Kovno, Russia (now Nemakšciai, Lithuania)
Arrived N.Y. May 13, 1922, aboard the *Reliance* from Hamburg as Meier Hering
Married Frances "Fannie" Kohm (1916-1989) in March of 1954 in Honolulu, Hawaii
Died August 2, 1991, in Spokane; buried Mount Nebo Cemetery, Spokane

Meyer first joined his cousin, Paul Herring, in New York, and worked as a clerk. In 1940 he lived in Chicago, near his sister, Esther (Herring) Guttman/Goodman. He served in the military, then married Fannie in Hawaii. The couple moved to Tacoma in 1956. Fannie immediately became a member of the Sinai Temple Sisterhood and the Council of Jewish Women. Meyer managed the M & M Junk Company until they moved to Spokane about 1959. There he worked in sheet metal fabrication.

David "Dave" Isadore Holzman, son of Moses and Sallie (Herman) Holzmann
Born May 17, 1893/4, in Filipkowce, Galicia/Austria (now Pilipche, Ukraine)
Arrived N.Y. February 2, 1914, aboard the *Pretoria* from Berlin as Isie
Married Lena Lee Lyons (1898-1973) in Texas about 1921, daughter of Morris and Ida Lyons
Parents of Philip "Phil" Holman (1922-2001), and Gertrude "Trudy" Holzman (1923-2006)
Died November 13, 1948, in San Francisco

David worked most of his life as a clothing salesman, often for a different store nearly every year. Before his marriage he lived in Beaumont, Texas. He then lived in Galveston, Dallas, Denver, and Oakland. Although he was only in Tacoma for two years, he was installed as Talmud Torah president in December of 1941. Several times during 1942 he assisted Rabbi Treiger in leading services, and participated in activities of the Jewish Welfare Board.

David Hyman, born April 23, 1909, in London, England
Arrived N.Y. December 28, 1919, aboard the *Adriatic* from London
Married Ada Leona Rackmil (1911-1999) daughter of Bernard and Rose (Friedman) Rackmil
Died November 19, 1981, in San Francisco, California

David studied pharmacy at the University of California, Berkeley. In 1931 he lived in Tacoma, worked as a pharmacist, and played basketball with the Young Hebrew Moderates. David married Ada Rackmil in 1936 and the couple moved to Los Angeles. The marriage ended and Ada resumed her maiden name. Her widowed mother, Rose, lived with her in Los Angeles. David moved to San Francisco and continued working in pharmacy. In 1949 he married Ione Collins (1915-1968).

Mendel "Max" Jacobson, son of Hilel and Guta Jakobsohn
Born August 16, 1873, in Friedrichstadt, Russia (now Jaunjelgava, Latvia)
Married Esther Stusser (1871-1957) on January 16, 1896, in Libau, Russia (now Latvia)
Parents of Abraham "Alfred" (1897-?), Anna Santiago (1900-1988), Rosa (1902-1987), and
    Melville (1904-1951)
Arrived N.Y. November 10, 1901, on *Lake Manitoba* from London and Quebec
Died January 30, 1950, in Seattle; buried Bikur Cholim Cemetery, Seattle

Tacoma 1907 city directory

Max worked his entire career as a tailor. He came to Tacoma with his family in the fall of 1903. His wife was Esther Stusser, youngest of the twelve children born to Abraham and Mollie (Friedman) Stusser. Max

> JACOBSON MAX, Tailor, Suits Made to Order, Cleaned and Repaired, 609 S 11th, h same

was noted as the president of Chevra Talmud Torah in the fall of 1907, and was one of the incorporators in 1908. Max also assisted with High Holy Day services in 1909. Around 1913 the family moved to Seattle.

Max and Esther had four children. Their eldest son, Abraham, was born in Libau and in the Fifties lived in Chicago. Their eldest daughter, Anna, married John Santiago and died in San Francisca. Their younger daughter, Rosa, died unmarried in Seattle. Their younger son, Melville, was born in Tacoma. He worked as a jeweler and died in Puyallup.

Morris Jaffe, son of Benjamin and Fanny (Sentner) Jaffe
Born June 9, 1920, in Seattle; younger brother of Harry Aaron and Yetta (Jaffe) Shapiro
Married Edith Brodsky (1926-2017) in Tacoma on November 3, 1946
Parents of Sandra, Susan, Steven (1952-1979), and Jerry
Died February 2, 2009, in Tacoma; buried Home of Peace Cemetery

Morris was born and raised in Seattle, but after his service in World War II he married a Tacoma girl. He spent the rest of his life in Tacoma, managing the Brodsky store started by her father, Philip Brodsky. In 1977 the name of the firm was changed to Brodsky's Men's Wear and Uniforms. Edith was active in Jewish women's groups and took frequent leadership roles in Hadassah. Morris was president of B'nai B'rith in 1962, and in 1972 was appointed to serve on the Selective Service board.

Walter Israel Jung, son of Adolph and Ida (Kauder) Jung
Born November 25, 1900, in Wien/Vienna, Austria
Married Margarethe "Grete" Korngut (1902-1988), daughter of Rudolph and Resi (Adler) Korngut
Arrived N.Y. November 17, 1939, on the *Saturnia* from Trieste, Italy
Parents of Ilse (1932-2010)
Died January 5, 1969, in Tacoma; buried Home of Peace Cemetery

Walter and Grete obtained passports on October 19, 1939, and one month later joined her uncle in New Jersey. Grete's mother, Resi, followed just a few weeks later. The family lived briefly in Seattle, then settled in Tacoma. Their daughter, Ilse, participated in holiday programs at Talmud Torah in 1942. They became U.S. citizens in May of 1945. The following year a newspaper notice in Seattle asked for help in locating the family in order to pass on a message from Carola Stahl of Austria. Walter managed a grocery and later held an office management position on Fort Lewis. Their daughter, Ilse, graduated from the College of Puget Sound and became a school teacher.

Henoch "Harry" Kantoff, son of Shmuel and Gertrude (Petersile) Kantoff
Born March 1870/72/74, in Warsaw, Russia (now Warszawa, Poland)
Married Regina Zuckerkorn (1874-1918) in Warsaw about 1895
Parents of Anna (1896-1973) and Adell Foff (1899-1969)
Arrived N.Y. January 27, 1904, aboard the *Rotterdam* from Rotterdam with brothers Yankel and Abram
Died January 10, 1931, in San Francisco; buried Eternal Home Cemetery, Colma, California

Harry and Regina had two daughters in Warsaw, then followed her brother, Max Zuckerkorn, to New York. Five years later they followed him to Tacoma. In 1909 Harry worked in Max's clothing store, then started his own. His niece, Regina Stetiner, married Aaron Silver in Tacoma in 1912. Harry and his wife attended the Shapiro anniversary party in 1913. Also that year Harry became a U.S. citizen. His nephew, Albert Wacholder, was born in Tacoma in 1914. A year later the extended families moved to San Francisco.

Tacoma city directory ad 1910

Max "Mickey" L. Kaplan, son of David Samuel and Lena (Abramovitz) Kaplan
Born September 5, 1905, in Chicago, Illinois; brother of Joe, Bessie, Ida, Rose, and Bernice
Married Betty Gorman (1907-1982) in Los Angeles on February 4, 1928
Parents of Adrienne, Eunice, and David Kenneth
Married second to Elsa Alice Schlesinger Altschul about 1951
Died March 12, 1998 in Los Angeles, California; buried Hillside Memorial, Culver City

Mickey was born and raised in Chicago and learned to work as an auto mechanic. He lived a few years in Los Angeles, where he met and married Betty Gorman, formerly Eska Bessie Gorbmann, daughter of Morris and Dora (Shapiro) Gorbmann. They lived briefly with his parents in Chicago, then moved to Tacoma about 1931. Both of their daughters were born in Tacoma. Betty was active in the Talmud Torah Auxiliary in the Thirties. Mickey operated the West Coast Investment Company, selling used cars from 2150 Pacific Avenue. In the early Forties he also partnered in the Turf Smoke Shop, and invested in an apartment building with Ben Etsekson. Max and Betty returned to Los Angeles, where their son was born.

David Kaplow, son of Jacob Naphtoly and Chana (Berman) Kapelov
Born February 28, 1879, in Kiev, Russia (now Kyiv, Ukraine)
Arrived Seattle March 2, 1907, by rail from Vancouver
Married Dora Metzger (1890-1966) in Seattle on April 9, 1911
Parents of Marian Schneider (1912-2008), Samuel (1913-2012), and Libby Malvin (1918-1992)
Died in Pierce County on February 20, 1932; buried Herzl Cemetery, Seattle

Dora came to the U.S. in 1906 with her parents, Shraga Faival and Manie (Neustadt) Metzger, and moved to Seattle in 1908. Morris Werbisky served as a witness at Dora's marriage to David. All three of their children were born in Tacoma, where David operated the American Junk Company with Morris Warnick and was active in the Knights of Maccabees. In 1917 they attended a social event with Frank Spigal, and in 1919 they contributed to the war relief fund as members of Talmud Torah. In the Twenties Dora managed a Well Worth dry goods store. The family returned to Seattle about 1928. David was killed in an automobile collision near Fort Lewis in 1932.

1918 Tacoma city directory ad

Jacob "Jack" Karp, son of Morris and Sophia (Kind) Karp
Born January 21, 1905, in Manhattan, New York
Married Rosalie Cone (1906-2006) in Seattle on May 27, 1928
Parents of Coralee and Myra
Died April 8, 1950, in Seattle; buried Herzl Cemetery, Seattle

Jack and Rosalie were married in Seattle and lived briefly in Spokane and San Francisco before coming to Tacoma about 1934. Jack managed Ideal Manufacturing, run by his father-in-law, Sam Cone. Rosalie managed the Betty Lou Dress Shop. Throughout the Thirties both were active at Talmud Torah. Jack served on the board of trustees in 1938 when Sam was treasurer. Rosalie was treasurer of the Women's Auxiliary in 1939, the year her mother was president. The family moved to Seattle after the war and Jack worked as a fur salesman. After Jack's death Rosalie operated apparel shops in White Center and Burien. She survived serious injuries suffered in a 1954 fall down an elevator shaft.

Max Leon Karsh, son of Israel and Eva Chana (Thal) Karsch
Born May 25, 1921, in Onikshty (now Anyksciai, Lithuania)
Arrived N.Y. November 10, 1922 aboard the *Aquitania* from Southampton as Motel Karsch
Married Audrey Rosenblatt (1926-2007) in 1948 in Chelsea, Massachusetts
Parents of Sue and Evan
Married second to Lucille Baran in King County on June 28, 1969
Died December 31, 1993, in Seattle; buried Seattle Sephardic Brotherhood Cemetery

Max grew up in Bellingham, graduated from the University of Washington, and served in the U.S. Army during World War II. He earned a master's degree at Oregon State and taught at the Boston College of Pharmacy. Max and Audrey moved to Tacoma about 1955. She was immediately active in Jewish women's groups, serving as president of the Sinai Temple Sisterhood in 1957 and 1958. Max was an officer in the Tacoma Federated Jewish Fund and the B'nai B'rith. During the Fifties he operated the Sixth and K Drug Store. Audrey taught for many years at Stadium High School. Max later remarried and moved to Seattle, and Audrey and her children moved to California.

David Klegman, son of Max and Bessie (Tonkonogy/Tonkon) Klegman
Born July 1, 1883, in Poltava, Russia (now Ukraine)
Arrived in Vermont from Liverpool via Quebec on September 7, 1897, with his mother and siblings
Married Helen Gevurtz (1889-1951) in Portland, Oregon, on July 4, 1909
Parents of Milton (1910-1972), Samuel Herman (1912-2003), and Bessie (1918-2010)
Died January 17, 1959, in Tacoma; buried Home of Peace Cemetery

David came to Portland with his family as a teenager. He started his career working with his father, selling secondhand furniture. After his marriage he joined his older brother, Ben, in Tacoma and opened the aptly named Portland Furniture Store. Unlike many Jewish merchants on Commerce Street who switched locations regularly, David stayed in business for nearly fifty years at 1136 Commerce. In 1918 he and Helen bought a home at 1429 North Prospect and lived there for the remainder of their lives.

SEE
Honest Dave Klegman
The Portland Furniture Store
1136 Commerce.

Tacoma News Tribune November 7, 1921

Like many parents, David and Helen were active in Talmud Torah when their children were in school. David served as Talmud Torah president in 1919 and 1920, and was treasurer in 1931. Their sons celebrated their bar mitzvahs in 1923 and 1925. Helen was a participating member of Hadassah and the Destiny B'nai B'rith auxiliary. She frequently held positions of leadership in Talmud Torah's Women's Auxiliary, serving as treasurer in 1931-1932, and then as president in 1933-1934. Helen again stepped in as president in the spring of 1937, and as vice president in 1940. Helen also supported the Sisterhood of Temple Beth Israel, serving as vice president in 1928. David donated the linoleum for Temple Beth Israel's kitchen in 1922. David and Helen were particularly close with Harry and Lena Rotman, hosting their 25th wedding anniversary celebration in 1935.

Helen and David's eldest son, Milton, taught school in Tacoma and Roy before moving to California. There he married Lucille Bloom (1919-1995) in 1957. He was buried in the same cemetery in Oakland as his uncle, Sam Klegman. Helen and David's younger son, Samuel Herman, married Thelma Korklin (1914-1990) in 1936. Samuel and Thelma observed the *Pidyan ha ben* ritual of "redeeming" their firstborn son in a ceremony at Talmud Torah, along with grandparents Helen and David Klegman, and Sarah and Julius Korklin. That same child, Marvin, was killed by falling debris at Lowell School in the 1949 earthquake. They later belonged to Temple Beth Israel. Helen and David's only daughter, Bessie, did not marry.

HOLD TIDYONHABEN

Mr. and Mrs. David Klegman and Mr. and Mrs. Julius Korklin will be hosts Monday evening at 7:30 o'clock for the traditional celebration of Tidyonhaben for their grandson, the small child of Mr. and Mrs. Samuel Klegman. All friends are cordially invited for the ceremony at the Talmud Torah synagogue.

Tacoma News Tribune January 7, 1938

Max Klegman, born November 23, 1859, in Russia, son of Max Sr. and Mary Klugman
Married Bessie Tonkonogy Tonkon (1861-1914)
Parents of Ben (1881-1932), David (1883-1959), Fannie Wise (1892-1961), and Sam (1893-1955)
Bessie arrived in Vermont from Liverpool via Quebec on September 7, 1897, with her children
Died May 23, 1919, in Portland, Oregon; buried Neveh Zedek Cemetery, Portland, Oregon

Max and Bessie lived in Portland in 1900. There Max operated M. Klegman and son, selling secondhand clothing and junk with his eldest son, Ben. David stepped in as the "and son" when Ben moved to Tacoma in 1905. Sam did the same after David moved to Tacoma in 1910. In 1913 Max and his remaining family also moved to Tacoma. Max briefly operated the Chicago Furniture Company, but his business failed after his wife's death in 1914. He stayed in Tacoma through 1917, then returned to Portland where he died in 1919.

Max and Bessie's eldest son, **Ben Klegman**, and his wife Mary Weinstein (1883-1966) lived in Tacoma from 1906 to 1910, and again from 1912 to 1914. In between he operated a store in Bellingham, and later sold clothing in Juneau. Ben and Mary returned to Portland in 1917. Their three children, Samuel, Dorothy, and Beatrice, were all born in Portland. Max and Bessie's son David Klegman married Helen Gevurtz in 1909. (See separate sketch for David Klegman) Max and Bessie's daughter Fannie married Harry Wise (1884-1940) in 1915. They had two daughters, Bessie Wikoff and Miriam Spigal. Max and Bessie's youngest son, Sam, grew up in Portland. After moving to Tacoma with his parents he worked as an insurance agent. In 1917 Sam married Fannie Fleisher in California and lived there the rest of his life. In 1937 he remarried to Madeline Wolf. Sam died in California in 1955.

Norman "Norm" Stanley Kleinman, son of Rabbi Philip and Yetta (Kirschenbaum) Kleinman
Born April 27, 1921, in Saint Paul, Minnesota; brother of Matthew and Solomon
Married first to Hermia Engelberg in Chicago on August 12, 1945
Parents of Lynnel, Ruth, and David
Married second to Goldina "Dena" Shirley Simon Siegel (1924-2008) on May 19, 1968
Died December 15, 2015, in Tacoma; buried Home of Peace Cemetery

Norman's father, Philip, emigrated from Austria as a child and grew up in New York in a family of Hebrew teachers. He earned the title of rabbi in 1918 and took his growing family to Saint Paul from 1917 to 1926, and then to Milwaukee. In 1937 Rabbi Philip and his family settled in Portland, Oregon, where he led the congregation Neveh Zedek. In 1942 Norman's brother, Solomon, married Shirley Rickles, daughter of Seattle's "Pinkey" Rickles. All three brothers served in the armed forces during World War II. Matthew worked as a dentist and Solomon later became a Reform rabbi.

Norman attended Oregon State College in Corvallis before and after the war. In 1945 he married Hermia Engelberg in Chicago, daughter of George and Mollie (Spilky) Engelberg. Norman and his wife moved to Tacoma around 1949. They operated Stadium Toy and Craft and in addition Norman ran a hot dog vending machine service. By 1960 they were both solely involved in the toy store. Norman often spoke at preschool and PTA groups about suitable toys for children. Hermia's mother, Mollie Engelberg, died in Tacoma in 1957 and was buried in Home of Peace Cemetery. In 1962 the couple opened a second toy store in Federal Way. Within a few years they parted ways and both remarried. In 1968 Norman opened another store in Villa Plaza in Lakewood.

Both Hermia and Norm were involved at Sinai Temple. Hermia served on the Sisterhood board in 1953 and 1954, and Norman taught in the Sunday school. Their eldest daughter was confirmed in 1960 and was involved in BBG. Norman was an officer in B'nai B'rith in 1965 and 1966, and served on the board of Temple Beth El in the Seventies. His second wife, Dena, was an officer of the National Council of Jewish Women in the Seventies and continued her participation for decades. Norman and Dena were still officers when the chapter was closed.

Everything for the Child But the Parent

Stadium Toy & Craft

2 Great Stores to Serve You Better
Tacoma Avenue at Division — Federal Shopping Way

Tacoma News Tribune December 12, 1963

Arthur A. Lamken, son of Shloime and Chana (Cohon) Lemchen
Born October 15, 1887, in Sassmacken, Russia (now Valdemarpils, Latvia)
Arrived N.Y. January 31, 1907, aboard the *Teutonic* from Liverpool as Abram Lemchen
Married Fanny Dorothy Sussman (1890-1936) in Seattle on August 17, 1913
Parents of six children
Died February 16, 1939, in Tacoma; buried Home of Peace Cemetery

Arthur applied for a junk license in Tacoma in July of 1909, and stayed in the same industry until his death thirty years later. The company was Milwaukee Junk, then Milwaukee Machinery, and later Arthur Lamken Junk. Until his marriage Arthur lived with newlyweds Lena Lamken and Harry Rotman. His wife, Fanny, was

a member of Hadassah and the Talmud Torah Auxiliary. Their daughters, Molly and Estelle, were confirmed in the Thirties and participated in the Young People's League activities. After Arthur and Fanny died their son Floyd continued the junk business and aided his siblings. Floyd's wife, Rose, took many leaderships roles in Sinai Temple and Hadassah.

Children of Arthur and Fanny:
- Phyllis (1914-2004) married 1939 to Harold Brotman (1906-1982)
- Floyd (1916-2007) married 1942 to Rose Greenberg (1920-2005)
- Joseph Wilbur (1917-1919)
- Molly (1918-2016) married 1939 to Gerald Cone (1915-2017)
- Evelyn (1921-2003) married 1956 to Howard Henderson (1905-1976)
- Estelle (1924-2021) married 1946 to Abraham Allen Farber (1920-1988)

Several of Arthur's siblings also lived in Tacoma. **Victor Lamken** (1885-1964) emigrated a year before Arthur and initially worked with him in Milwaukee Junk. Victor married Carolyn Goldstein (1893-1976) in Seattle on December 22, 1913. He was a contributor to the 1919 war relief campaign as a member of Tacoma's Talmud Torah, but joined Temple Beth Israel later that year. Their four children were all born in Tacoma: Gordon, Mildred, Jeanne, and Dorothy. Victor sold railway supplies and equipment. Around 1925 the family moved to Seattle for a decade with other Lamken siblings, then lived the remainder of their lives in Sacramento.

Arthur's brother, Frank Lamken (1892-1965) didn't emigrate until 1912. He married Pansy Goldstein (1899-1951) in Seattle on September 28, 1919. Their sons, Gerald and Cecil, were also born in Tacoma. Frank moved back to Seattle and worked for Alaska Junk, then moved to Centralia.

Arthur's younger sister, Lillian Lamken (1894-1969), was married by Rabbi Slotnik in Tacoma in 1925 to Harry H. Bear (1889-1947). They had two children, Shirley and Stanley. Lillian died in Seattle in 1969. Although her birth was recorded in Sassmacken on December 31, 1893, her Washington death certificate carried a later birth date of October 8, 1903.

Another brother, Abraham H. Lamken (1887-1946), emigrated in 1904. He married Sarah Small and raised his family in New Jersey. The eldest brother, Baruch Zelig Lemchen, was born in Sassmacken in 1881. He perished with his entire family in Latvia in 1941.

Louis Lamken, son of Itsak and Devorah Lemchen
Born December 25, 1892, in Sassmacken, Russia (now Valdemarpils, Latvia)
Arrived N.Y. July 14, 1907, aboard the *Saratov* from Libau as Liebe Lemchen
Married widowed Elizabeth "Lizzy" (Kaufman) Roseman (1892-1977) in Tacoma on October 28, 1919
Died August 28, 1979, in Portland, Oregon; buried Home of Peace Cemetery, Tacoma

Louis first lived in Seattle, then came to Tacoma just in time to be drafted. He served in the Army from July of 1918 to February of 1919. After his marriage he briefly worked as a cattle stockman, then operated a fleet of buses as the Olympia-Tacoma Stage Company. His next ventures included running the American Furniture Company, making burlap bags, and selling ice cream. In 1924 Louis started selling concessions at the fair in Puyallup. At one time he operated twenty-five fast food stands and was the fair's exclusive ice cream vendor. He was most remembered for the burgers at Louie's Place.

His wife, Lizzy, was active in Talmud Torah and chaired several anniversary banquets. She regularly led Hadassah activities and received her life membership pin in 1969. Her daughter, Marion, was married to Jack Weinstein at Talmud Torah in 1937. Louis was noted as a past president of Sinai Temple. He and Lizzy celebrated their 50th anniversary at Temple Beth El in 1969.

*(Left) 28 Flavors Ice Creamery, 8922 Gravelly Lake Drive
June 2, 1958, Tacoma Public Library Richards A114903-1*

AWAIT ANNIVERSARY—Mr. and Mrs. Louis Lamken and their children will be hosts at a reception next Sunday to observe the golden wedding anniversary of the Lamkens. They extend an open invitation to all of their many friends to attend.—Jess Snyder photo.

*(Right) Golden wedding anniversary
Tacoma News Tribune December 7, 1969*

Pincos Lampart, son of Chaim David Lampart
Born July 17, 1892, in Zareby, Ostrow, Lomza, Russia (now Poland)
Arrived Halifax, Nova Scotia, July 21, 1920, aboard *Uranium* from Rotterdam
Married Esther Greenberg (1901-1986) on November 28, 1920, in Victoria, British Columbia
Parents of Blanche Dauber (1922-1984) and Doris Siegel (1928-2005)
Died January 10, 1962, in Los Angeles; buried Hillside Memorial, Culver City, California

Pincos came directly to Tacoma to work for Hyman Greenberg, lived with the family, and seven years later married his daughter. His 1914 naturalization was witnessed by Abraham Rose and Morris Friedman. Pincos was a 1919 war relief donor as part of Talmud Torah. That year he operated the Lampart Bag and Burlap Company. Pincos and Esther moved with the Greenbergs to San Francisco in 1921 and lived most of their married life in Los Angeles.

BAGS AND BURLAP

LAMPART BAG & BURLAP CO., 2511 So. G. Main 9358. Dealers in grain and potato bags. We are always in the market for buying and selling.

Tacoma Daily Ledger February 24, 1919

Aaron Lazerson, born April 20, 1877, in Russa
Married Hana Kaplan (1884-1969) on August 28, 1902, in Marinsk, Russia
Parents of Norman (1903-1978), Agnes Gruener (1905-1986), and Bella Katz (1914-2014)
Arrived Seattle January 12, 1917, aboard the *Asaki Maru* from Kobe, Japan
Died August 31, 1959, in Oakland, California; buried Home of Eternity, Oakland

Aaron spent his entire American career working as a tailor, even though he had suffered the loss of several fingers on his right hand. Hana and the children joined Aaron in Tacoma in 1920, three years after his emigration. Agnes was a member of the Young Hebrew Moderates in 1925, Norman was active in B'nai B'rith in 1928, and Bella was an officer of the Jewish Juniors in 1933. Aaron operated his own tailoring firm during the Twenties, and in the Thirties worked for others, including Joseph Rome. In 1937 Norman married and moved to Walla Walla, and Aaron and the women moved to San Francisco.

Tacoma Daily Ledger September 14, 1931   A. Lazerson   1139 Commerce

Max Benjamin LeBid, son of Benjamin and Beila LeBid, brother of Rose (LeBid) Dobry
Born March 25, 1892, in Tomsk, Russia
Married Nura Godesoff (1894-1978) in Russia on February 27, 1909
Parents of Sam (1911-2002), Miriam/Marion Crevin Painter Davis (1912-2007), and Lillian Winters
Arrived N.Y. May 12, 1913, aboard the *George Washington* from Southampton as Mendel Lebed
Died January 4, 1963, in Los Angeles, California

After their arrival in the United States Max and Nura lived in Bridgeport, Connecticut, for fifteen years. Max worked as a barber and Nura operated the Charm Beauty Shoppe. They moved to Tacoma about 1928, joining Max's sister, Rose (LeBid) Dobry. Max first sold used cars, then founded Tacoma Auto Wrecking in 1930. He expanded to selling wholesale auto parts with his son, later operating several locations of the Top Auto Store. The family was first affiliated with Talmud Torah, with Nura participating in the Women's Auxiliary and Sam playing on the Young Hebrew Moderates' sports teams. Later Nura was active in the Sisterhood of Temple Beth Israel. In 1956 she was noted as a founder of the Tacoma chapter of City of Hope. After the family moved to Seattle she helped found City of Hope chapters in Spokane, Aberdeen, and Alaska. Their son, Sam, expanded the auto parts companies and later had a career in real estate investing and development.

Morris Shapiro Levinson, son of Benjamin and Rachel (Mongoss) Shapiro
Born April 15, 1877-79, in Parichi, Minsk, Russia (now Belarus)
Married Jennie Shimen Friedman (1880-1942) daughter of Jacob and Rebecca Friedman
Parents of Harry (1900-1987), Sam (1901-1996), Benjamin (1906-1974), and Robert (1908-1996)
Arrived Philadelphia July 10, 1905, aboard the *Kroonland* from Liverpool
Died May 26, 1919, in Soap Lake, Washington; buried Home of Peace Cemetery

Morris and Jennie lived several years in London, where their first two sons were born. Their third son was born in New York in 1906. Six weeks later the couple joined Jennie's Friedman siblings in Tacoma, where their fourth son was born in 1908. Morris first operated a secondhand store on Commerce Street, but became insolvent in 1910. Jennie continued the secondhand store. Morris worked as a meat cutter, sold jewelry and junk for a few years, and then worked as a bond broker. Jennie contributed to the 1919 war relief fund as a member of Talmud Torah just months after the early death of Morris.

Their eldest son, Harry, served in the Navy, then married Rose Goodglick (1900-1996) sister-in-law of Julius Shafer. The couple moved to Los Angeles for a decade. He operated several prominent stores in Spokane in the Thirties and early Forties, then returned to Los Angeles. There his family took the surname Sheridan, the name his actor son, John, was using in Hollywood.

Morris and Jennie's son, Sam, married Elsa Kaufman (1901-1979) in Tacoma in 1924. He worked for seventy years as a lawyer in Seattle, becoming an expert in maritime law and a specialist in trial law. Both Sam and Elsa were community activists and served on dozens of boards. Sam was a mainstay of the Seattle Symphony and the Children's Home Society.

Morris and Jennie's son, Benjamin, was a member of the Young Hebrew Moderates in 1925. He married Florence Witenberg (1906-1987) in Los Angeles in 1930. She was the youngest daughter of S.N. Witenberg. Benjamin worked as a retail manager in Seattle for a decade, then started his own business as a manufacturing agent. They lived for many years in the San Francisco area and were active in Jewish organizations and charities.

Robert married Alberta Myerson (1910-1974) in 1928 and lived with her family in San Francisco for a decade. Then the couple joined his brother, Harry, in Spokane, where Robert worked as a clothing store manager. The family returned to California in 1940. After Alberta's death Robert twice remarried and died in Las Vegas.

Solomon "Saul" Levy, son of Sam and Ida Chaie Levy (formerly Sam Wilensky)
Born May 4, 1913, in Augusta, Georgia; brother of Harry, Yetta Cohen, and Rosa Goodglick
Married Ruth Witenberg (1917-1980) in Tacoma on June 28, 1942; daughter of Bernard and Charlotte
Parents of Larry, Sherry, and Lynn
Died July 31, 2001, in Seattle; buried Home of Peace,
Tacoma

(Left)
Saul and Ruth (Witenberg) Levy

(Right)
American Surplus Sales c. 1970

Courtesy of Lynn Levy

Saul's parents emigrated as Sam and Chaie Wilensky and lived first in New York. They changed their surname to Levy about 1911 when they moved to Georgia. Sam's sister, Rosa, married Seattle's Dr. Samson Goodglick in 1932. Before the decade was out Saul had joined her in Seattle, working for her father-in-law at the Pioneer Paint Company. Saul married Ruth Violet Witenberg in 1942. The couple lived five years in Seattle before moving to Tacoma. Saul operated American Surplus Sales on South Pine Street and South Tacoma Way for more than three decades. The two-acre emporium sold a wide variety of government surplus materials; from amphibious "Ducks" and postal trucks, to military clothing, mess hall supplies, mattresses and bedding, and even wooden spoons. To encourage browsing Saul enjoyed sending customers to look for an elevator to a mythical fourth floor. He also donated surplus autos to the Wilson High School car smash. Saul and Ruth's children celebrated their bar and bat mitzvahs at Sinai Temple. Ruth served as treasurer of Sinai Sisterhood in 1952 and was also active in Hadassah. She was Tacoma chapter president in 1953 and was a regional officer over much of the next thirty years. Ruth died on Yom Kippur, September 20, 1980.

Moses Lewinson, born August 20, 1879, in Mikhalishki, Kovno, Russia (now Mikaliskis, Lithuania)
Married Olga Fradenheim (1889-1974) on May 27, 1911, in Vilna, Russia (now Vilnius, Lithuania)
Parents of Rachel Hunt (1912-2005), Saul (1916-2007), Annie, Arthur, and Martin
Arrived Seattle October 7, 1916, aboard the *Tacoma Maru* from Kobe, Japan
Olga arrived Philadelphia August 26, 1920, aboard the *Haverford* from Liverpool
Died February 1, 1934, in Tacoma; buried Chevra Kadisha Cemetery, Home of Peace

Moses declared his intention to become a citizen in Tacoma in 1919, with Solomon J. Farber as his witness. He operated a secondhand furniture store for nearly fifteen years at 1133 Tacoma Avenue South, across from the public library. In 1919 Moses contributed to the war relief campaign as a member of Talmud Torah, and his daughter, Annie, was in a school play there in 1932. After his death his widow and children moved to Seattle and then to Los Angeles.

Harry Lorber, son of Henry and Esther (Samuels) Lorber
Born August 8, 1901, in Manhattan, New York
Married Vera (Goldstein) Yewdall (1905-1988) in New York on May 22, 1926
Parents of Sigmund "Kenneth" (1928-1987)
Died March 6, 1974, in San Francisco, California; buried Salem Memorial, Colma, California

Harry spent his entire career in Tacoma working as an auctioneer for the West Coast Fur Company, a division of West Coast Grocery. Vera became involved with the Destiny auxiliary in the fall of 1936 and served several terms as president in the early Forties. She also participated in activities of Hadassah and the Council of Jewish Women. Harry was president of the B'nai B'rith lodge in 1937, and their son Kenneth celebrated his bar mitzvah at Talmud Torah in June of 1941. He served in the Navy during the war, and around 1948 the entire family moved to San Francisco. There Kenneth married Florence Berger (1929-2000) in 1950.

Harry Lorber inspecting silver fox pelts
Tacoma News Tribune December 14, 1935

Abraham "Abe" Lyon, son of Solomon and Gussie Lena Luboschitz (brother of Morris)
Born July 15, 1873, in Pruzhany, Grodno, Russia (now Belarus)
Married Mildred Witenberg (1881-1954) in Chicago on December 5, 1899
Parents of Ezra Phillip (1901-1999), Lester Victor (1902-1983), and Leonard Zalman (1914-1980)
Died June 23, 1947, in Los Angeles

Abe lived in Chicago for a decade before coming to Tacoma around 1908. He managed Witenberg Manufacturing with his brother-in-law, Bernard Witenberg. His son, Ezra, was "confirmed" in 1914. Abe and his sons were donors to the 1919 war relief campaign as members of Talmud Torah. In 1920 Abe briefly operated a salvage shop, then moved to Los Angeles.

Emanuel Henry Lyon, son of Samuel M. and Rosa (Cohen) Lyon
Born December 10, 1861, in Portland, Oregon
Married Amelia Slimmon (1877-1922) in Olympia on May 17, 1905
Parents of Harry S. (1901-1918)
Died April 30, 1924, in Tacoma; buried Home of Peace Cemetery

Emanuel grew up in a pioneer family in Portland and worked in real estate in San Francisco in the 1890s. He and Amelia moved to Tacoma in 1907. He sold real estate and worked as clothing salesman. Late in life he became known as Tacoma's "Sandwich Man," for carrying sandwich-board advertising signs in downtown. In 1918 his teenage son, Harry, died while climbing Narada Falls. After Amelia's death a few years later Emanuel became a recluse and died in a house fire. His obituary noted that he had served as the Orthodox congregation's "mourner," saying prayers over the deceased.

Tacoma News Tribune April 30, 1924

> Harry was a constant companion of the old "sandwich man," and when only a tiny toddler would walk with his father until he would be too tired to go further, and then he would be carried together along with the advertising sign.
>
> When the boy was about 6 years old he was given a small sign, which he would carry along several feet behind his father. As the boy grew larger the sign was made bigger, until after a number of years he took over his father's work at times.

Morris Jacob Lyon, son of Solomon and Gussie Lena Luboschitz (brother of Abraham)
Born December 25, 1884/5, in Pruzhany, Grodno, Russia (now Belarus)
Arrived N.Y. May 11, 1904, aboard the *Rotterdam* from Holland
Married Rae Levine (1892-1976) in Portland, Oregon, on October 14, 1917
Parents of Victor Lester (1918-1990) and Griselda "Babe" Lehrer (1921-2015)
Died June 10, 1942, in Tacoma; buried Home of Peace Cemetery

Morris joined his older brother, Abe, in Chicago, when he came to the US in 1904. He followed Abe to Tacoma in 1912, and lived with him until he married. Morris worked first as a salesman for Joe Weinstein's New York Outfitting. In 1916 Morris briefly partnered with Henry Zeidell, then president of Talmud Torah. In 1919 Morris donated to the war relief campaign as a member of Talmud Torah. After his marriage, he and his wife participated in Temple Beth Israel events and held several board positions. For many years Morris operated Lyon's Sample Shop, selling women's clothing. After his death his daughter ran the company. His widow, Rae, remarried in 1946 to Adolph Auslander.

Sam Sydney Mackoff, son of Joseph and Bertha (Baker) Mackoff
Born July 4, 1905, in St. Paul, Minnesota; brother of Charles and Mildred
Married Elizabeth "Bettie" Anne Warnick (1903-1950) in Tacoma on July 4, 1928
Parents of Judith Faye
Died December 24, 1935, in Tacoma; buried Home of Peace Cemetery

Sam was raised in Spokane, where his father ran Liberty Dye Works. He attended the University of Washington and took additional courses in the chemistry of dry cleaning. After his marriage to Bettie the couple lived five years in Spokane. He was active in B'nai B'rith and taught in the synagogue's religious school. The couple moved to Tacoma in 1932. Sam was elected president of Tacoma's B'nai B'rith in 1935. He died that year of blood poisoning from the chemicals he used in his daily work. His widow, Bettie, was the only daughter of Harris and Fannie (Weinstone) Warnick. After her husband's death she continued her activities in the Council of Jewish Women and enrolled her daughter in Talmud Torah programs. Bettie married again in 1939 to Nathan Mosler and moved to Seattle.

Haskel Levitt Maier, M.D., son of Samuel Jacob and Anna (Levitt) Finkelstein
Born Haskel Maier Finkelstein on October 7, 1912, in Brooklyn, New York
Married Dorothy Brodsky (1917-1997) in Utica, New York, on November 24, 1940
Parents of Stuart and Charles (1948-2001)
Died September 29, 1993, Tacoma; buried Home of Peace Cemetery

Haskel was born in Brooklyn and grew up in Utica, New York. He graduated from the University of Michigan Medical School in 1937 and did his residency in Chicago. After his marriage he practiced in Chicago before moving to Tacoma in 1943. As an Eye, Ear, Nose and Throat specialist he was on the staff of all Tacoma hospitals for over 35 years. Haskel was elected president of Sinai Temple in October of 1946. Dorothy was active in Hadassah and Sinai Sisterhood, often chairing events. She worked as a hospital dietician. At the time of his death Haskel was also the owner of Narrows Marina.

George Martin, son of Abraham and Eva (Garb) Martin, formerly Avraham Machtchin
Born August 17, 1913, in St. Louis, Missouri; youngest of five boys
Married M. Beatrice "Bea" Goldberg (1917-2010) in Boston, Massachusetts, about 1943
Parents of Roberta and Avraham Alan
Died February 13, 1996, in Tucson, Arizona; buried Evergreen Memorial, Tucson, Arizona

George's parents emigrated in 1898 from Bobruisk, Minsk, Russia; now Belarus. George's father, Abraham, worked his entire life as a tailor. When he applied for citizenship in 1940 Abraham made his mark with an "X." Yet his youngest son, George, a college graduate and a chemist, was recruited to Tacoma in 1946 to work for the new Parker Paint Company. George was chief chemist in the Fifties and vice president and general manager in the Sixties. He was president of the family-owned company when he arranged for its sale in 1982. George was equally involved in Sinai Temple activities, co-chairing the 1953 anniversary banquet, and serving as president from 1956 to 1958. Bea joined the Sisterhood board shortly after arriving in Tacoma, served several terms as secretary, and was vice president in 1956. Their daughter, Roberta, celebrated her bas mitzvah at Sinai Temple in 1957. Their son made *Aliyah* and moved to Israel.

Arthur Meier, son of Jacob/Yankel and Adalaya Droyan/Drujan, brother of Max and William
Born March 15, 1885, in Dagda, Davinsk, Russia (now Latvia)
Arrived N.Y. March 16, 1911, aboard the *Zieten* from Bremen, Germany, as Ascher Drujan
Married Bertha "Berdie" (Tat) Backer (1895-1971) on February 25, 1924, in Seattle
Parents of Joseph Backer (1912-1976) and Leon Meier (1924-2007)
Died August 15, 1945, in Tacoma; buried Bikur Cholim Cemetery, Seattle

Arthur followed his older brother, Max. He followed him in changing his surname to Meier, inspired by Portland's prominent Meier and Frank advertising. He followed him to Everett and worked with him as a pawnbroker and clothing dealer. And in 1919 Arthur followed Max to Tacoma. There he partnered with his younger brother, recent veteran William, in operating a jewelry firm. After his marriage Arthur sold clothing, then operated a dry goods store in Wenatchee in the late Twenties. On his return to Tacoma in the Thirties he sold secondhand goods from several locations on Pacific Avenue, near the stores of his brothers. In the Forties he worked as a pawnbroker, still on Pacific Avenue.

Arthur's wife, Berdie, served as the first treasurer of the new Hadassah chapter in 1926 and 1927, and was president in 1928. After she and Arthur moved to Wenatchee the chapter dissolved. On their return, their son, Leon, celebrated his bar mitzvah at Talmud Torah in 1937. In 1943 Arthur was Talmud Torah treasurer, and served as vice president of the congregation in 1946. After his death, Berdie joined her sons in Hayward, California.

Max Meier, son of Jacob/Yankel and Adalaya Droyan/Drujan, brother of Arthur and William
Born April 15, 1881, in Dagda, Davinsk, Russia (now Latvia) as Mandel Drujan
Arrived N.Y. September 6, 1904, aboard the *Rotterdam* from Rotterdam
Married Bessie Nagel (1888-1974) on November 11, 1906, in Portland, Oregon
Parents of Dorothy Schwartz (1909-1984), Wilbur (1912-2001), Bertram (1913-2001) and
    Gerald (1923-2011)
Died May 7, 1964, in Tacoma; buried Home of Peace Cemetery

Max and Bessie lived in Everett after their marriage, where their first three children were born, and where Max sold clothing. In 1916 they moved to Tacoma, joining Bessie's sister, Esther, wife of Benjamin Thompson. In 1919 Max contributed to the war relief campaign as a member of Talmud Torah. Bessie actively participated in women's groups at both Temple Beth Israel and at Talmud Torah. Their children celebrated their bar and bas mitzvas at Temple Beth Israel in the Twenties and Thirties, yet Max was treasurer of Talmud Torah in 1940 and 1941. He operated a clothing store on Pacific Avenue for over forty years. Max partnered with his son, Wilbur, and his son-in-law, Ben Schwartz, in running Bert's Men's Wear. He previously had been the owner of Red Front Clothing. In 1971 Bessie was honored as a charter member of the Tacoma chapter of the Council of Jewish Women, on the occasion of its 50th anniversary. Her daughter, Dorothy Schwartz, was also a member.

Bert's Men's Wear at 1156 Pacific, January 17, 1944
Tacoma Public Library Richards Collection A-16793-3

William D. Meier, son of Jacob/Yankel and Adalaya Droyan/Drujan, brother of Max and Arthur
Born November 8, 1892, in Dagda, Davinsk, Russia (now Latvia)
Arrived in U.S. on November 10, 1914, by rail from Montreal
Married Anna Brenner (1898-1980) in Everett on June 1, 1919, daughter of Robert and Dora
Parents of Jordan (1921-1959) and Adelyn Barde (1926-2013)
Died July 2, 1968, in Tacoma; buried Home of Peace Cemetery

Meier and Brenner families on June 3, 1944, ordered by Anna (Brenner) Meier
Standing left to right:
Dave Brenner, Lou Sherman, Oren Rabin, Stan Rabin, Jordan Meier, Miriam Rabin, Bill Sherman, William Meier
Seated left to right:
Jean Brenner, Liz Sherman, Sarah Rabin, Dora Brenner, Anna Meier, Adelyn Meier, Rose Sherman
Courtesy of Tacoma Public Library Richards Collection A17649-2

William worked as a peddler and junk dealer in Everett before his military service in the First World War. After his discharge from Camp Lewis late in 1918 he returned to Everett, where he sold jewelry. Anna and William moved to Tacoma shortly after their marriage, and William briefly sold jewelry with his brother, Arthur, as Meier Brothers. William then operated his own jewelry store, added a line of trunks, and operated the London Loan Office. In the late Forties he brought his son-in-law, Warren Barde, into the firm, renamed Randy's Jewelry.

William served as president of Talmud Torah both in 1931, and again in 1935 when the mortgage was burned. Anna served on the board of the Council of Jewish Women and was active in the Sinai Sisterhood in the Forties. Both Anna, and her daughter, "Addie," were active in Jewish activities throughout their lives. (See separate Barde biographical sketch.)

Tacoma News Tribune May 28, 1937

Samuel B. Mesher, son of Benjamin and Dora Rose (Cooperstein) Mesheretsky/Mesher
Born July 4, 1884/6, in Ekaterinoslav, Russia, (now Dnipro, Ukraine) as Ezrael Mesheretsky
Arrived Bellingham March 15, 1906
Married Sophie Cohn (1889-1947)
Parents of Irving Henry (1910-1989) and Frances Klatzker (1914-1998)
Died May 9, 1952, in Kirkland; buried Herzl Cemetery, Seattle

We Offer You

Plumbing Supplies and
Pipe at Wholesale Prices

YOU do not have to be a plumber to
buy from us.

MESHER PLUMBING
SUPPLY CO.

1352 COMMERCE.   MAIN 534
Tacoma, Wash.

Samuel and Sophie lived in Bellingham, Spokane, and Portland, before coming to Tacoma in 1922. Samuel first worked for his nephew, Norman, in Mesher Plumbing Supply. Then Ben Rashbam managed the plumbing company while Sam operated his own general merchandise firm for a few years. His son, Isadore (later Irving) participated in the Young Hebrew Moderates in 1925. The family moved to Aberdeen in the late Twenties and then settled in Seattle. Norman and Moe's sister, Sarah Mesher, married Max Rosen, who continued selling wholesale plumbing supplies.
Tacoma Daily Ledger January 22, 1922

Adolph Miller, son of Harold and Dorothy Miller
Born April 15, 1885, in Warsaw, Russia (now Warszawa, Poland)
Married Eva Marylander (1892-1981) on December 22, 1915
Parents of Dorothy Rosengarten Wittenberg (1916-2009) and Harold (1918-1979)
Died September 15, 1933, in Tacoma; buried Chevra Kadisha Cemetery, Home of Peace Cemetery

Adolph emigrated about 1905 and married Denver's Eva Marylander in 1915. The next year Eva's sister, Fannie, married Joseph Buchner in Tacoma. Adolph and Eva had two children in Denver, then joined the Buchners in Tacoma around 1919. They briefly joined Temple Beth Israel in the fall of 1919. Adolph worked as a watchmaker and a jeweler. After his death Eva and her children moved to California.

Isaac "Ike" Moses, born August 19, 1875, in Davinsk, Russia (now Latvia)
Died December 25, 1934, in Portland, Oregon; buried Home of Peace Cemetery

Isaac came to Tacoma from New York in the late 1880s and worked as a junk sorter for Henry Winkleman. In 1895 Isaac briefly partnered with Julius Friedman in a clothing store. In 1908 he was an incorporator of Talmud Torah, along with Raphael Winkleman. Then Isaac served on the board of Temple Beth Israel from 1919 to 1920. Throughout the Teens and mid-Twenties he continued as a junk dealer. In 1928 Isaac went a step farther in recycling, operating the Standard Bag and Burlap Company on Commerce Street. He lived in Tacoma through 1933, then joined the adult Winkleman siblings in Portland as his health failed.

1929 Tacoma city directory

Moses Isaac (Standard Bag & Burlap
Co) r710 S 15th

Saul Ronald Naimark, son of Moses and Bessie (Seltzer) Naimark
Born March 11, 1917, in Portland, Oregon
Died June 1989 in Forest Hills, New York

Saul's parents both died before he was ten, and he lived with his grandparents, Noe and Sarah Naimark. His grandmother was a trustee of Portland's Neighborhood House, where Lena Farber worked. Saul and several of his relatives attended the Portland Hebrew School in the Twenties when Bert Treiger was principal. After Saul graduated from high school he lived briefly in Tacoma, and was a member of the Talmud Torah choir in 1938 as "Ronald." He moved to Seattle a year later and worked as a riveter at the Boeing aircraft plant. His 1940 marriage to Ethel Kramer was officiated by Rabbi Treiger. Saul returned to Portland and divorced in 1946. Two years later he moved to Boston and married Grace Herbert.

Harry L. Nemetz, son of Charles and Annie (Levison) Nemetz (brother of Hymie)
Born May 10, 1916, in Watrous, Saskatoon, Saskatchewan, Canada
Married Lena "Lee" Gula (1913-1992) on April 3, 1938, in Hamilton, Toronto, Canada
Parents of Tobyann and Charlene
Died May 27, 1970, in Tacoma; buried Home of Peace Cemetery

Harry's family moved to Vancouver, British Columbia, when he was a teenager. Harry and Lee had two daughters in Vancouver, then came to Tacoma in 1951. Harry first worked for his brother's Army and Navy Store. Then he opened his own army surplus store, the Work-N-Man's Family Store on South Tacoma Way. His wife, Lee, attended Sisterhood events at Sinai Temple and was elected president in 1955. They lived the remainder of their lives in Lakewood.

*Extended Nemetz Family
July 21, 1956*

Bar Mitzvah of Louis Nemetz, son of Hy and Edith (Levin) Nemitz

*Courtesy of Tacoma Public Library Richards Studio
D100571-19*

167

Hymie "Hy" Nemetz, son of Charles and Annie (Levison) Nemetz (brother of Harry)
Born November 20, 1919, in Watrous, Saskatoon, Saskatchewan, Canada
Married Edith Levin (1919-2011) the former Mrs. Robert Abramovitz, about 1947
Parents of Louis Abramovitz Nemetz, Edward Abramovitz Nemetz, Mark, and Gary
Died November 1975 in Santa Clara, California; buried Home of Peace Cemetery, San Jose

Hy said his fraternity life at the University of Washington prepared him for service in World War II. He served in France and Germany, arranging supplies for POW camps. After the war he continued along the same lines, selling military surplus goods. He operated a store in Fife called the Duffle Bag, selling everything from wool sleeping bags to toilets and automobiles. With his brother's arrival he opened a second Army and Navy Store on South Tacoma Way in 1951. After a major fire in Fife in 1953 Hy ran Bargain Mart and then Admiral Furniture. Edith was president of the Sinai Sisterhood in 1955. In July of 1956 their son, Louis, celebrated his bar mitzvah at Sinai Temple. (See previous photo.) The family moved to Oregon in 1959, where Hy briefly managed the Pendleton Hotel with his father. Hy and Edith eventually settled in California.

Max Solomon Novikoff
Born February 25, 1892, in Perelaz, Chernigov, Russia (now Chernihiv, Ukraine)
Arrived Baltimore, Maryland, January 15, 1913, aboard the *Neckar*
Arrived Washington State January 1, 1918, from Lethbridge, Canada, via railway
Married Emma Esther Yudelson (1894-1986) in Tacoma on February 25, 1918
Parents of Mollie Cohen (1918-1985), Bea Goldfarb (1920-2009), Melvin (1922-1987), and
     Harold (1926-2020)
Died June 17, 1972 in San Jose, California; buried Home of Peace Cemetery, San Jose

Max's first year in Tacoma was a busy one. He arrived in January after working several years in Canada. In February he married Emma, youngest daughter of Peter and Bluma (Stusser) Yudelson. In April he was swindled out of $50 at his secondhand clothing store, Bob's Place. In June he registered for the draft, signing his name with an "X." And in December his first child was born. He would continue his store on Commerce Street for fifteen years, before moving to an upstairs pawn and jewelry shop on Pacific Avenue. In the meantime Emma was busy raising children and participating in Talmud Torah events. She chaired the 1934 spring lunch and assisted at many others. Both of their boys celebrated their bar mitzvahs at Talmud Torah and Melvin was AZA president. Both sons also served in the Navy during World War II. Max declared his intent to become a U.S. citizen in 1921, 1924, 1929, and again in 1938, and was finally admitted in 1942. In 1949 Max and Emma built a twelve-unit apartment house, moved in, and operated Julianna Court for nearly twenty years. He and Emma joined their married children in California in the late Sixties.

(Right)
Tacoma News Tribune
July 20, 1938

*(Left) Current street
view of Julianna Court
314 North G Street*

**Announce Bar
Mitzvah Rites**

Mr. and Mrs. Max Novikoff, of 3021 North 9th street, announce the Bar Mitzvah ceremony of their second son, Harold, to be held in the Talmud Torah synagogue, South 4th and I streets, Saturday, at 9:30 o'clock. Immediately following the ceremony Mr. and Mrs. Novikoff and their son will hold a reception in the vestry room, to which all friends are invited.

Samuel L. Nudelman, son of David and Eva (Schreiber) Nudelman
Born May 22, 1900, in New York, brother of Edward and Pearl
Married Tillie Witenberg (1900-1990) in Tacoma on August 31, 1924
Died September 14, 1941, in Clatsop, Oregon; buried Neveh Zedek Cemetery, Portland, Oregon

Samuel was born in New York shortly after his parents' immigration, and raised in Portland, Oregon. There his father was a junk peddler and a founder of congregation Neveh Zedek. His brother, Edward, married Jennie Waldocks in Tacoma in 1911. Samuel moved to Tacoma about 1921 and managed the Fashion Cloak and Suit store. In 1924 he married Tillie Witenberg, daughter of S.N. Witenberg, and became involved with Temple Beth Israel. Samuel remodeled a storefront at 1132 Broadway and opened Nudelman's in 1927, selling women's apparel. For two years Tillie was president of the Tacoma Hebrew School. By the early Thirties the Depression forced Samuel to close his business. He and Tillie moved to Astoria, Oregon, and continued selling women's clothing. After his early death Tillie moved to California and married Leon Rosenbaum.

Tacoma News Tribune March 19, 1931

Gives Old Aluminum

Tacoma "Dealer" Backs City Defense Drive

Time was when Sam Offerman, 3210 South Tacoma avenue, added to his earnings by buying old aluminum and selling it at a profit. But right now Offerman, learning that an aluminum drive is on here and throughout the country for defense purposes, not only is foregoing his profit, but is donating his investment in the aluminum to the cause.

Mayor Harry P. Cain said Monday that Offerman came to him with seven sacks of aluminum pots and pans he had purchased in a house to house canvass in the city, with the statement he was going to add it to Tacoma's collection.

The current aluminum drive also

Samuel "Sam" Offerman, son of Israel and Eva (Finer) Offermann
Born January 12, 1886, in Warsaw, Russia (now Warszawa, Poland)
Arrived N.Y. July 27, 1906 on the *Pretoria* from Hamburg as
    Simcha Offermann
Married Frieda Zuckerkorn (1890-1939) in Manhattan, August 30, 1908
Parents of Eva Keyser (1909-1984), Sadie Chapman Patton (1909-1988),
    Frances Shaw Nelson (1913-1987), and Doris Clifton (1921-1986)
Died March 5, 1957, in Los Angeles, California; buried Hollywood
    Forever Cemetery, Los Angeles

(Left) Tacoma News Tribune July 22, 1941

Sam began his naturalization process in New York, where he married and became the father of twins. He moved to Tacoma in 1911 but his business failed in 1913. Next he sold clothing in the coal town of Wilkeson, and became a U.S. citizen in 1916. During the First World War Sam operated Offerman Dry Goods in Ruston, just north of Tacoma, with his sister, Sadie. That ended in a small war of their own. Sam ran Cut Rate Grocery during the Twenties, and in 1930 built a store on Center Street for his junk business. Frieda was active in the Talmud Torah Auxiliary in the Thirties. In 1935 Sam appealed to the city council to reclassify his business as secondhand, which would reduce his annual license. He stated that he mostly picked up bottles, jars, and burlap sacks. Nearly five hundred sacks were stolen from his truck in 1938, after he was distracted by some clever youths. That same year he bought a building on Tacoma Avenue, and his wife's Greenbaum relatives lived upstairs. When Frieda died in 1939 she was buried in the Chevra Kadisha Cemetery. After her death Sam served as secretary of the local Workmen's Circle chapter and in the fall of 1940 was elected vice president of Talmud Torah. He led an aluminum drive for defense purposes the following year. Sam moved to Los Angeles in 1945 and remarried. His obituary identified him as a past president of Tacoma's B'nai B'rith and Chevra Kadisha Cemetery.

Peter "Pit" Olswang, son of Israel and Schindle (Kirschbaum) Olswang
Born Feivel Alswang about 1865 in Sassmacken, Russia (now Valdemarpils, Latvia)
Arrived Philadelphia April 1887
Married Rebecca Sussman (1877-1939) in Seattle on December 11, 1895
Parents of Samuel (1896-1986), Harry (1898-1972), Abe (1900-1981), Joseph (1904-?), and
     Edward (1911-1996)
Died January 27, 1951, in Tacoma; buried Bikur Cholim Cemetery, Seattle
(Additional information on page 14)

Peter did some adventuring before coming to Tacoma. He farmed in Devil's Lake, North Dakota, with his brother, Jacob, in the late 1880s. Then he operated a grocery store with his brothers on the Ocean Dock in Seattle. In 1895 Peter married Rebecca Sussman, eldest daughter of Lipman and Yeta Sussman. He likely was working in his store on the dock in 1897 when the *Portland* steamed in with a ton of gold from Alaska, and six months later he set off for Skagway. By 1900 he had returned and moved his family to Bellingham. Peter sold junk there until about 1904.

In Tacoma Peter operated a secondhand business in a cluster of Sussman stores at South 23rd and Pacific. During the Twenties he sold hardware with his middle son, Abe. Peter and Rebecca's sons celebrated their bar mitzvahs at Talmud Torah. Rebecca was active in Auxiliary activities and chaired a Hadassah benefit in 1926. Peter lived in Tacoma until his death in 1951. Their eldest son, Sam, worked as a dentist in Beverly Hills and took the surname Osborne.

Abraham "Abe" A. Plotkin, son of Tzvi, brother of Sam, uncle of Ann and Abram
Born February 20, 1878, in Bykhov, Mogilev District, Russia (now Bykhaw, Ukraine)
Arrived Baltimore June 30, 1904, on the *Brandenburg* from Bremen, Germany
Married Lena Monesevitch (1889-1943) in Chicago in December of 1907
Parents of Morris (1908-1968) and Leo (1913-1978)
Died December 8, 1950, in Santa Monica, California; buried Herzl Cemetery, Seattle

Abraham and Lena lived three years in Seattle before moving to Tacoma in 1911. Abraham began his career as a tailor, but also operated a fruit ranch and chicken farm near Long Branch. During the First World War he did additional tailoring work at Fort Worden, near Port Angeles. In the Twenties he operated a secondhand store on Commerce Street. In 1928 he ran a pawnshop at 1348 Pacific, later called the Star Loan Office. His son, Morris, participated in the Young Hebrew Moderates in 1925, and his wife, Lena, was a member of the Talmud Torah Women's Auxiliary. Abraham was an active member of the Workmen's Circle and served as toastmaster of the 1931 convention held in Tacoma. Later his son, Leo, also ran a pawnshop and partnered with Morris. After Lena's death Abraham moved to California.

Abram Plotkin, son of Sam and Mary (Dovshitz) Plotkin, nephew of Abraham A. Plotkin
Born September 24, 1901, in Magilew, Mogiliovsky, Russia
Arrived Seattle October 26, 1916, aboard the *Sado Maru* from Yokohama, Japan
Brother of Anne Brodsky, Ethel Nash, Rose Berliner, Ida Efron, and Lillian Fotheringham
Died December 4, 1979, Tacoma; buried Home of Peace Cemetery

Abram said that he was conscripted into the Russian army as a teen and held at Harbin, Manchuria, before escaping to the U.S. in 1916. He lived several decades in Seattle with his parents. He also worked for his brother-in-law, Philip Brodsky, as a uniform tailor at Fort Lewis. Abram enlisted in the U.S. Army in November of 1942. After the war he continued working for Brodsky's Uniforms. He died unmarried.

Morris "Morrie" Plotkin, son of Abraham and Lena (Monesevitch) Plotkin
Born in Seattle on October 20, 1908
Married first to Sallie Rios on December 21, 1938, in Yuma, Arizona; divorced in 1944
Married second to Sonya "Sonny" (Jaffe) Pinch (1908-1981) on April 30, 1944, in Seattle
She was the mother of Barbara Arlene (Pinch) Rosenthal Ladd (1932-2020) and Mitzie Pinch
Morris died May 6, 1968, in Lake Tahoe, California; buried Herzl Cemetery, Seattle

(Below) Tacoma News Tribune August 11, 1951

Morris worked first in Tacoma in his father's pawnshop. In 1944 he operated Western Loan with George Jaffe, while his brother, Leo, continued Western Loan. In the Forties his wife, Sonya, participated in programs at Sinai Temple and in Hadassah and Council of Jewish Women events, then joined Morris in his ventures. They had a small upstairs store on Broadway called the Diamond Shop, and in 1951 moved into a large store at 1126 Broadway. They also had a costume jewelry store called the Jewel Box. In 1958 Morris and Sonya left downtown and opened a pancake house on Steilacoom Boulevard. They added an early Colonel Sanders fried chicken franchise and eventually ran multiple restaurant locations.

3701 Steilacoom Boulevard on January 28, 1959
Courtesy of Tacoma Public Library Richards Studio A119376-7

Abraham Polisky, son of David and Guta/Gerta (Wexler) Polisky
Born March 15, 1877, in Mogilev, Russia (now Mahilyow, Belarus)
Married Sarah Weinstone (1885-1950) on February 12, 1930, in
    Glasgow, Scotland
Arrived Montreal, Quebec; October 4, 1904, aboard the *Sicilian* from Glasgow
Arrived Detroit, Michigan; March 4, 1908, by railway from Montreal
Parents of Morris Pollard (1903-1977), Gertrude Kailin (1905-1986), and
    Rose Vehon Sarno (1907-1996)
Died October 13, 1959, in San Francisco,
    California; buried Hills of Eternity, Colma
(Left) Polisky family c. 1915, courtesy of Jack Warnick
(Right) Tacoma city directory ad 1917

Abraham lived with his married sister, Sarah (Kurcik/Carrick), in Glasgow in 1901. Two years later he married Sarah Weinstone, daughter of Froem and Bertha (Kurash) Weinstone. Abraham and Sarah had a son in Glasgow. Then they followed the extended Carrick, Weinstone and Warnick families to Montreal, where they had two daughters. They all came to Tacoma in 1908. Abraham first worked as a cabinet maker, then opened a grocery. During the First World War he partnered with Ben Slotnick in the Puget Sound Junk Company, and would sell junk for the rest of his career. His wife, Sarah, briefly operated her own grocery. Their daughter, Rose, was a charter member of the Young Hebrew Moderates and organized several dances. Their daughter, Gertrude, participated in the Jewish Juniors in 1927. In 1928 their son, Morris, changed his name to Maurice Pollard and the entire family moved to San Francisco. Abraham's obituary identified him as a charter member of Workmen's Circle.

Samuel Portnoy, born December 25, 1881/5 in Smiela, Kiev, Russia (now Smila, Ukraine)
Married Rose/Ruchla (1885-1964) on May 10, 1909, in Smiela
Parents of Boris (1910-2003), Clara Friesen (1911-1993), and Dianah Dickstein (1915-2009)
Arrived Seattle on October 2, 1915, from Kobe, Japan, aboard the *Chicago Moru* as Avram Portnoi
Wife Rose and children arrived N.Y. May 22, 1922, aboard the *Constantinople* from Rumania
Died May 5, 1932, in Tacoma; buried Chevra Kadisha Cemetery, Home of Peace

LIBERTY JUNK CO (S Portnoy, E Lewison) Junk of All Kinds, Second Hand Goods Bought and Sold, We Pay Highest Prices, 1918 Jefferson Av, Tel Main 2378

Portnoy Boris clk Liberty Malt Store r2518 Fawcett av
" Saml (Rachel R) (Liberty Malt Shop) h2518 Fawcett av

(Above) 1920 and 1931 Tacoma city directory ads
(Left) Liberty Malt Store 1918 Jefferson
Boris and Samuel Portnoy c. 1930
Courtesy of Mickey Portnoy

Samuel did wartime labor in Seattle before moving to Tacoma. He celebrated the end of the First World War by opening Liberty Junk, which evolved into Liberty Furniture in the early Twenties. His son, **Boris Portnoy**, joined him in running the Liberty Malt Store, selling bottling supplies during Prohibition. Boris had played on the Young Hebrew Moderates basketball team and later was a member of the B'nai B'rith bowling team. He was most passionate about boxing and helped form local boxing teams. Boris had two children with his first wife, Myrna (1913-1990), then served in the Navy during World War II. After the war he had six children with his second wife, Audrey (1928-2007). Boris operated pawn shops for forty-five years, including Crown Jewelry and Loan. In 1978 he was acting secretary of the Chevra Kadisha Cemetery when it was merged into the Home of Peace Cemetery. After his father's early death his mother, Rose, lived with her married daughters in Seattle. In 1965 Rose married Harry Dickstein, father-in-law of her daughter, Dianah Dickstein.

George Posner, son of Isadore and Freida (Cohen) Posner, formerly Israel Peisner
Born September 25, 1919, in Akron, Ohio; brother of Harry Posner
Married Julie Mossafer (1917-2001) on January 21, 1945, in Seattle
Parents of Terry and Debbie
Died March 2, 1954, in Tacoma; buried Home of Peace Cemetery

George married Julie after completing his service in the Army medical corps during World War II. He operated Bender's for five years, then remodeled and re-opened as Cole's Ladies' Apparel. In 1950 George served as president of the Tacoma B'nai B'rith chapter. His wife, Julie, helped with Sinai events in 1948 and was consistently active in Hadassah. That year she and George sponsored a contest to name her new maternity clothing store, selecting Taco-Ma-Ternity as the winner. Their son, Terry, earned the Boy Scouts' exclusive Ner Tamid Award in 1960, the first in Tacoma to do so.
Tacoma News Tribune December 11, 1959

Sizes 8 to 30   *Open Mon. thru Fri. Till 9*   Sizes 38 to 52
TACO-MA-TERNITY SHOP
APPAREL FOR EXPECTANT MOTHERS
(Everything and Anything for the Expectant Mother)
765 Broadway

Harry Posner, son of Isadore and Freida (Cohen) Posner, formerly Israel Peisner
Born August 22, 1912, in Youngstown, Ohio, brother of George
Married Rose Sonia Zaner (1915-1999) in Norfolk, Virginia, on March 29, 1935
Parents of Barry (1939-2022) and Linn
Died September 6, 1963, in Tacoma; buried Home of Peace Cemetery

The first decade of Rose and Harry's married life took them from Virginia to Arkansas, Iowa, and North Carolina. In 1945 they settled in Tacoma, where Harry and his brother, George, both sold women's clothing. Harry ran Barry Frocks in the Forties and in the Fifties owned and operated the Helen Davis store. He served as president of Sinai Temple in 1951. He also made time to participate in B'nai B'rith events, especially the golf tournaments. His wife, Rose, was a steadfast member of Hadassah, serving several terms as treasurer and several as president in the Fifties. Rose and Harry also hosted many AZA and BBG events in their home. Their son, Barry, served as treasurer of the Sinai Teen group in 1956. After Harry's death Rose continued operating the Helen Davis store and opened a Tacoma Mall location with Rose Friedman. A youth leadership award is presented annually at Temple Beth El in honor of Harry and Rose.

Harry and Rose Posner, publicity for Hadassah 50th anniversary benefit "Every Bit Helps"
Tacoma News Tribune March 25, 1962

Nathan Rabstoff, born September 25, 1885, in Slutsk, Minsk, Russia (now Belarus)
Married Gertrude "Gertie" Carrick (1883-1955) in Scotland about 1905
Arrived N.Y. December 24, 1909 aboard the *Lusitania* from Liverpool
Gertie arrived N.Y. November 11, 1910, also aboard the *Lusitania,* as G. Rabstaff
Parents of Alex (1906-1985), Morrie (1910-1989), and Sam (1911-1990)
Died June 1, 1961, in Tacoma; buried New Tacoma Cemetery

(Above) November 1910 Lusitania passenger list   *(Below) Tacoma Daily News December 30, 1916*

Nathan immigrated directly to Tacoma, joining the Carrick, Warnick and Weinstone families. He traveled with his sister-in-law, Jennie Carrick, and her children. Nathan left his son and pregnant wife in Scotland. Gertie came the following year, traveling with her brother, Harry.

TAILORING, PRESSING, REPAIRING
MOOSE TAILORS, N. RABSTOFF,
PROP., Cleaning, Pressing and Repairing. All Work Guaranteed. 1339
Broadway. Main 2292.

Nathan worked as a tailor for fifty years in Tacoma. He partnered briefly with Leon Farber, worked for Drury and for Fashion Craft, and operated his own firm for decades. Their younger sons belonged to the Young Hebrew Moderates in 1925. Nathan was an incorporator of the Chevra Kadisha Cemetery in 1930, and his mother-in-law, Esther Carrick, was buried there in 1933.

Morris Raphalowitz, born April 12, 1884, in Liutsin, Vitebsk, Russia (now Ludza, Latvia)
Arrived N.Y. May 2, 1905, aboard the *Ryndam* from Rotterdam as Moisch Rafalowicz
Married Sara "Sadie" Rashbam (1886-1924) in Tacoma on January 30, 1916 (sister of Ben Rashbam)
Parents of Alice Farber Matin (1916-2004), Abe (May 1918-Nov 1918), and Arthur Rolfe (1921-2011)
Married second Alice Edith Koorse (1895-1967) on July 25, 1926 in Brooklyn, N.Y.
Died August 3, 1964, in Tacoma; buried Home of Peace Cemetery

Morris lived briefly in New York and Cincinnati before coming to Washington in 1908. He sold junk and secondhand furniture in Tacoma for over fifty years. In 1933 Morris refused to accept city garbage service at forty cents per month. He ended up paying over fifty dollars in fines and spent a night in jail over the issue, but held fast to his position. His son, Arthur, joined the Naval Reserve in 1938, was active in AZA in 1940, and entered active military service after graduation from Stadium High School. He was working as a radioman on the *SS California* at Pearl Harbor at the time of the 1941 attack. Arthur worked his entire civilian career for the Boeing Company. Morris and Sadie's daughter, Alice, married Kenneth Farber in 1941, and after his death married Harmon Matin. She was an active member of many Jewish organizations. When Morris died in 1964 he was the proprietor of the Independent Tool and Furniture Company, and known as the business owner with the most longevity on Commerce Street.

INDEPENDENT TOOL & FURNITURE CO, Morris Raphalowitz), New and Second Hand Furniture, Household Goods and Mechanical Tools 1334 Commerce, Tel Main 1149

1928 Tacoma directory

Benjamin "Ben" Rashbam, son of Abram Hirsh and Feige (Grochov) Raschbam
Born April 5, 1889, in Grodno, Russia (now Hrodna, Belarus)
Arrived N.Y. September 12, 1910, aboard the *George Washington* from Bremen as Boruch Raschbann
Married Sadie Farber (1890-1974) in Seattle on June 18, 1911
Parents of Dorothy Epstein (1912-2008) and Frieda Steinberg (1917-1980)
Died July 20, 1966, in Seattle; buried Bikur Cholim Cemetery, Seattle

Ben traveled to the U.S. with his younger sister, Anna, and his future bride, Sadie Farber. Rounding out the group was Sadie's brother, Leon, who would later marry Anna. Ben and Sadie first lived in Seattle, where he worked as a jeweler and polisher. They moved to Tacoma about 1914 and sold secondhand goods from a shop on Commerce Street. During the First World War Ben partnered with in-laws Solomon Farber and Solomon Epstein in the Independent Junk Company. Then he worked nearly a decade for Mesher Plumbing Supply before starting his own firm, Central Plumbing Supply, in 1931. His next job as a salesman for Sherman Plumbing Supply took him to Seattle. There he was active in Jewish organizations and served a dozen years as director of the Seattle Hebrew School. His younger daughter's 1939 wedding was held in Rabbi Treiger's study.

Tacoma News Tribune July 29, 1931

Samuel "Sam" H. Reibman, son of Moshe Charles and Goldie (Geffen) Reibman
Born April 5, 1887, in Kovno, Russia (now Kaunas, Lithuania)
Arrived N.Y. March 18, 1898, aboard the *Frederick der Grosse* from Bremen, as Scholem Reibmann
Married Bessie Friedman (1890-1952) in New York on January 9, 1910
Parents of Morris (1911-2000), Irving (1913-2000), Phillip (1918-2000), and David (1928-2009)
Died June 15, 1971, in Seattle; buried Bikur Cholim Cemetery, Seattle

Samuel immigrated with his older brother, Jacob, when he was just 11 years old. He immediately went to work as a cutter in the garment district, even though he only had vision in one eye. Samuel married Bessie Friedman, daughter of Philip B. and Rose (Landsman) Friedman. Bessie had immigrated in December of 1905 with her middle siblings, Harry and Jennie. Samuel named his first son after his father, who had died in 1904. Samuel and Bessie moved to Tacoma around 1912, where two more sons were born. Samuel worked as a clerk in her brothers' clothing stores. He donated to the 1919 war relief fund as a member of Talmud Torah. The couple briefly lived in Connecticut in the early Twenties, then moved to Ballard and had a fourth son.

Their eldest son, Morris, stayed in Tacoma and finished school at Stadium. He lived with his grandmother, Rose (Landsman) Friedman, worked as a jewelry clerk, and participated in Young Hebrew Moderates events at Talmud Torah. In the Thirties Morris performed in Tacoma as part of the HaLevy Singers, directed by composer Samuel E. Goldfarb. His brothers, Irving and Phillip, both served in the military in World War II.

Morris Reibman, 1928 Stadium High School yearbook

Benjamin "Ben" Richlen, son of Jacob and Frieda (Spector) Richlen, brother of Harry
Born February 27, 1895, in Kishinev, Bessarabia, Russia (now Chisinau, Moldova)
Married Reba Gloveshivitsky/Rebecca Goodman (1898-1990) in Russia on October 26, 1918
Parents of David (1919-2010), Jack (1920-2015), and Charles
Arrived Halifax, Nova Scotia, on November 27, 1920, aboard the *Canada* as Benjamin Rachlin
Arrived Seattle on April 20, 1921, from Montreal, Canada
Died September 27, 1978, in Seattle; buried Bikur Cholim Cemetery, Seattle

Ben and Reba arrived in Montreal just in time for the birth of their second son. Less than a year later they joined Ben's older brother, Harry, in Tacoma. The brothers worked in tandem industries. Ben ran an auto wrecking company and Harry sold auto parts. They were able to bring their mother from Russia about 1930. Ben and Reba's older sons, David and Jack, celebrated their bar mitzvahs at Talmud Torah. In 1936 their family moved to Seattle, where Ben continued selling scrap metal and auto parts. He later owned Royal Jewelers.

AMERICAN AUTO WRECKING CO (B Richlen, S Epstein), We Specialize in Buying Wrecks and Selling Automobile Parts, 2309 Jefferson av, Tel Main 721

1925 Tacoma city directory ad

Harry Richlen, son of Jacob and Frieda (Spector) Richlen
Born January 23, 1881/3, in Kishinev, Bessarabia, Russia (now Chisinau, Moldova)
Arrived Victoria, British Columbia, on February 25, 1907, aboard the *Titan Blue* as Hime Richlen
Arrived Tacoma April 4, 1908, from Vancouver, British Columbia, as Hime Richlen
Married Sarah Singer (1894-1962) in Tacoma on November 9, 1913
Parents of Ethel Levy Minkin (1914-1994)
Died September 5, 1941, in Tacoma; buried Bikur Cholim Cemetery, Seattle

Harry first worked in Tacoma for the Sussmans in their junk business, and in 1910 worked as a blacksmith for a lumber company. Then he was a junk dealer for nearly a decade. Around 1919 Harry started an auto wrecking company. The following year his brother, Ben, came from Montreal to continue the auto wrecking, and Harry transitioned to selling auto parts. He would work in that trade for nearly two decades, advertising his business as "The House of a Million Parts." His wife, Sarah, attended Talmud Torah Auxiliary events during the Twenties, and their daughter was married there in 1931. Harry and Sarah divorced in the late Thirties and Harry returned to dealing in junk. Sarah and Ethel moved to California, where in 1957 Sarah married Henry Nadel.

RICHLEN AUTO WRECKING CO Harry Richlen Propr, Automobile Used Parts, Cash Paid for Wrecked Cars, 2502-6 Jefferson Av, Tel Main 9510 (See left bottom lines and Auto Dept)

Tacoma Daily Ledger March 20, 1927

1920 Tacoma city directory

Joseph Benjamin Robinson, son of Louis and Carrie (Benjamin) Robinson
Born December 28, 1891, in Portland, Oregon; eldest of five children
Married Anna M. Cohen (1901-1985) in Tacoma on June 1, 1919
Parents of Clarissa Joyce Mory (1928-1994)
Died August 28, 1960, in Tacoma; buried Bikur Cholim Cemetery, Seattle

Joseph lived in Seattle in 1913 when his mother died. His father and siblings moved to California, and Joseph came to Tacoma. He married Anna Cohen, daughter of Jacob and Sarah Cohen. (See Cohen biographical sketch.) Anna operated her mother's clothing store, and bought her interest in 1924. Joseph managed the Cohen family's Army Supply Store, Robinson's Out-Door Store and later the Outlet Store, all selling military surplus clothing and supplies. In the Thirties his brother, Samuel, came to manage Robinson's Army Goods Store. Joseph sold and financed used cars under the company name Northern Finance. Anna participated in several Talmud Torah Auxiliary events in the Thirties, and their daughter, Clarissa, was enrolled in the school. In the Fifties the couple lived with their married daughter in Los Angeles.

Robinson's Out-Door Store
1310 Pacific Ave.
The Store With the Orange Front

Tacoma News Tribune ad June 3, 1925

Joseph Rome, son of Hillel and Esther Romanowsky
Born August 21, 1885, in Chernigov, Russia (now Chernihiv, Ukraine)
Married Brame "Rose" Gurevich (1890-1965) in Russia on June 16, 1912
Arrived N.Y. June 21, 1913, aboard the *Adriatic* from Liverpool as
    Josef Romanowsky
Parents of Boris "Ben" (1913-1995) and Hillyard "Harold" (1919-2017)
Died January 9, 1971, in Tacoma; buried Home of Peace Cemetery

(Left) Rose and Joseph Rome, courtesy of David Rome

(Below) June 1913 Adriatic passenger list

Joseph and Rose emigrated together in 1913 with their infant son. They lived in Seattle for several years, then moved to Tacoma. Joseph worked at Camp Lewis during the First World War, and again at Fort Lewis during the second. Later he operated his own firm, Rome The Tailor. At the time four other tailoring companies had similar name structures, capitalizing "The." Joseph briefly belonged to Temple Beth Israel in the Twenties and was an officer in Workmen's Circle in 1931. He was secretary of Sinai Temple in 1951 and recognized as a past president. Joseph is remembered for creating a custom short-waist jacket for Dwight Eisenhower that later became a popular garment style.

Rome Ben (Freida; Rome Co) r440 Berk-
  eley av (Fircrest)
ROME COMPANY
  HAROLD ROME, OWNER
  BEN ROME, OWNER
  DESIGNERS, BUILDERS
  CONTRACTORS
  COMMERCIAL, RESIDENTIAL
  INDUSTRIAL CONSTRUCTION
  BRICK, FRAME, STUCCO,
  CONCRETE and CONCRETE BLOCK
    STRUCTURES
  3721 SOUTH TACOMA WAY
  TELEPHONE HAwthorne 9166
--Harold (Reta W; Rome Co) h434 Buena
  Vista av (Fircrest)
--Jos (Rose B) tailor Peoples h2508 N
  Cedar

(Left) Tacoma city directory listing 1953
(Above center) Eisenhower Jacket
(Above right) Armed Forces Day ad Tacoma News Tribune May 18, 1956

Both of Joe and Rose's sons worked in construction. The eldest, **Ben Rome**, celebrated his bar mitzvah at Talmud Torah in 1926. A decade later he married Freida Fuchson/Fuxon (1916-2005) and moved to Fircrest. Freida participated in Women's Auxiliary activities and raised three children. Ben studied architecture and operated Rome Concrete Products, then partnered with his brother in Rome Construction.

Harold Rome married Reta Weinstein (1926-2011) in 1947. She served several terms as Sinai Sisterhood president in the Fifties. Harold worked for Boeing, then operated Rome Construction with his brother for nearly forty years. Harold and Reta also raised three children, and retired in Las Vegas.

Abraham Rose, son of Simon and Fanny (Klinburg) Rose
Born September 22, 1879, in Plovna, Russia (now Pietrekof, Poland)
Married Sadie Shapiro (1891-1952) in Tacoma on November 8, 1908
Parents of Fannie Rubin (1914-2002) and Simon (1921-2011)
Died February 17, 1958, in Tacoma; buried Home of Peace Cemetery

Abraham Rose July 10, 1955 Tacoma News Tribune

Abraham lived briefly in New York and San Francisco before making Tacoma his permanent home in 1905. He first owned the Silver Dollar Pawn on Pacific Avenue, then operated a jewelry and loan business at several nearby Pacific Avenue locations over the next fifty years. Abraham married Sadie Shapiro, daughter of Barney and Dora (Kraft) Shapiro, in 1908. He was the secretary and treasurer of the Chevrah Ahavas Israel group in 1912 and 1913, and in 1914 was a founder of the Chevra Kadisha Cemetery. In 1922 he was able to purchase 1328 Pacific Avenue for $25,000 cash. Abraham was an active member of Workmen's Circle in the Thirties. In July of 1955 he celebrated the 50th anniversary of his arrival in Tacoma. Sadie was a member of Hadassah and both belonged to Sinai Temple.

Abraham and Sadie's daughter, Fannie, married Sam Rubin. (See separate Rubin sketch.)

Abraham and Sadie's son, **Simon "Si" Rose**, celebrated his bar mitzvah at Talmud Torah in 1934 and was confirmed in 1937. He was active in AZA and a lifelong member of B'nai B'rith. Simon joined his father's jewelry firm, then served three years in the Army during World War II. During his military service Simon was in an anti-aircraft gun battalion in twelve different European countries. After his military discharge he married Florence "Flo" Ostrow (1923-2018) in San Francisco. Her sister, Monia (Ostrow) Katz had operated a clothing store in Tacoma in 1941 and 1942. Both Si and Flo were active in Sinai Temple activities. They were the parents of Eddie and Bernard (1947-1996) Rose.

In 1920 Abraham installed a freestanding clock outside his jewelry store at 1328 Pacific Avenue. Simon remembered watching a truck back into it, sending it crashing into pieces. Nearly seventy years later the Farber family had it restored. Steph Farber maintains the clock, now in front of LeRoy Jewelers.

Simon Rose checking clock for earthquake damage, April 1949
Tacoma Public Library Richards Studio Collection D41863-3

Isadore Rosenbaum, son of Josef Rosenbaum
Born August 10, 1880, in Konin, Russia (now Poland)
Married Frances Jacobs (1887-1973) daughter of Aaron and Bertha (Baumgart) Jacobs/Jacobovsky
Arrived N.Y. November 2, 1911, aboard the *President Lincoln* from Hamburg
Parents of David Rosenbaum Ross (1912-1981)
Died January 9, 1922, in Tacoma; buried Home of Peace Cemetery

Isadore came to the U.S. with his wife and her father and sister, Esther Jacobs. They came directly to Tacoma where her brother, Herman Jacobs, operated Eastern Outfitting. Isadore and Frances then went on to Nevada in time for their son's birth in January of 1912. They returned to Tacoma late the next year and Isadore operated a jewelry store for nearly a decade. In 1919 he was a war relief donor as a member of Talmud Torah. After his death his widow stayed active in Talmud Torah and the Council of Jewish Women, but also worked as a cashier for her brother. Isadore and Frances' son, David, participated in youth activities at Talmud Torah while he attended Stadium High School. In the Thirties they joined her married sister, Esther Lipman, in Seattle, and then moved to California.

Frank S. Rosenberg, born about 1862 in Russia
Died January 21, 1926, in Tacoma; buried Home of Peace Cemetery

Frank likely lived in Tacoma at the time of the 1893 banking panic, as he had some financial difficulties in 1894. He never married, but he attended the 1899 wedding of Julius Friedman and Augusta Stusser. He also operated a fruit and tobacco store at 1514 Jefferson, near Julius' store. Frank moved up to Tacoma Avenue around 1907. His store at 1022 Tacoma Avenue doubled as an election polling place. Frank was a contributor to the 1919 war relief fund as a member of Talmud Torah.

Rabbi George Rosenthal, son of Max and Bessie (Horowitz) Rosenthal
Born February 10, 1925, in Washington, D.C.
Died March 20, 2016, in West Hartford, Connecticut; buried Ados Israel Cemetery, West Hartford

George Rosenthal was a lifelong learner. He grew up in the District of Columbia and at age sixteen enrolled in the Orthodox Yeshiva of Ner Island Rabbinical College in Baltimore, Maryland. He was ordained in June of 1949, and led Tacoma's Sinai Temple from 1951 to 1953. Rabbi George Rosenthal then volunteered as an Army chaplain, serving two years in Germany. He worked the rest of his career as a Reform rabbi. He led several congregations in New York and Connecticut and served as president of the

local Zionist Organization of America. He stated that he had become a Zionist when he was just thirteen, and during his lifetime visited Israel at least thirty times. He earned a doctorate from Hebrew Union College in 1968. Rabbi George Rosenthal retired in 1985, and fifteen years later returned to college to study macro economics. A 1956 biography mentioned that he had a wife and infant son.

Hartford Courant March 22, 2016

179

Harry Rotman, son of Meyer and Gnondle (Kant) Rotman
Born October 13, 1883, in, Kamenets, Russia (now Kamyanets Podileskyy, Ukraine)
Arrived N.Y. January 4, 1905, aboard the *Ivernia* from Liverpool as "Hirsh," destination Winnipeg
Married Lena Lemchen/Lamken (1882-1986) in Seattle on March 31, 1910
Parents of Rose Goldie Friedman (1910-1993)
Died May 2, 1946, in a Seattle hospital; buried Home of Peace Cemetery, Tacoma

Harry and Lena Rotman circa 1910, courtesy of Harold Friedman

Harry immigrated with a large group of fellow Russians headed to a Society of Baron deHirsch farming community near Winnipeg, Manitoba, Canada. Within a year he made his way to Seattle. There he married Lena Lamken, daughter of Feivel and Yochvid (Salmanovitz) Lemchen. She had arrived in 1908, joining her Olswang relatives from Sassmacken. Harry and Lena immediately established their home in Tacoma, in time for the birth of their daughter.

Like many others in Tacoma's Jewish community, Harry started as a junk and rag dealer. By 1912 he had opened his Oregon Furniture Company, 1122 Commerce Street, next to the store of his soon-to-be best friend, David Klegman. Harry served on the Talmud Torah board and was a charter member of B'nai B'rith #741. In 1923 Harry and Lena built a home at 810 North J Street, and enjoyed several large housewarming parties. Over the next twenty years they hosted many more occasions.

Silver wedding bells rang this week for Mr. and Mrs. Harry Rotman, of 810 North J street, when friends gathered to surprise the two Tacomans, who have made a special place for themselves in the life of the town. With the assistance of Dr. and Mrs. Abedeaux Friedman (Rose Rotman), the surprise was made complete, as arranged by Mrs. David Klegman and Mrs. P. Olswang. Fifty shared the evening, bringing a gift of silver and many flowers, with telegrams and letters added by many friends, both from Tacoma and away. Notable among them were messages from the presidents of Talmud Torah synagogue and its auxiliary, both personal and official, W. D. Meier and Mrs. S. Farber, writing of the warm appreciation of service given the organization during all the 25 years Mr. and Mrs. Rotman have been connected with them, and bespeaking a like period of time for the two to continue their service.

810 North J Street in 1977, Tacoma Public Library BU-695

In 1934 their daughter, Rose, married Abedeaux Friedman. He was the son of Julius and Augusta (Stusser) Friedman. (See separate biographical sketch.) In 1935, on Harry and Lena's silver wedding anniversary, the couple was described as having "made a special place for themselves in the life of the town."

(Left) Tacoma News Tribune April 4, 1935

Harry lived to meet his first grandson, but not his second. After his death Lena continued her lifelong work for the Tacoma Jewish community. Her efforts as a fund raiser for Talmud Torah and Sinai were legend: she solicited ads, arranged ticket sales, cooked for suppers and banquets, and chaired rummage sales. She was also an active member of Destiny auxiliary of B'nai B'rith, Hadassah, and the Council of Jewish Women.

Carl Rubenstein, son of Mordecai, born March 2, 1883, in Mielec, Galicia, Austria (now Poland)
Arrived in Washington April 24, 1916, from Vancouver, British Columbia
Married Dora Tiefenbrun (1887-1959)
Parents of Samuel (1917-2007) and Rosa Jacobs (1919-1978)
Died March 25, 1947, in Seattle; buried Herzl Cemetery, Seattle

Carl lived in Tacoma briefly during the booming economy at the close of World War I. He partnered with Sol L. Lewis in the firm of Lewis and Rubenstein, selling clothing from 1328 Pacific. Carl contributed to the 1919 war relief fund as a member of Talmud Torah. Previously he had lived in Seattle and partnered in the People's Store. In the early Twenties he returned to Seattle and was successful in a wide variety of ventures including brokering canned salmon, running Trinity Packing Company, and producing dog food. In 1930 Carl was president of the Herzl congregation. He later returned to an earlier spelling of his surname, Rubinstein.

Seattle Star December 25, 1937

Sam Rubin, son of Harry and Sophie (Holtzman) Rubin
Born August 31, 1910, in Springfield, Illinois; twin brother of Max
Married Fannie Rose (1914-2002) in Tacoma on November 5, 1943
Parents of Sharon, Harry, Chuck, and Diane
Died December 23, 1997, in Seattle; buried Home of Peace Cemetery, Tacoma

SAT., OCT. 13, 1956

Sinai Teenagers Found New Club

Rabbi Joseph Wagner of Hertzel Temple, Seattle, was guest speaker at a meeting in which Sinai Temple teen-agers organized for cultural, religious, social and athletic purposes, it was announced today.

Rabbi Ralph Carmi, spiritual leader of Tacoma's Sinai Temple, said the organizational meeting was held at the home of Sam Rubin. Sharon Rubin was elected president; Steven Weinstone, vice president; Jules Friedman, secretary, and Barry Posner, treasurer.

Another meeting is scheduled at 7 p.m. Oct. 21 in the home of Irving Farber.

Sam was born and raised in Springfield, Illinois, and worked there as a chiropodist in the Thirties. He served in the Army Air Corps during World War II. When he married Fannie he was stationed at McChord Field. Fannie was the daughter of Abraham and Sadie (Shapiro) Rose, and the sister of Simon Rose. Sam and Fannie lived in Springfield when their first son was born, then returned to Tacoma. Sam worked in retail sales at Nordstrom's until his retirement, then worked another twenty years for the Duffle Bag surplus store. Fannie was active in Hadassah and in Sinai Temple Sisterhood, especially in the Fifties when her children were in school. Sharon was in the 1954 confirmation class and in 1956 was elected president of the new Sinai Teens group.

*(Left) Tacoma News Tribune
October 13, 1956*

*(Right) Sam and Fannie (Rose) Rubin
Courtesy of Chuck Rubin*

Ellis Harry Ruden, son of Hersh and Lime (Levin) Rudenski
Born June 8, 1880, in Volozhin, Vilna, Russia (now Valozhy, Belarus)
Arrived N.Y. May 5, 1904, on the *Pennsylvania* from Hamburg, as Elis Rudenski
Married Anna Rovsky/Rovan (1890-1974) on November 7, 1913, in Toronto, Canada
Parents of Simon Julian (1915-2017) and Arthur Wallace (1919-1999)
Died May 7, 1959, in Los Angeles, California; buried Sholom Memorial, Sylmar, California

    Ellis lived briefly in Pittsburgh, Pennsylvania, then worked in Spokane, Washington, in 1908. By 1910 he was living with Jacob and Liebe Friedman in Tacoma and working for Julius Friedman. Nathan Witenberg served as his citizenship witness in 1911. Ellis then went to Toronto, Canada, to marry. The couple lived a few years in Michigan, where their first son was born. By 1917 Ellis was back in Tacoma, operating a store in South Tacoma. He was a 1919 war relief donor as a member of Talmud Torah. In 1920 his advertising asked customers not to support the "High Rent Profiteers" in downtown. He briefly belonged to Temple Beth Israel from 1922-1923. In 1923 Ellis built a three-storefront brick building that still stands at 5441 South Tacoma Way. He lived in South Tacoma through 1925, then moved to Seattle and manufactured "Men's and Boys' athletic patented No-Button Underwear." Later he and his family moved to California.

Tacoma News Tribune May 19, 1920

Sigmond "Sam" Seinfeld, born August 1, 1881/3, in Solotwina,
    Galicia, Austria (now Solotvyn, Ukraine)
Married Celia Neiman (1885-1976) in Chicago on January 23, 1910
Parents of Lester (1911-2001) and Sam (1915-1915)
Died February 29, 1964, in Los Angeles, California

S. SEINFELD'S
1318 Broadway
"WHERE YOUR $$$ BUY MORE"

(Left) Tacoma News Tribune ad
December 20, 1929

(Right) Sam and Celia Seinfeld and grandson Denny, April 1942
Courtesy of Karen Seinfeld

    Sigmond and Celia lived the first five years of their married life in Chicago, where their son, Lester, was born. The family spoke only Yiddish in their home. A second son died in infancy in 1915. The couple moved to Tacoma after investing in a business, but learned that their unscrupulous partner had disappeared, forcing them to start over. Sigmond first operated a company called the Chicago Junk and Second Hand Store, then the Tacoma Bargain Store, and later simply Seinfeld's. In 1926 their son, Lester, served as treasurer of the Young Hebrew Moderates. Sigmond, now Sam, joined the board of trustees of Talmud Torah in the winter of 1931, and Celia was active in the Women's Auxiliary for twenty years. Their son, Lester, passed his bar exam in 1935 and married Sylvia Moises (1915-2002.) Sylvia participated in Council of Jewish Women and Sisterhood programming at Temple Beth Israel, where they felt there were more young couples. Lester was prominent in B'nai B'rith, serving as president in the late Thirties. Sam and Celia still lived in Tacoma when their granddaughter married in 1956, then moved to California. In 1959 and 1960 their son, Lester, served as attorney for the merger of Tacoma's Temple and Shul.

David Shafer, son of Abraham and Sarah (Jacobs) Schofowitch
Born September 15, 1863, in Poland
Married Celia P. Abrams (1879-1963) in Tacoma on September 8, 1901
Parents of Herbert David (1902-1988) and Hortense (1907-1999)
Died October 2, 1942, in Tacoma; buried Home of Peace Cemetery

David lived in Tacoma in 1895 as Schofiwitch, then as Schafowitch, Schaefer, and Schafer; and by 1911 was Shafer. For many years he operated a clothing store at 1338 Pacific Avenue, at one time known as Red Front Clothing. David was president of the short-lived Chevrah Ahavas Israel congregation in 1912 and 1913, then joined Temple Beth Israel. His thirteen-year-old son celebrated his "confirmation" there in 1914, and David served several terms on the board during the Teens. David and Celia contributed to the 1921 building campaign, and were still members in 1942 when members of Temple Beth Israel celebrated its 50th anniversary. His wife, Celia, was the youngest daughter of Isaac and Esther (Isaacs) Abrams. Both had many pioneering family members in Tacoma and Seattle.

Jacob "Jay" Shain, son of Michael and Ida (Bobrotsky) Shainsky/Shain
Born October 8, 1881, in Tarocher, Russia
Arrived N.Y. December 22, 1901 aboard the *St Louis* from Southampton as Jakob Shainsky
Married Anna Alt (1879-1946) in Chicago on June 10, 1906
Parents of Dorothy Hurwitt (1907-1980) and Max (1908-1971)
Died August 2, 1930, in Tacoma; buried Home of Peace Cemetery

Jacob and Anna lived several years in Chicago, where they married and their children were born. They next lived several years in Seattle. Jacob became a U.S. citizen and worked as a tailor. Then they joined his parents and siblings in the Home colony near Lakebay. Jacob and Anna farmed there during the first war, then moved to Tacoma. Like many others he sold secondhand goods, in 1919 as the Camp Lewis Second-Hand Store, and for several years in partnership with Louis Freedman. During the Twenties Jacob operated Tacoma Egg Supply, likely in conjunction with his father's Lakebay chicken ranch. A disastrous fire in the summer of 1930 destroyed the Tacoma warehouse and 10,000 chickens. Jacob died just a few months later and his newly married son took over the poultry concern.

WAREHOUSE, POULTRY CO, LOSS HEAVY

Old Graystone Hotel Building Fire Victim for Third Time; 10,000 Chickens Cremated or Smothered by Smoke

Tacoma Daily Ledger June 18, 1930

Jacob and Anna's children were both in leadership roles in Talmud Torah in the Twenties. Dorothy was secretary of the Young Hebrew Moderates in 1925 and president of the Council of Jewish Juniors in 1929. She married Gene Hurwitt (1906-1988) in 1931 and moved to California.

Max Shain was treasurer of the Young Hebrew Moderates in 1925 and played on the Moderates sports teams. In the Thirties he managed several of the city's intramural sports leagues and continued playing on the B'nai B'rith team. Just before his father's death Max married Marie Sussman (1908-1988), daughter of Charles and Gustie (Stusser) Sussman. Their sons, Jerry and Marvin, participated in Talmud Torah's children's events. In the Fifties Max moved to Seattle and operated a restaurant. Marvin was principal at Stadium High School from 1980 to 1995 and finished his career at Foss High School.

Charles Zody Shallit, son of Chaim and Sarah Shallit
Born December 1, 1871; or November 19, 1873, in Russia
Married Bertha Siegel (1881-1946) in Seattle on April 28, 1908
Parents of Rebecca Turtletaub (1909-1999), Aben (1910-1999), Myra Kurshan (1912-2009), Bernard
        "Barney" (1914-1993), and Fred (1915-1990)
Died June 11, 1945, in Seattle; buried Machzikay Hadath Cemetery, Seattle

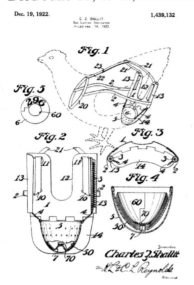

The birthplaces of Charles and Bertha's children echo their travels, including Nome, Alaska; Port Angeles, Washington; Vancouver, British Columbia; and Seattle. Charles worked in mining, sold shoes for his brother-in-law at Pike Place Market, and briefly manufactured mattresses in Seattle. He and his family lived in Tacoma from 1923 to 1938. During that time he was granted several patents relating to collecting eggs from chickens. His eldest son, Aben, served in the Navy in World War II and worked as a mining engineer in Alaska. His younger son, Barney, was president of Talmud Torah's Young People's League in the fall of 1937 and later spent his career as a shoe salesman. Charles' wife, Bertha, worked in Tacoma as a cashier for Fashion Bootery. After her husband's death she joined her married daughters in New York.

Shallit egg-laying indicator invention 1922 patent approval

Barney Shapiro, son of Aaron Jacob and Ethel (Hoidericker) Shapiro, brother of Samuel
Born September 6, 1869, or September 10, 1872, in Russia
Married Dora Kraft (1870-1947) in February of 1888, sister of Isadore
Parents of Aaron Jacob (1889-1921), Sadie Rose (1891-1952), and Ethel Stein (1908-1969)
Died June 26, 1945, in Tacoma; buried Chevra Kadisha, Home of Peace Cemetery

Barney and Dora's first two children were born in Ostrava, Russia, now Poland. Barney immigrated first, and Dora followed several years later. Barney was an early member of Chevra Talmud Torah and had High Holy Day tickets available at his store in 1907. The following year his teenage daughter, Sadie, married Abraham Rose. (See separate biographical sketch.) Barney worked as a shoemaker and secondhand dealer, was a jewelry clerk with Abraham, and worked several decades as a junk buyer. By 1913, when Barney and Dora celebrated their twenty-fifth wedding anniversary, they had a long list of relatives living in the area. In 1914 Barney was an incorporator of the Chevra Kadisha Cemetery. They briefly belonged to Temple Beth Israel in 1920.

Their only son, Aaron "Jake," married Kate Sidelsky in 1917. Their grandson, Stanford, celebrated his bar mitzvah at Talmud Torah in 1930. Barney and Dora's daughter, Ethel, married Maurice Stein in 1947 and lived the remainder of her life in Portland. In 1941 Barney and Dora were photographed with their great-granddaughter, granddaughter of Abraham and Sadie Rose.

Tacoma News Tribune August 10, 1941

Morris Shapiro, born November 29, 1914, in Chicago, Illinois
Married Manya Vera Shochatt (1910-2000) in the Forties
Parents of Steven and Susan Shapiro
Died August 27, 1997; buried Willamette National Cemetery, Portland, Oregon

Morris grew up in Chicago and later lived in Baltimore, Maryland. His wife, Manya, emigrated from Schoikoff, Russia, in 1922 and also lived in Baltimore. Morris served in the U.S. Army. The couple lived in Germany in the early Fifties before moving to Tacoma. Manya joined the Sinai Sisterhood in the fall of 1956. The family lived for decades in Lakewood, south of Tacoma.

William Jerome Sherman, son of Louis and Elizabeth (Brenner) Goldstein/Sherman
Born November 15, 1917, in Everett, Washington
Married Rose Touriel (1921-1990) in Seattle on September 10, 1944 (sister of Gabriel)
Parents of Robert, Michael, and Joni
Died October 5, 1994, in Tacoma; buried Home of Peace Cemetery

William was born and raised in Everett, among many Brenner, Sherman, and Meier relatives. He came to Tacoma in 1939 and worked at London Loan. He lived with his aunt and uncle, W.D. and Anna (Brenner) Meier. After graduating from the University of Washington William married Rose Touriel, daughter of Morris and Hannula (Hasson) Touriel. During the Forties Rose frequently held office in both Hadassah and the Council of Jewish Women. She joined the Sinai Sisterhood in 1949 and helped with several events. During the Fifties Rose was a staple of Hadassah fundraising events. William was an officer in Talmud Torah's new Brotherhood group in 1946. His parents lived briefly in Tacoma in the late Fifties and participated in Sinai Temple activities. William continued to operate London Loan, and added a second location nearby called Diamond Jim Jewelers. At the time of the 1959-1960 temple merger he was president of the board of trustees of Temple Beth Israel.

PAWNBROKERS

Arts's Loans 1209 Pacific av
Century Loan & Jewelry 1316 Pacific av
Diamond Jim Jewelers 1318 Pacific av
Eagle Loan & Jewelry 1356 Pacific av
Jack's Jewelry & Loan 1334½ Pacific av
London Loan Office 1310 Pacific av
OK Loan & Jewelry Co 1154 Pacific av
Pacific Loan & Jewelry Co 1312 Pacific av
Western Loan Co 1308 Pacific av

(Left) 1958 Tacoma city directory

(Right) London Loan at 1310 Pacific Avenue in 1977
Tacoma Public Library BU-2292

Morris Siegel, son of Joseph Leo and Rose (Berger) Zeigelstein
Born December 15, 1890, in Egrsky, Hungary (now Czech Republic)
Arrived N.Y. August 1, 1905, from Austria
Married Etla/Ethel Cherevatskaya/Chain (1902-1987) on October 25, 1921, in San Francisco
Parents of Helen Weiss (1923-2019) and Joe George (1928-1980)
Died March 15, 1955, in Seattle; buried Bikur Cholim Cemetery, Seattle

  Morris lived several times in Tacoma. In 1911 he operated a secondhand store at 1325 Commerce. He served in World War I, and on his return promptly donated to the war relief fund as a member of Talmud Torah. Morris worked the rest of his career as a tailor. He married in San Francisco, then moved to Seattle. He again lived in Tacoma from 1925 to 1930, then returned to Seattle.

Stanley "Buddy" A. Sigel, son of David and Sarah (Glazer) Sigel
Born September 18, 1921, in Everett, brother of Bernice
Married Iris Arlene Woolfe (1928-2015) in Seattle on March 26, 1949
Parents of Debby, Jeri, and Diane
Died April 6, 2011, in Tacoma; buried Home of Peace Cemetery
1949 wedding photo of Buddy and Iris, courtesy of Diane Sigel Steinman

  Buddy attended Seattle's Garfield High School and the University of Washington before enlisting in the military in 1943. At the time his father was already in the Army, in addition to being a veteran of World War I. After their marriage Buddy and Iris lived several years in Aberdeen before moving to Lakewood in the mid Fifties. Iris joined the Sinai Sisterhood in the fall of 1956. She also taught in the religious school. However, her lifelong passion was supporting Hadassah. Iris served multiple terms as president and held several other offices. Buddy founded the Duffle Bag Army Navy Department Store on South Tacoma Way in March of 1955. He operated the business for over fifty years, until 2007. His daughter, Diane, managed the business for the latter twenty-five of those years.

Joseph Simon, son of Philip and Bessie Simon
Born January 6, 1895, in Dorben, Russia (now Lithuania)
Arrived in Washington November 15, 1923, from Glasbay, Nova Scotia
Married Rebecca "Betty" Jacobsen (1901-1993) in Seattle on July 23, 1926
Parents of Philip (1927-2008), Norman, Shirley Olson (1935-2007), and
  Herbert
Died March 12, 1972, in Seattle; buried Home of Peace Cemetery

  Joseph declared his intention to become a U.S. citizen four months before his marriage. He worked his entire career in Tacoma as a wholesale junk dealer. As his sons married and joined him the company name was changed from Simon Junk to Joseph Simon and Sons. He also founded Economy Steel and Supply. His wife, Betty, was active in Talmud Torah Sisterhood in the Thirties and in the Forties. In 1940 their eldest son, Philip, was confirmed just weeks before his bar mitzvah. Their youngest son, Herbert, celebrated his bar mitzvah at Sinai Temple sixteen years later.

Tacoma News Tribune January 23, 1936

Ben Dovedovsh Slotnick, son of David and Rosa (Baker) Slotnick
Born August 13, 1893/4, in Irkutsk, Siberia, Russia
Arrived Washington December 1, 1915, on the *Shidzuoka Maru* from Yokohama, Japan
Married Lena Kosokoff (1901-1982) in Seattle on June 11, 1923
Parents of Roy (1924-1993) and David
Died August 1, 1967, in Tacoma; buried Home of Peace Cemetery

Ben lived in Harbin, Russia, before immigrating to the Pacific Northwest. His first business venture was Puget Sound Junk, in partnership with Abe Polisky. Abe stayed in the junk business and Ben moved to selling furniture. In 1922 Ben founded Puget Sound Furniture and Hardware at 1320 Commerce. By 1930 his furniture store was on Broadway. Expansions over the years included adding upper floors so that the store had frontage both on Broadway and on Commerce.

(Left) Puget Sound Furniture upper mezzanine March 1949, Tacoma Public Library Richards A41139-2
(Right) Puget Sound Furniture at 1309-1311 Broadway in 1966, Tacoma Public Library BU-14998

After her children were born Lena was active in four Jewish women's groups: Hadassah, the Council of Jewish Women, the B'nai B'rith Destiny auxiliary, and the Talmud Torah Auxiliary. She regularly held multiple board positions and assisted with programs. Both boys were enrolled in school programs and in confirmation classes. Ben served as vice president of Talmud Torah in 1937 and again in 1943. In 1961 he was recognized as a 25-year member of B'nai B'rith.

Their eldest son, **Roy B. Slotnick**, attended the University of Washington and served in the South Pacific during World War II. He married Hilde Mohrer (1926-2001) in Seattle in 1948. She was the daughter of Alexander and Betty (Buchbinder) Mohrer. After his marriage Roy worked with his father and eventually took over the furniture store. Hilde was a respected teacher and a leader in Sinai Temple activities. She was later a president of Temple Beth El. Roy and Hilde were the parents of four sons: Nathan, Larry, Drew and Douglas.

Ben and Lena's younger son, David, served in the military in the Fifties. He married Charmain Goodkin in 1956 and moved to Los Angeles, and later lived in Bellevue.

Rabbi Jehuda Leib "Leo" Slotnik, son of Schlioma Zlotnik
Born November 5, 1874, in Shkudy, Kovno, Russia (now Skuodas, Lithuania)
Married Lea/Lina Shereshevski (1875-1947) about 1900, likely in Russia
Parents of Rhea Volotin (1902-1983), Morris (1903-1927), Cecille Moskovitz (1905-?),
     Myer (1905-1980), and Jack (1909-2006)
Arrived Seattle August 6, 1921, aboard the *Princess Victoria* from Vancouver, British Columbia
Died May 27, 1966, in Philadelphia, Pennsylvania; buried Mt. Lebanon Cemetery, Collingdale, PA

Although Leib and his wife were both born in Shkudy, their children were born twenty-five miles northwest in Libau, now Liepaja, Latvia. Leib immigrated to Tacoma in 1921 via Vancouver, British Columbia. He served as Talmud Torah's rabbi for just over a decade. His eldest son, Morris, stayed in Vancouver and died of tuberculosis in 1927. Tacoma's Jewish community joined together the following year in a fundraiser to support the West Coast's Jewish consumptive sanitarium. Leib and his family lived in Seattle in the early Thirties. In 1937 he officiated at the marriage of Leslie Sussman and Sophie Rothstein in Vancouver, British Columbia. Rabbi Slotnik then moved to Pennsylvania. His obituary identified him as Yehuda Leib Slotnik, rabbi of Congregation B'nai Abraham in Philadelphia.

Their youngest son, **Jack Slotnik**, stayed in Washington. He joined the Young Hebrew Moderates in 1925 and became good friends with Irving Farber. (See Farber biographical sketch.) They roomed together in college. Then they operated a successful jewelry business in Eastern Washington, where the Grand Coulee Dam was under construction. Jack's brother, Myer, operated a restaurant nearby. Jack and Irving moved back to Tacoma in 1941 and opened LeRoy Credit Jewelers together. After serving in the military in World War II Jack married Irving's sister, Ethel (Farber) Slavin (1911-2001). Jack and Ethel later ran OK Loan and Jewelry, and Garland Jewelers. Ethel was a member of Hadassah and Council of Jewish Women, and served on the board of the Sinai Sisterhood in 1954. Jack died in Bellevue on July 9, 2006, and was buried in the Bikur Cholim Cemetery, Seattle.

Jack Slotnik and Irving Farber 1941 store opening at 951 Broadway
Courtesy of the Farber family

Israel Sohn, born April 15, 1889, in Kovno, Russia (now Kaunas, Lithuania)
Arrived N.Y. March 19, 1909 aboard the *Graf Waldersee* from Hamburg
Married Rose Tone (1896-1972) in Tacoma on March 8, 1920
Parents of Arthur (1921-2010) and Theoline "Toby" Cohn (1923-1986)
Died August 30, 1984, in Tacoma; cremated

Israel lived in Spokane when he registered for the draft in 1917, drawing a high number. He lived in Seattle in 1920 when he married Rose, eldest daughter of Abraham and Jennie (Friedman) Tone. Israel and Rose lived briefly in Raymond, Washington, where he worked as a tailor with Jacob Blechman, his future brother-in-law. They lived in Tacoma when their children were born in the early Twenties. In the Thirties Rose was active in the Destiny B'nai B'rith auxiliary and the Talmud Torah religious school, which their children attended. The couple divorced about 1935. Israel moved to Sacramento and continued working as a tailor. Rose had a career in real estate, managed apartments, and built a medical building. Her son-in-law, Shelton Cohn, served in the military in the Second World War. Israel returned to Tacoma in the Seventies.

Itzehak "Ivar" Spector, Ph.D., son of Vladimir and Maria Spetorsky
Born October 13, 1896, in Stavishche, Kiev, Russia (now Ukraine)
Arrived N.Y. October 26, 1920, aboard the *Pesaro* from Naples, Italy; last residence Palestine
Married first to Clara, born Palestine, divorced before 1920
Married second to Margaret Marion Mitchell (1904-1977) in Tacoma on April 2, 1937
Died March 11, 1989, in Seattle; buried Lopez Union Cemetery, San Juan Islands, Washington

Ivar Spector first lived in the Chicago area after emigrating to the U.S. He was naturalized there in 1927. His doctoral dissertation on the ethics of Jewish dietary laws was first published by the University of Chicago in 1928, and republished in Tacoma in 1930. In Tacoma he taught at the Tacoma Hebrew School and at the College of Puget Sound. Dr. Spector's time in Tacoma was subsidized by Morris Kleiner, who provided housing in his Avalon Apartments in exchange for Hebrew tutoring for his son, Herman. Morris also helped fund publication of Dr. Spector's book, "Out of the Fog." Dr. Spector then moved to Seattle and taught International Studies at the University of Washington. Over the next several decades he wrote more than a dozen books on Russian history and language. His second wife, Marion, was a 1926 graduate of the University of British Columbia and in 1934 held the travelling fellowship of the Canadian Federation of University Women. When they married she was a professor of history at the University of Washington. Dr. Spector retired from teaching in 1969. His obituary noted that he was a longtime member of the University United Methodist Temple in Seattle's University District.
Dr. Ivar Spector 1957 press photo

Joseph Abraham Spellman, son of Abraham and Clara (Abramowitz) Zonenshine/Spellman
Born April 25, 1893, in Perry, Iowa
Married Anne Nemerovsky (1893-1965) in Portland, Oregon, on June 26, 1921
Parents of Jerry (1924-1986) and JoAnne Rae
Died April 10, 1958, in Tacoma; buried Neveh Zedek Cemetery, Portland, Oregon

Joseph's family lived in Iowa and Nebraska before coming to Portland. He worked as a clerk in his father's grocery before serving in the First World War. His younger brothers, William and Jack, bought a Buster Brown shoe store in Vancouver, then bought a Tacoma store in 1933. (William had married Sadye Olswang in 1924, niece of Peter Olswang.) Joseph moved to Tacoma in 1934 and managed the store for decades, while his brothers added locations in other cities. His son, Jerry, joined Rabbi Treiger's Junior League at Talmud Torah. He was confirmed in 1938, participated in several AZA activities, and attended the 1941 "Reconsecration." After his military service Jerry entered the family business in Tacoma. He married Rachel "Blossom" Hodes (1924-2012) in Portland in 1946. His parents, Joseph and Annie, lived in Portland in the late Forties and moved back to Tacoma in 1951.

Spellman Brothers in their Buster Brown Shoe Store, 1122 Broadway, March 9, 1953
(Left to right) Jack and William Spellman, Eugene Pease, Jerry Spellman, and Joseph Spellman
Tacoma Public Library Richards Studio D73667-2

Feivel "Frank" Spigal, born July 12, 1880/2, in Solotwina, Austria (now Solotvyn, Ukraine)
Arrived N.Y. March 16, 1902, aboard the *SS Moltke* from Hamburg, Germany
Married Dora Yallon/Yelin (1889-1964) on May 25, 1910, in Everett, Washington
Parents of David (1915-1991)
Died July 22, 1941, in Tacoma; buried Chevra Kadisha Cemetery, Home of Peace

(Below) 1913 Tacoma city directory advertisement

F. SPIGAL

Tacoma Second Hand Store
FURNITURE and TOOLS Bought, Sold and Exchanged

WE BUY ALL KINDS OF JUNK

Phone Main 6371   1526 Commerce Street

Frank operated the St. Louis Junk Company in Tacoma in 1906 with John Smith. Over the next thirty years he transitioned from owning the Tacoma Second Hand Store to dealing in hardware. Frank was an incorporator of Chevrah Ahavas Israel in 1913 and lived near Barney Shapiro for much of his life. He contributed to the 1919 war relief fund as a member of Talmud Torah. That same year Frank took delivery of a new Hudson seven-passenger touring car. He served on the board of Talmud Torah in 1931 and Dora was part of the Women's Auxiliary in 1937.

Their son, **David Spigal**, married Miriam Wise (1918-1978) at Talmud Torah in 1942, daughter of Harry and Fannie (Klegman) Wise and sister of Bessie (Wise) Wikoff. David served in the navy in World War II. Bessie participated in Sisterhood activities and their sons attended Sinai school programs.

Max Stern, son of Ernest and Jennie (Katzeneldogen) Stern
Born May 5, 1890, in Denver, Colorado
Married Sadie Weinstone (1900-1986) in Tacoma on August 6, 1916
Parents of Frances Lorraine Flaks (1918-2012) and Martin M. Stern (1923-2007)
Died August 26, 1954, in Tacoma; buried Home of Peace Cemetery

Max grew up in Seattle. He married the daughter of Kopel and Libby (Averback) Weinstone in Tacoma in 1916. Max and Sadie's daughter was born while he was serving in the Army in the First World War. The couple lived most of their married life in Seattle and moved to Tacoma in the early Fifties, after the death of his parents and her father. Sadie immediately joined the Sinai Sisterhood and was elected second vice president in 1955. She also was a member of Hadassah. Max worked as a salesman.

Charles Israel Stusser, eldest son of Hugo and Jennie (Stusser) Stusser
Born October 15, 1881; in Libau, Russia (now Liepaja, Latvia) as Srol
Married Ada Friedman (1889-1980) in Seattle on February 14, 1909
Parents of Samuel Millard Stusser (1910-1994) and Tybe Hoda Reibstein Greenberg (1920-1995)
Died December 15, 1968, Seattle; buried Bikur Cholim Cemetery, Seattle

Charles came to Tacoma with his family as a teenager. He worked as a store clerk for relatives, and in 1908 briefly operated his own leather goods store. He was one of the incorporators of Chevra Talmud Torah in 1908 and partnered with his younger brother, Benjamin, in Stusser Brothers, pawnbrokers. Then he married and moved to Seattle, where he lived the remainder of his life. His bride, Ada, was the eldest child of Samuel and Richla/Rose (Golomb) Friedman. Charles and Ada operated Western Leather Works in 1916, and in 1930 ran Stusser Canvas Goods. The sleeping bag manufacturing firm was later known as S.M. Stusser Textile Manufacturing, in partnership with their son, Samuel.

Hirsch "Herman" Stusser, eldest son of Abraham and Mollie (Friedman) Stusser
Born March 15, 1857, in Libau, Russia (now Liepaja, Latvia)
Married Ita "Betty" Ulman (1860-1948) on August 10, 1879, in Gazenpot (now Aizpute, Latvia)
Died September 9, 1921, in Tacoma; buried Home of Peace Cemetery

When Herman married Betty her dowry was 1000 silver rubles. Their nine children born in Russia were:
1. Zalman (1880-?)
2. Ida (1883-1965) m. Max Friedlander
3. Gustie (1888-1954) m. Charles Sussman
    (See separate biographical sketch)
4. Samuel (1889-1951) m. Eva Emanuel
5. Abram Samuel (1891-1962) m. Dorothy Davison
6. John Zisel (1893-1984) m. Celia Valansky
7. Sophia Bluma (1896-1968) m. Nathan Mozorosky
8. Verna (Jan 1897-1988) m. Morris Molin
9. Leslie (Dec 1897-1964) m. Elizabeth Waxman

Herman sold clothing at 1313 Pacific Avenue, and in 1908 was an incorporator of Chevra Talmud Torah. During the last decade of his life he sold jewelry at 1317 Pacific Avenue. After his death most of his children lived in Seattle.

Hirsch "Hugo" Stusser, eldest son of Jacob and Hoda (Loev) Stusser
Born in September of 1856 in Libau, Courland, Russia (now Liepaja, Latvia)
Married Jennie Stusser (1861-1928) about 1879, daughter of Abraham and Mollie (Friedman) Stusser
Parents of: Augusta (1880-1942) m. Julius Friedman; Charles Israel (1881-1968) m. Ada Friedman;
    Bessie (1883-1937) m. Isidore Kaplan; Samuel (1884-1966) m. Birdie
    Hecht; Benjamin (1886-1967); Julius Jay (1888-1974) m. Hazel Frankford;
    and Lena "Ella" (1890-1974) m. Louie Pearl
Died August 21, 1929, in Hoquiam, Washington; buried Home of Peace Cemetery, Tacoma

Stusser's Clothing House
1140 Pacific Avenue — 1140 Pacific Avenue
NEXT DOOR TO VIRGIS' DRUG STORE

(Right) Hugo Stusser, FindAGrave.com

(Left) Tacoma Daily News January 19, 1906

Hugo's arrival in Tacoma in 1891 was likely a factor in the 1892 decision to hold Orthodox High Holy Day services separately. He initially worked as a tailor, adapting to the secondhand business after the 1893 banking panic. By 1900 he was able to open a clothing store on Pacific Avenue, likely in partnership with his sons. During the Teens his store was on Commerce Street. Hugo was one of the initial incorporators of Chevra Talmud Torah in 1908. His obituary described him as "the father of the Orthodox church in Tacoma."

Hugo Stusser family in Libau c. 1891, *courtesy of Harold Friedman*
Hugo seated on the left, with Julius on his knee, and Charles and Augusta standing on his left. Jennie seated with infant Lena on her lap and Bessie standing on her left. Samuel seated on front left, and Ben seated front center

Schlaime "Solomon" Stusser, son of Abraham and Mollie (Friedman) Stusser
Born November 8, 1866, in Libau, Courland, Russia (now Liepaja, Latvia)
Married Yetta/Jennie Kagan/Kahn (1872-1925) in Libau on October 27, 1888
Arrived N.Y. July 25, 1906, aboard the *SS Smolensk* from Libau
Died October 27, 1949, in Seattle; buried Bikur Cholim Cemetery, Seattle

Parents of:

Isidor (1889-1943) m. Anne Levy
Augusta S. (1892-1981) m. Julius Jaffe
Abram (1894-1895)
Schloime Joshua (1896-1897)
Julius Samuel (1898-1981) m. Beulah Hmara
and Esther Germaise

Hazel (1900-1982) m. Michael Grieff
Charlotte (1901-1991) m. N. Nathan and ? Soll
Samuel Abram (1903-1989) m. Eva Skaletar
Max (1906-1975) m. Gussie Nelson
Mary (1908-1909) born and died in Tacoma

Solomon and Yetta immigrated together with seven small children. He worked as a shoemaker in Tacoma until 1923, then lived several years in Vancouver, British Columbia. After his wife's death Solomon worked as a jeweler in Seattle. His son, Julius Samuel Stusser, was a donor to the 1919 war relief fund as a member of Talmud Torah, and left memoirs of his pioneering great-uncle, Adolph Friedman. Julius later lived in Vancouver, British Columbia.

Sussman Family

While brothers Philip and Lipman Sussman never lived in Tacoma, their children and grandchildren certainly impacted the community. Like many families, they sent their eldest children to America first, and others followed in a chain of immigration. And like the Friedmans, their large families married and gave their children similar names honoring ancestors, as seen in the following chart.

Yossel/Joseph and Fega/Frances Sussmann, parents of:

1. Feive Shrage/Philip Sussmann (1837-1912), immigrated March 1911
Married first to Sarah
        1. Benjamin Leo (1868-1945), immigrated 1904, married Anna Greenberg (1880-1951)
Married second to Pessi Hanna Kahan (1853-1938), immigrated March 1911
        2. Joseph S. (1887-1982), immigrated 1906, married Rosie Kahn (1894-1972)
        3. Feige Dorothy (1890-1936), immigrated February 1909, married Arthur Lamken (1887-1939)

2. Lipman Sussman (1842-1919), immigrated August 1900
Married Yeta Israelson (1849-1915), immigrated August 1900
        1. Rebecca (1877-1939), immigrated 1894, married Peter Olswang (1865-1951)
        2. Frank Isaac (1880-1964), immigrated 1905, married Ida Yudelson (1892-1969)
        3. Charles (1883-1956), immigrated 1899, married Gustie Stusser (1888-1954)
        4. Joseph Aaron (1884-1957), immigrated 1900, married Minnie Esther Benson (1890-1963)
        5. Jennie Freida (1886-1921), immigrated 1899, married Aaron Rome (1883-1961)
        6. Celia (1891-1966), immigrated 1900, married Jacob Kaplan (1886-1974)
        7. Mollie (1892-1967, married Samuel Isaac Gross (1889-?) and Harry Sackman (1889-1951)

Charles Sussman, son of Lipman and Yeta (Israelson) Sussman
Born June 2, 1883, in Sassmacken, Russia (now Valdemarpils, Latvia)
Arrived Quebec July 15, 1899, aboard the *Californian* from Liverpool
Married Augusta "Gustie" Stusser (1888-1954) on February 25, 1907, in Tacoma
Parents of Marie Shain (1908-1998) and L. Sanford (1909-1988)
Died October 12, 1956, in Tacoma; buried Home of Peace Cemetery

Charles first worked for his Olswang relatives in Bellingham. In 1906 he worked briefly for his brothers, Frank and Joseph, in their Tacoma Junk Company. Then he founded Washington Furniture, selling secondhand furniture on Commerce Street. He ran the company for nearly fifty years. In 1908 Charles was an incorporator of Chevra Talmud Torah. Gustie was active in the Women's Auxiliary, especially in the Thirties after their children were married. Marie married Max Shain (see separate biographical sketch) and L. Sanford married Vivien "Frankie" Berolski (1907-1990.) Gustie often hosted club picnics at their summer home on Day Island.

Isaac "Frank" Sussman, son of Lipman and Yeta (Israelson) Sussman
Born February 16, 1880, in Sassmacken, Russia (now Valdemarpils, Latvia)
Arrived in Washington August 4, 1895
Married Ida Yudelson (1892-1969) in Tacoma on July 11, 1910
Parents of Philip (1912-1995), Mollie Grunbaum (1914-1988), and Lorraine Braverman (1923-2020)
Died December 18, 1964, in Tacoma; buried Home of Peace Cemetery

(Below right) Tacoma city directory ad 1910

Frank first lived in Seattle with his Olwang and Sussman relatives and worked for the Seattle Junk Company. In 1903 he operated Tacoma Junk with his brothers Charles and Joseph. In 1910 he married Ida Yudelson, daughter of P.J. and Bluma (Stusser) Yudelson. Frank served as president of Talmud Torah in 1913. When he applied for naturalization in 1914 the judge asked why he had two names, Frank and Isaac. He told the judge that he didn't like when the ladies called him "Ikey," so he decided to call himself Frank. He formed the Frank Sussman Company in 1920. Frank was treasurer of Talmud Torah when the new synagogue was constructed, and their son Philip's 1925 bar mitzvah was noted as the first in the new building. Frank built a three-story business block in 1930 that still bears his name across the upper façade.

WAREHOUSES:
119 Puyallup Av., Tel. A 2029

BARNS:
2148 Pacific Av., Tel. Main 3529

Tacoma Junk Co.

FRANK SUSSMAN, PROP.

WHOLESALE JUNK DEALERS

Buy and sell all kinds of Machinery, Scrap Iron, Metals, Rubber, Sacks, Bottles, Hides, Pelts, etc. City orders solicited. Country orders given prompt attention. Goods hauled from wharves and depots free of charge.

2135 South C Street.

Tels., Ind. A 4135, Main 7312

The Frank Sussman Steel Company was the first local firm to earn a merit award for collecting scrap during the Second World War.

A.F. Blangey (left) presenting to Frank Sussman, center, and Philip Sussman, right, September 29, 1942

Courtesy of Tacoma Public Library
Richards Studio D13484-2

Joseph Aaron Sussman, son of Lipman and Yeta (Israelson) Sussman
Born October 22, 1884, in Sassmacken, Russia (now Valdemarpils, Latvia)
Arrived St. Albans, Canada, August 18, 1900, aboard the *SS Parisian* from Liverpool
Married Minnie Esther Benson (1890-1963) on September 9, 1913, in Detroit, Michigan
Parents of Leslie Phillip (1914-2000), Jean Vivian (1918-1921), Rhoda Lewis (1922-2014),
   Beatrice Friedman (1924-1977) (see separate biographical sketch), and Joanne Arfin
Died December 22, 1957, on visit to Vancouver, BC; buried Home of Peace Cemetery

Joseph came to Tacoma from Seattle in 1903. He first partnered in Sussman Brothers, then Tacoma Junk and Tacoma Steel and Equipment, and later Tacoma Metals. He was an incorporator of Talmud Torah in 1908, served as treasurer in 1913, and was president in 1917. In 1925 he served on the building committee of the new synagogue. Joseph and Minnie presented a curtain on the occasion of their son's bar mitzvah in 1927. During the early Thirties Minnie was active in the Council of Jewish Women, serving four terms as president. During the late Thirties she resumed her participation in the Talmud Torah Auxiliary and was president in 1937-1938. Her daughter, Rhoda, was president of the Junior League in 1936. Joseph again joined the Talmud Torah board of trustees in the spring of 1943.

(Left) Joseph A. and Minnie (Benson) Sussman, courtesy of Joann Arfin
(Below right) Leslie Sussman in 1984, courtesy of Joann Arfin

Their son, **Leslie Sussman**, entered the family metal business and with his father founded Tacoma Steel. In 1937 he married Sophie Rothstein (1916-2012) in Vancouver, British Columbia. Their wedding ceremony was officiated by Rabbi J.L. Slotnik, formerly of Tacoma. Leslie and his father earned a merit award in 1942 for donating over 465 tons of scrap metal to the war effort in just one month. That process went full circle in 1956 when Leslie formed a division of General Metals to salvage tons of materials left in the Aleutians by the military after World War II. Leslie and Sophie stayed active in Tacoma's Jewish community and were known for their philanthropy across the region. They were the parents of Paula Jean Rose (1940-2010) and Alan Sussman.

Joseph S. Sussman, son of Philip and Pessi Hanna (Kahan) Sussman
Born January 18, 1887, in Sassmacken, Russia (now Valdemarpils, Latvia)
Arrived N.Y. November 23, 1906, aboard the *Smolensk* from Libau as Yossel Sussmann
Married Rosie Kahn (1894-1972) in King County on March 11, 1917
Parents of Philip (1918-2010) and Shirlee Haupt (1920-1998)
Died March 4, 1982, in Tacoma; buried Home of Peace Cemetery

Joseph lived and worked for a decade in Everett before joining his sister, Dorothy (Sussman) Lamken, in Tacoma. He worked for his cousin, Joseph A. Sussman, in Tacoma Junk, then sold secondhand goods. He later worked for his cousin's firm of General Metals. Joseph and Rose's son, Philip, was confirmed in Talmud Torah in 1931, and served in the military in 1942.

Benjamin Thompson, son of Abram Tomsinsky
Born February 25, 1871, in Sebezh, Russia (now Kaunas, Lithuania)
Married Esther Nagel (1873-1953) on March 18, 1896, in Rezekne, Russia (now Latvia)
Arrived St. Johns, Nova Scotia, on December 5, 1903, as Baruch Tunczynski
Esther arrived N.Y. December 4, 1905, aboard the *Umbria* from Liverpool, with four children
Died January 14, 1956, in Portland, Oregon; buried Neveh Zedek Cemetery, Portland, Oregon
Parents of:

Marie Loeb/Eisenberger/Reiser (1897-1982)	Sanford (1906-1913)
Anna Zusman (1898-1990)	Robert (1908-1995)
Helen Silberman (1900-1987)	Dorothy Berman Horenstein (1913-1993)
Jack (1901-1952)	Eileen Tarshis Bonasera (1917-1989)

Benjamin and Esther lived in New York in the early 1900s, then moved to Tacoma about 1910. Benjamin sold secondhand merchandise on Commerce Street, and later sold clothing. His 1921 naturalization included his name change. Benjamin was vice president of Talmud Torah in 1925 when the new synagogue building was constructed. In the early Thirties the family moved to Portland, Oregon, joining several of Esther's Nagel sisters. Another sister, Elizabeth (Mrs. Max Meier), stayed in Tacoma. Benjamin and Esther celebrated their 50th wedding anniversary in Portland in 1945.

(Right) Esther (Nagel) Thompson and children c. 1910, courtesy of Bootsie Hennessy

Robert Tone, eldest son of Abraham and Jenny (Friedman) Tonne
Born August 9, 1894, in Mitava, Courland, Russia (now Jelgava, Latvia)
Arrived N.Y. July 5, 1907, aboard the *Andalusia* from Hamburg, with Jack Bender
Married Sarah Lewis (1894-1975) in Tacoma on January 14, 1923
Parents of Alvin "Al" (1930-2020) and Wilmont "Bill" (1933-1998)
Died April 4, 1949, in Tacoma; buried Home of Peace Cemetery

Robert came to the U.S. with his Bender cousins when he was just twelve years old. He lived with his uncle, Julius Friedman, and other relatives while he attended Central School. His mother and three sisters joined them in 1912 and 1913. Robert briefly ran a grocery business, then opened his own clothing store in 1921. He married two years later. Unlike many who married other recent immigrants, Robert married a second-generation American. His wife, Sarah, was the youngest daughter of William and Lucy (Martin) Lewis. She was active in the Destiny auxiliary of B'nai B'rith, serving several decades as treasurer. Robert was president of Talmud Torah in 1940 and 1941, and both boys celebrated bar mitzvahs. In the Forties Robert bought out his clothing partner, Edward Denzler, and continued his own firm, Tone's,

at 940 Pacific Avenue. Robert also learned the power of real estate investing from his Uncle Julius. He built a two-story brick on South 56th Street in 1929. In 1938 he owned the Sierra Apartments on Sixth Avenue. After Robert's death Sarah continued in a leadership role in multiple Jewish organizations for several more decades.

Sierra Apartments, 1310 Sixth Avenue in 1977
Courtesy of Tacoma Public Library BU-13

195

Gabriel "Gabe" Touriel, son of Morris and Hannula (Hasson) Touriel
Born November 9, 1929, in Seattle
Married Gerda "Trudie" Aschkenazi (1932-2017) in Seattle on June 27, 1954
Parents of Morris, David, and Betsy
Died February 15, 2019, in Seattle; buried Home of Peace Cemetery

Gabe was born and raised in Seattle and attended Garfield High School. He served in the U.S. Navy from 1947-1951, the last two years during the Korean War. On his return he worked in Tacoma for the London Loan Office with his brother-in-law, William Sherman. Gabe and Trudie married just three weeks after they met, later bringing her Vienna-born parents, Freidrich and Gisela (Herzfeld) Aschkenazi from La Paz, Bolivia. Trudie joined the Sinai Temple Sisterhood in 1956 and held leadership roles in Hadassah for decades. Gabe became the owner of the London Loan Office, first on Pacific Avenue, and later on South Tacoma Way. He also ran Hit Processing, developing photographic film.

Rabbi Baruch Israel Treiger, son of Israel L. and Ethel Rebecca (Brezner) Treiger
Born August 12, 1895, in Demidovca, Volhynia, Russia (now Demydivka, Ukraine)
Arrived St. John's, New Brunswick, aboard the *Montrose* on December 23, 1913
Married Lena/Leah Farber (1906-1972) in Tacoma on May 27, 1928
Died November 12, 1954, in New York City; buried Bikur Cholim Cemetery, Seattle
(Additional information in Chapter Eight)

(Above left) Treiger family Canadian alien arrival card, December 23, 1913
(Above right) Bert Treiger c. 1930, principal of Portland Hebrew School, courtesy of Seattle Jewish Transcript

Baruch's father, Israel Treiger, immigrated to the U.S. in 1910, leaving his wife and five children behind while he found work and housing. They joined him in Portland, Oregon, three years later. During the interim his eldest son, Baruch, was not able to attend school. In Portland young Baruch adopted the American nickname of Bert and attended self-paced classes, completing grammar school courses in just two years. He worked as a Hebrew teacher to support his education at Reed College, then earned a Masters at Columbia. Bert led the Portland Hebrew School for five years and on his departure was awarded the title of Honorary Principal for Life. In 1928 he married Tacoma's Lena Farber, daughter of Solomon and Goldie (Elyn) Farber. Also a scholar, Lena was a graduate of U.W. and the N.Y. School of Social Work. At the time of their marriage she was director of girls' work at Portland's Neighborhood House. In 1930 the couple moved to New York where Bert, again Baruch, worked toward a Ph.D. at Columbia and was ordained at the Jewish Theological Seminary. He led the large Toronto Hebrew School before coming to Tacoma in the fall of 1936. He later served congregations in Reno, Nevada; and in Altoona, Pennsylvania. After his death his widow, Leah, married Samuel Schimmel (1893-1978) and was buried in Israel.

Rabbi Leo Trepp, son of Maier and Selma (Hirschberger) Trepp
Born March 4, 1913, in Mainz, Germany
Married first to Miriam (1916-1999) on April 27, 1938, in Oldenburg, Germany
Parents of Susan
Married second to Gunda after 2001
Died September 2, 2010, in San Francisco, California; buried Santa Rosa, California

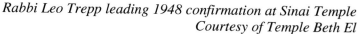

Rabbi Leo Trepp leading 1948 confirmation at Sinai Temple
Courtesy of Temple Beth El

Leo Trepp was ordained as a rabbi in Germany in 1936. Two years later he was arrested during Kristallnacht and imprisoned in the Sachsenhausen concentration camp. His wife, Miriam, helped gain his release and the couple found safety in London. Then they moved to Boston and Rabbi Trepp earned a

degree from Harvard. After leading a congregation in Greenfield, Massachusetts, Rabbi Trepp and Miriam came to Tacoma in the fall of 1946. He was active in the Zionist Organization of America, frequently traveling and lecturing in support of the movement. In 1948 he took a position in Berkeley, California, and later worked in Napa and Santa Rosa. His wife, Miriam, taught elementary school for several decades. Rabbi Trepp frequently returned to Germany, teaching and lecturing about reconciliation. He was also involved in the restoration of the Weisenau Synagogue. At the time of his death in 2010 he was the last living pre-Holocaust German rabbi. After his death his second wife, Gunda, compiled his notes and published his autobiography, "The Last Rabbi." He was the subject of a documentary by the same title.

Rabbi Leo Trepp, courtesy of FindAGrave

Napoleon Isadore Turenne, son of Clovis and Alicia (Dufault) Turenne
Born April 24, 1888, in Arnprior, Ontario, Canada
Married Sarah Hait (1893-1990) in Shanghai, China, on January 25, 1916
Parents of Abraham (1916-2007), Alice Goldblatt (1918-2009), Anna Greenberg Van Buskirk (1920-?),
    Bernard (1921-abt 1922), Edward (1922-2012), David (1924-2015), Esther Utman (1925-1998),
    and Louise Smith (1929-1980)
Died November 19, 1952, in Tacoma; cremated

Napoleon met Sarah while he was serving in the U.S. Navy in Shanghai, China. After his discharge he stayed in China and worked in advertising. Their first five children were born there, before they moved to Washington about 1923. In Tacoma Napoleon worked as a school custodian, a job often given to veterans. He also ran the Ideal Repair Shop. The couple divorced about 1931. Esther enrolled her younger daughters in Talmud Torah school programs in 1940. After the Second World War Esther moved to California. Her son, Edward, served in the Navy in both World War II and Korea.

(Above left) Sarah H. Turenne passport photo April 27, 1922

(Above right) Edward Turenne Tacoma News Tribune August 1, 1943

Louis Wacholder, born June 2, 1882, in Warsaw, Russia (now Warszawa, Poland)
Arrived N.Y. January 1904, aboard the *Philadelphia* from London
Married Zissel "Sophie" Kantoff (1889-1941) likely in N.Y. about 1907
Parents of Helen (1909-1918), Albert (1914-1976), and Arthur (1916-1944)
Died February 24, 1924, in San Francisco, California; buried Eternal Home Cemetery, Colma

Louis and Sophie lived in Brooklyn before moving to Tacoma about 1911. They joined her brother, Harry Kantoff, and his wife, Regina Rose Zuckerkorn. In 1912 Louis was one of the trustees who incorporated the Chevra Ahavas Israel. He declared his intention to become a citizen in Tacoma in June of 1915, then moved to San Francisco. In 1935 his widow, Sophie, married again to Joseph Stoler.

Rabbi Haskell Armin Wachsmann, son of Abraham and Drezel (Taub) Wachsmann
Born September 30, 1917, in Munkacsevo, Czechoslovakia
Married Friedel (1921-?) in London about 1947
Parents of Vivien Ruth and Abraham Herschell
Died November 4, 2001, in Fort Lauderdale, Florida

Haskell was born in Czechoslovakia and attended schools in Holland, Netherlands; and London, England. There he married Friedel and was ordained as a rabbi in 1947. His first congregation was in Regina, Saskatchewan, Canada. He also worked in Sacramento, California; and Council Bluffs, Iowa. Rabbi Wachsmann led Tacoma's Sinai Temple from the fall of 1953 until the summer of 1955, then returned to Regina. After a dozen years in Canada he lived and worked in Florida and Illinois.

Emanuel Waldocks, son of Philip and Edessa Waldocks
Born about 1862 in Krakow, Austria (now Poland)
Married Yetta Hoffman (1867-1924) in January of 1890 in Leavenworth, Kansas
Parents of Hannah Weinstein (1890-1975) and Jennie Nudelman (1892-1983)
Died February 17, 1921, Tacoma; buried Home of Peace Cemetery

Emanuel Waldocks was a career military man. In the 1880s he worked in canteen services with the 14th Infantry at Fort Leavenworth, Kansas. There he married Yetta Hoffman, daughter of Jacob and Hannah (Froenh) Hoffman. She had immigrated via New Orleans in 1888 as Henrietta, and lived with her brothers, David and Samuel, in Leavenworth. Emanuel and Yetta's first daughter was born in Kansas, the second in Portland, Oregon. Emanuel left Yetta in Portland and enlisted in the Marines. He re-enlisted several times over the next decade, and was stationed in Sitka, Alaska, and at Mare Island, California. He served several years in the Philippines and was in Peking at the time of the Boxer Rebellion. By 1905 he was in charge of the mess at Marine brigade headquarters. Yetta had divorced her absent husband in 1896. He returned to Portland and they remarried in 1906 and moved together to Tacoma. Emanuel first worked as a bookkeeper for another brother-in-law, Harry Hoffman, and later had his own wholesale liquor business. He was noted as a founding member and the third president of Chevra Talmud Torah. After both daughters married, the couple again divorced. Hannah married clothier Joseph Weinstein in 1909 and he became prominent in Temple Beth Israel. Jennie married Edward Nudelman in 1911, brother of Samuel Nudelman.

1912 Tacoma city directory listing | **Waldocks Emanuel whol liquors 1139 Commerce r 1143½ Commerce**

Harris Warnick, son of Jacob and Lizzie (Greenberg) Warnock, younger brother of Morris
Born December 31, 1880, in Dzwinogrod, Kiev, Russia (now Zvenyhorod, Ukraine)
Married Fannie Dorothy Weinstone (1880-1940) in 1902 in Glasgow, Scotland
Arrived Halifax N.S. on February 27, 1904, aboard the *Bavarian* from Glasgow
Parents of Elizabeth "Bettie" Mackoff Mosler (1903-1950), Jack (1905-1916), and Robert (1907-1976)
Died January 10, 1950, in Tacoma; buried Home of Peace Cemetery

Harris and Fannie (Weinstone) Warnick in 1910
with children Betty, Bob, and Jack
Courtesy of Jack Warnick

In December of 1930 Harris Warnick celebrated his 50th birthday. In an interview with the *Tacoma News Tribune* he revealed that he had been apprenticed to a cabinet maker at the age of nine to help support his widowed mother. He left his little town near Odessa when he was 20. He quipped that he first worked in Germany, where he knew the language, and then in Glasgow, where he did not.

Harris fell ill shortly after arriving in Glasgow. He was taken in by Froem and Bertha (Kurash) Weinstone, also immigrants from Odessa. In 1902 Harris married Fannie Weinstone, Froem's eldest daughter. Two years later the couple moved to Montreal, Canada, where their sons were born.

Harris was recruited to work for the Wheeler-Osgood Company, at the time the largest door manufacturer in the world. He trained first in Portland, Oregon, then came to Tacoma. After living in five countries in ten years, Harris chose to stay in Tacoma. A cluster of Weinstone and Warnick relatives followed. Harris opened his own firm, Puget Sound Manufacturing, in 1919.

Harris was vice president of the short-lived Chevrah Ahavas Israel congregation in 1912-1913, and joined Temple Beth Israel in 1922. Then, in the Twenties he took a leadership role in Talmud Torah. He served on the board of trustees in 1925 and his son, Robert, was a member of the Young Hebrew Moderates. Harris was recognized as a major contributor at the 1930 rededication, and Fannie chaired the banquet. He was vice president of the congregation in 1931. Fannie was active in multiple Jewish women's groups and chaired several banquets in the late Thirties. Harris' grandchildren remembered that he spoke without an accent and that the family spoke no Yiddish. He received a "Silver Beaver" award from the Boy Scouts for his work in establishing the Mount Rainier Council in Pierce County, complete with a commendation certificate signed by President Franklin D. Roosevelt.

Seven years after Fannie's death Harris remarried to Phyllis Leah Harris, of the Harris Department Stores in San Bernardino. Their first Tacoma residence was in the Hotel Winthrop, which Harris had supplied woodwork for in the early Twenties. Twenty-five years later he still recalled his bitter disappointment that all of his carefully matched mahogany was painted before the hotel opened.

Harris and Fannie's eldest son, Jack, died in 1916. Their daughter, Bettie, married Samuel Mackoff on July 4, 1928. (See separate biographical sketch.)

Their younger son, **Robert Warnick**, was "confirmed" at age thirteen at Talmud Torah in 1924 and was the first president of the Young Hebrew Moderates in 1925. He married Phreda Soss (1909-1994) in Spokane on March 31, 1929. They were the parents of four children; Alan (1931-1984), Jack M, Frederick and Elsa. Phreda was president of the Council of Jewish Women in 1937 and was active in the Women's Auxiliary of Talmud Torah. Later the family joined Temple Beth Israel. Robert continued his father's firm, Puget Sound Manufacturing, retiring just before his death. Warnick descendants would have tremendous community impact. One worked in Tacoma to cast out corrupt city officials and fought against housing discrimination. Another became a nationally known female cantor and rabbi.

Morris Warnick, son of Jacob and Lizzie (Greenberg) Warnock, older brother of Harris
Born either May 1, 1877, or January 6, 1878 in Kiev, Russia
Married Bessie Yablovsky/Yablonovich (1883-1967) about 1902
Parents of Wray Scott (1903-2005), John "Jack" Bertrand (1907-2006), and Robert Fredrick (1911-1999)
Died November 20, 1963, in San Francisco, California; buried Salem Memorial, Colma, California

The birthplaces of Morris and Bessie's children mirror their travels. Their first son was born in Kiev, the second in Montreal, and the third in Tacoma. Morris worked as an "expressman," first driving a wagon and then operating a truck. In that capacity he made rounds as a buyer for Tacoma's secondhand stores. He later worked as a delivery driver for his brother's manufacturing firm. His wife, Bessie, was prominent in the B'nai B'rith Destiny auxiliary. She was a steady helper at Talmud Torah activities, especially in the Thirties, often chairing spring banquets and coordinating fall rummage sales. Their eldest son enlisted in the Navy in 1942 from Seattle, and their youngest son enlisted from San Francisco in 1943. Morris and Bessie moved to California in the mid Forties.

Samuel Wasserman, born November 20, 1888; or February 20, 1889/90; in Irkutsk, Siberia, Russia
Formerly Izai Vaserman
Arrived Seattle December 28, 1915, aboard the *Chicago Maru* from Yokohama, Japan
Married Milly Joslowitz/Joslow (1890-1983) in Seattle on July 24, 1923
Parents of Leonard L. (1925-1957) and Marjorie
Died August 28, 1951, in Fircrest; buried Home of Peace Cemetery

Sam's first job in Tacoma was peddling junk for the Tacoma Junk Company. By 1922 he had his own secondhand store, American Furniture, on Commerce Street. After his marriage he operated the Home Furniture Store for nearly thirty years. His wife, Milly, helped with several Talmud Torah banquets. She often accompanied their talented son, Leonard, as he gave violin performances in the late Thirties. He performed at a variety of Jewish and community events and at Rabbi Treiger's first lecture series. In 1945 Sam and Milly learned that their son was slightly wounded while serving in the Army in France. At the time of Sam's death in 1951 Milly was president of the Tacoma Chapter of Hadassah. She later joined her married children in California.

Leonard Wasserman's NJWB record card

Julius "Jay" Udie Wax, son of Campbell Israel and Blanche (Walter) Waxengeisser/Wax
Born May 14, 1917, in Seattle
Married Shirley Willens (1920-2019) in Los Angeles on June 16, 1946
Parents of Michael, Judy, and Barbara
Died May 4, 2000, Tacoma; buried Home of Peace Cemetery

*(Left) Tacoma News Tribune ad
June 28, 1951*

*(Right) Shirley and Jay Wax
Courtesy of the Wax family*

Jay was born and raised in Seattle and lost his father before his tenth birthday. After his service in the Army Air Force in World War II he worked for a steel and scrap company. Friends introduced him to Shirley, and they married six months later. The young family moved to Tacoma in 1950 when Jay partnered with Floyd Lamken in forming Northwest Pipe and Salvage. Shirley immediately joined the Sinai Sisterhood and was active in Hadassah and Council of Jewish Women. She served as Hadassah president in 1952, and as Sisterhood vice president in 1954 and 1957. The couple hosted many youth group events in their home. In 1965 Jay became sole owner of his business and changed the name to Northwest Steel and Pipe. He later passed the firm on to his son. Generations of Jay and Shirley's family celebrated life cycle events at Sinai Temple and later at Temple Beth El.

Ephraim "Froem" Weinstone, son of Morris/Moshe Aaron Wheinstone
Born May 15, 1854/5 in Kovno, Russia (now Kaunas, Lithuania)
Married Bertha Gertrude Kurash (1856-1920)
Arrived N.Y. December 2, 1912 aboard the *Cameronia* from Glasgow, Scotland
Died June 6, 1933, in California; buried Home of Peace Cemetery, Tacoma

Bertha (Kurash) Weinstone, couresy of Jack Warnick

Children of **Froem Weinstone** and
Bertha Kurash
1. Kopel (1874-1940) spouse Libby Averback
2. Ben
3. Charles
4. Fannie (1880-1940) spouse Harris Warnick
5. Mannie (1883-1918) spouse Rose Schwartz
6. Sarah (1885-1950) spouse Abraham Polisky
7. Rebecca (1890-1942) spouse Jack Cohen
8. Mildred (1892-1973) spouse David Good
9. Hannah (1895-1982) spouse Tom Goldfarb
10. Maurice (1897-1968) spouses Thea Bergman
        and Cecelia Abrams

Froem and his wife, Bertha, had ten children in Russia between 1874 and 1897. They followed their married children to Scotland and eventually to Tacoma. Froem worked as a tailor before and after the First World War, and during the war as a shipbuilder. In 1919 he was a donor to the war relief fund as a member of Talmud Torah. After Bertha's death Froem lived in Tacoma another decade, then spent the last few years of his life with his daughters in California.

Weinstone Family in Glasgow, Scotland, circa 1904, *courtesy of Jack Warnick*
(Standing left to right) Abraham Polisky, Harris Warnick, Rebecca, Emanuel?, and Kopel Weinstone
(Seated left to right) Sarah Polisky holding Maurice Polisky, Fannie Warnick holding Bettie Warnick, Froem
Weinstone, Bertha Weinstone, and Libby Weinstone holding Philip
(Front left to right) Hannah, Maurice, Milldred, Louis, and Sadie Weinstone

Kopel Weinstone, son of Froem and Bertha (Kurash) Wheinstone/Weinstone
Born July 8, 1874, in Odessa, Russia (now Odesa, Ukraine)
Married Lillian "Libby" Averback (1878-1958) in Odessa on June 10, 1898
Parents of Sadie Stern (1900-1986), Louis "Lew" Winston (1901-1996), Philip (1903-1989), and
      Harry "Scotty" (1905-1983)
Died March 2, 1940, in Tacoma; buried Home of Peace Cemetery

All four of Kopel and Libby's children were born in Glasgow, Scotland. The family came to Tacoma in 1911, one year after their brother-in-law, Harris Warnick. Kopel first worked as a tailor, then operated Alaska Junk and Second Hand. Kopel and Libby's only daughter, Sadie, married Max Stern in 1916. (See separate biographical sketch.) Kopel was a donor to the 1919 war relief fund as a member of Talmud Torah. In the Twenties he and his three sons operated Weinstone and Sons Clothing on Pacific Avenue. In the late Twenties the family formed Alaska Iron and Metal, Inc., with Philip as president. Libby volunteered with the Women's Auxiliary at Talmud Torah, mostly after her children married. Kopel was a delegate to the 1933 Workmen's Circle convention.

Kopel and Libby's eldest son, Louis, worked in Tacoma's shipyards during the First World War, and later worked in his father's businesses. Louis married Marie Mintz (1906-1995) in Spokane on January 17, 1926. He took the name Lew Winston and raised his family in California.

Lew's youngest brother, "Scotty," had two professional fights in the Twenties, then spent the remainder of his life supporting others in the sport, earning the nickname "Mr. Golden Gloves." He married Minnie Carrick (1908-1973) in Tacoma on February 15, 1931. She was a daughter of David and Jennie (Galon) Carrick, and sister of Alice (Carrick) Bender. Scotty and Minnie had two daughters. (See Carrick biographical sketch)

Kopel and Libby's middle son, **Philip Weinstone**, also was a boxer in the Twenties. Under the name "Scotty O'Brien" he earned the nickname of the "Fighting Irishman" and was a sparring partner of the boxing great Freddy Steele. In addition he worked in his father's clothing business, and was later president of Alaska Iron and Metal. Philip married Frances "Fanny" Sussman (1909-1978) in Everett on December 31, 1934. She was a daughter of Benjamin Leo Sussman, cousin of Tacoma's Sussman brothers. Fanny was a member of Hadassah and the Council of Jewish Women, and helped with Women's Auxiliary events at Sinai Temple. Their son celebrated his bar mitzvah there, and in 1957 she co-chaired the school board. In the Fifties Philip also operated the Blue Note Ballroom.

1929 Tacoma city directory listing   " **Iron & Metal Inc Philip Weinstone pres Lillian Weinstone v-pres Kopel Weinstone treas Harry Weinstone sec 2301 So C**

Alex Weiser, born July 10, 1876, in Russia; son of Abraham and Ida Minnie Weiser
Married Rose Apflebaum (1873-1938) on July 25, 1896, in Ramsey County, Minnesota
Parents of Julie "Bud" Herbert (1898-1989), Abraham Jackson (1900-1971), and
      Rose Bloomberg/Nadler (1903-1979)
Died February 23, 1941, in San Francisco; buried Eternal Home Cemetery, Colma, California

Alex and Rose lived in Minnesota and North Dakota when their children were born. Both sons served in World War I. The family moved to Tacoma about 1920 and briefly belonged to Temple Beth Israel. Alex and his eldest son first operated a clothing store, A. Weiser and Son, on Pacific Avenue. His success allowed for the purchase of a new Buick sedan in 1923 and a new home in 1924 that tempted a burglar a month later. Their younger son, Abe, opened a clothing store and a candy store in South Tacoma in 1925. Alex ran the Midway Fruit Market in the late Twenties, located midway between his two sons. His eldest son Julie, nicknamed "Bud," operated a Haberdashery at 924 and later 934 Pacific. Rose participated in several Talmud Torah war relief events, and Bud was a guest at Abedeaux Friedman's 1928 birthday party. Alex and Rose lived briefly in Portland in 1930, then settled in San Francisco.

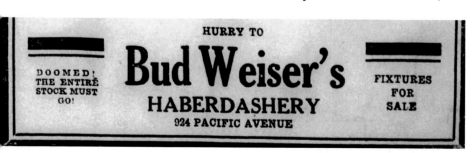

Tacoma News Tribune ad
May 5, 1928

Morris Werbisky, born March 18, 1883/5/6, in Kamenka, Kiev, Russia (now Kamyanka, Ukraine)
Arrived Montreal 1907 aboard the *Mount Temple* from Antwerp
Married Viola Elizabeth Hecht (1896-1942) in Seattle on November 10, 1918
Parents of Harry (1919-1940), Jeanette Walden (1922-1992), and Frank C. (1929-2014)
Died August 7, 1958, in Puyallup; buried Home of Peace Cemetery, Tacoma

Morris worked as an iron and metal buyer in Tacoma for over forty years, all with Frank Sussman and Tacoma Junk. In 1918 he married Viola Hecht, daughter of Charles and the late Jennie Hecht, and sister of Berdie Hecht Stusser. When Morris and Viola first married they lived with her father in Regents Park, later known as Fircrest. In 1919 the newlyweds donated to the war relief fund as members of Talmud Torah. Their eldest son, Harry, was an outstanding athlete at Stadium High School and at the College of Puget Sound. He died suddenly in 1940 from an infected tooth, leaving his team and his community in shock. His mother never recovered and died soon after. Harry's younger brother, Frank, was a student at Talmud Torah in the early Forties and was a member of the 1944 confirmation class. He served in the military in the Fifties and settled in Los Angeles. The Harry Werbisky Memorial Award presented by the University of Puget Sound recognizes outstanding students for their sportsmanship, citizenship, and scholarship.

1941 College of Puget Sound yearbook memorial

Harry Lemil Weston, son of Sam and Helen (Cassman) Weston
Born January 12, 1915, in Portland, Oregon
Married Beatrice "Bee" Elaine Klegman (1918-1995) in Tacoma on October 26, 1941
Parents of Barbara
Died November 17, 1987, Tacoma; buried New Tacoma Cemetery

Harry served two enlistments in the U.S. Army. The first was from July of 1937 to March of 1938. The second was from October of 1943 to January of 1946. In between he married Bee, daughter of Ben and Mary (Weinstein) Klegman, also of Portland. They had one daughter, Barbara. Harry spent his career working for the post office department, first as a route carrier and later as the Lakewood supervisor. Bee was a member of Hadassah and in the late Fifties was in the Sinai Temple Sisterhood.

Joseph Willner, son of Bene/Bernard and Clara (Halpern) Willner.
Born August 6, 1885/6, in Toporo, Galicia, Austria (now Toporiv, Ukraine)
Arrived N.Y. August 17, 1904, aboard the *Barbarossa* from Bremen, Germany
Married Rose Gesusinsky/Good (1890-1979) in Seattle on June 15, 1913 (Sister of David Good)
Parents of Ruth Shulman (1914-2006), Esther Cohen/Corben (1916-1993), and
        Caroline Leibowitz/Lewis (1921-2000)
Died July 14, 1973, in Tacoma; buried Herzl Cemetery, Seattle

Moses "Morris" Willner, son of Bene/Bernard and Clara (Halpern) Willner
Born April 12/15, 1895, in Toporo, Galicia, Austria (now Toporiv, Ukraine), brother of Joseph
Arrived Baltimore June 20, 1912 aboard the *Main* from Bremen, Germany, as Moses Willner
Married Julia Epstein (1893-1961) in Tacoma on July 4, 1917
Parents of Bernard (1918-1930) and Richard (1925-1996)
Died November 3, 1985, in Seattle; buried Herzl Cemetery, Seattle

WESTERN JUNK CO (Joseph and Morris Willner) Buyers of All Kinds of Junk, Furniture and Tools, Machinery, Scrap Metal, Sacks, Pipes, Barrels, etc, 406 Puyallup Av, Tel Main 1341 (See classified Junk Dealers)

The Willner brothers, Joseph and Morris, spent several decades together in Tacoma. They first operated the Chicago Junk and Second Hand Store in 1917, later known as Western Junk. In the Twenties they sold army goods as Willner Brothers. They transitioned to men's furnishings in the late Twenties. Morris' eldest son, Bernard, died in 1930, and shortly after the couple moved to Seattle. There Morris joined a third brother, William, and founded Willner's Department Store. Joseph and Rose stayed in Tacoma and continued operating Willner Brothers for three more decades. Joseph was secretary of Workmen's circle in 1939 and served several terms on the board of trustees of Talmud Torah. Rose belonged to the Women's Auxiliary and co-chaired a number of large events. They celebrated their fiftieth wedding anniversary in Tacoma in 1963, the same week as Sam and Mary Friedman.

Raphael Winkleman, eldest son of Henry Philip and Lottie (Raphael) Winkleman
Born January 28, 1881, in New York, New York
Died in Seattle on January 26, 1916; buried Home of Peace Cemetery

(Left) 1910 Winkleman Lumber business card
From the Freedman Collection
(Right) Raphael Winkleman c. 1905
Courtesy of Judith Parker Hindin

Raphael was born in New York, the eldest son in a family of eight children. They came to Washington Territory from Philadelphia about 1888 and operated a prominent junk and metal business. Raphael and his sister, Rose, organized Winkleman Lumber about 1906, doing business from the same location as their father's Winkleman Iron and Metal. Two years later Raphael was an incorporator of Chevra Talmud Torah. In 1914 he managed Winkleman Bag and Burlap, in addition to the other family companies. Raphael was killed in a warehouse fire in Seattle in 1916 when a stove exploded that was being used to dry out damaged strands of hemp. His remaining family members moved to Portland.

Harry Wiseblatt, son of Peter/Paltiel and Haye Sarah (Hirskevitz) Weisblatt/Wiseblatt
Born October 14, 1895, in Nikolayev, Russia (now Mykolayiv, Ukraine)
Married Rose Gussman (1904-1980) in Montreal, Canada, on December 20, 1936
Died March 9, 1952, in Tacoma; buried Home of Peace Cemetery

Harry's family moved to Montreal from Russia in 1904. He was drafted into the U.S. Army in April of 1918. Harry and Rose came to Tacoma in 1946, joining her brother, Irving Gussman. Harry worked at his brother-in-law's clothing store until just before his death in 1952. His obituary identified him as a member of Sinai Temple and of Workingman's Circle. Rose participated in Hadassah activities in Tacoma in the Fifties, and eventually returned to Montreal.

Bernard Jack Witenberg, son of Ezra Favius and Shayna Witenberg
Born October 15, 1887, in Marjampol, Suwalki, Russia (now Marijampoli, Lithuania)
Arrived N.Y. June 2, 1904, aboard the *Deutschland* from Hamburg
Married Charlotte Endelman (1886-1953) in Spokane in July of 1913
Parents of Favius "Fav" Ezra (1915-2008) and Ruth Levy (1917-1980)
Died December 4, 1967, in Tacoma; buried Home of Peace Cemetery

(Right) Charlotte and Bernard Witenberg
Courtesy of Toby (Witenberg) Israel and Bruce Witenberg

(Left) Tacoma Daily Ledger ad
June 13, 1915

(Below) Tacoma News Tribune ad
June 14, 1959

Canvas Gloves

Made in Tacoma by
WITENBERG MFG. CO.
Priced, the pair—
5¢, 10¢, 15¢ and **25c**

LIBERTY FINANCE COMPANY

Under Personal Management of B. J. Witenberg Since 1941

3425 So. Tac. Way   "BORROW WITH CONFIDENCE"   GR 4-0544

Bernard's first home in the U.S. was with his married sister, Mildred (Witenberg) Lyon, in Chicago. Another sister, Lillian (1885-1977), married Isaac Raban in Chicago in 1907 and then lived in Kentucky and Seattle. The same year Bernard and Mildred joined a fourth sibling, Samuel Nathan, in Tacoma. Bernard first worked in his brother's clothing store. Then the siblings partnered in a new venture, Witenberg Manufacturing. The company produced canvas gloves for the next thirty years with Samuel as president, Bernard vice president, Mildred secretary, and her husband, Abraham Lyon, as manager. The company frequently advertised for skilled sewing machine operators. Bernard and Charlotte built a substantial home on North Union Street in 1925. After Sam's death in 1941 Bernard established Liberty Finance. Although his siblings belonged to Temple Beth Israel, Bernard and Charlotte were active in Talmud Torah. She served as president of the Women's Auxiliary in 1938 and treasurer in 1940. Their daughter, Ruth, married Saul Levy in 1942. (See separate biographical sketch.) In 1958 the Tacoma chapter of Hadassah presented Bernard with a Man of the Year Award for his lifetime of service to his community.

Favius "Fav" Ezra Witenberg, son of Bernard Jack and Charlotte (Endelman) Witenberg
Born December 14, 1915, in Tacoma
Married Lillian "Lil" Smilovitz/Smiley (1916-1995) in Seattle on June 12, 1945
Parents of Bruce and Toby
Died May 14, 2008, in Tacoma; buried Home of Peace Cemetery

Fav enlisted in the Navy in December of 1941. He married Lil shortly before his discharge in 1945. For several years he operated a hardware and surplus materials yard near his father's finance company on South Tacoma Way. In 1951 his father, Bernard, was robbed and badly injured. Fav closed his business and joined Liberty Finance. He ran the company for the next fifty years. Lil was an active member of the Sinai Sisterhood, serving as secretary in 1952 and president in 1954-1955. Both were known for their dedication to their community.

Jacob Wolf, born May 6, 1877, in Russia, husband of Anna Meland
Parents of Richard (1904-1970) and Edward (1908-1976)
Died October 15, 1944, in Tacoma; buried Home of Peace Cemetery

Jacob and Anna lived most of their lives in New York, where Jacob owned a stationery store. In 1941 they joined their sons in Tacoma. Richard operated a large sporting goods store, Wolf and Gaines, on Pacific Avenue, and Edward worked as a surgeon. Both sons were members of Temple Beth Israel. Jacob's obituary identified him as a member of Talmud Torah and of Workman's Circle. After his death his sons both moved to Los Angeles.

Bernhard Yudelson, son of Hyman and Chane (Jaffe) Judelsohn/Yudelson
Born about 1862 in Libau, Russia, now Liepaja, Latvia
Died December 4, 1902, in Tacoma; buried Home of Peace Cemetery

Bernhard was an older brother of Peter J. Yudelson. He lived in Tacoma as early as 1896. Bernhard worked as a tailor and was employed by Hugo Stusser and Julius Friedman. He likely was one of the ten men needed to make up a minyan in the 1890s. Bernhard died unmarried.

Peter Julius/Pesach Yehudah Yudelson, son of Hyman and Chane (Jaffe) Judelsohn/Yudelson
Born April 6, 1860, Libau, Russia, now Liepaja, Latvia
Married Bluma Stusser (1854-1920) in Libau about 1883, daughter of
    Abraham and Mollie (Friedman) Stusser
Peter arrived N.Y. November 9, 1901, aboard the *Philadelphia* from Southampton
Bluma arrived N.Y. August 9, 1902, aboard the *St. Paul* from Southampton
Bluma died October 14, 1920, in Tacoma; buried Home of Peace Cemetery
Peter died July 8, 1939, while visiting Seattle; buried Home of Peace Cemetery

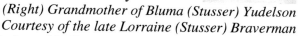

(Right) Grandmother of Bluma (Stusser) Yudelson
Courtesy of the late Lorraine (Stusser) Braverman

Peter and Bluma's arrival in Tacoma helped fill a vital need in Tacoma's Jewish community. They brought with them five daughters, all of whom would marry over the next two decades. After Bluma's death in 1920 many of her daughters gave their own daughters names starting with the letter "B" in her memory.

1. Augusta (1887-1983) married Henry Molin (1880-1939) on March 26, 1907
2. Betty (1891-1978) married Nathan Friedman (1880-1947) on June 7, 1909
3. Ida (1892-1969) married Frank Sussman (1880-1964) on July 11, 1910
4. Hazel (1893-1982) married Abraham Saperstein (1887-1971) on August 18, 1921
5. Emma (1894-1986) married Max Novikoff (1892-1972) on February 25, 1918

Peter worked as a tailor and dyed clothing, but for most of his career in Tacoma he sold secondhand goods on Commerce Street. In 1908 their home was burglarized and some of Peter's clothing was stolen, including his hat and a unique thimble. The burglar made the mistake of leaving his own battered hat, which bore his name and proved to be a condemning perfect fit at his trial. After Bluma's death Peter remarried in 1921 to Bessie Fisher.

(Left) Yudelson family in Libau circa 1897   *(Right) Yudelson family in Tacoma circa 1907*
Courtesy of Jim Friedman, from the late Lorraine (Sussman) Braverman

Henry Nathan Zeidell, born March 20, 1884, in Riga, Latvia
Married Rebecca "Bea" Eichenwald (1884-1956) in Oklahoma on August 1, 1907
Parents of Bernice Borah (1910-1983) and Myron (1916-1974)
Died February 23, 1968, in San Francisco, California; buried Hills of Eternity, Colma

Henry and Bea came to Tacoma in 1915 and briefly belonged to Temple Beth Israel. Over the next two years Henry sold millinery with Morris Lyon, served as Talmud Torah president, participated in a city billiards tournament, and celebrated the birth of a son. Several of Bea's Eichenwald sisters were also in the area. (See page 55.) Earlier the couple had lived in Ohio and California. After their time in Tacoma they lived in Fresno, California, where Henry was one of the cofounders of a new synagogue.

Max Adolph Zuckerkorn, son of Abraham and Higa Sarah (Weichenberg) Cukierkorn
Born May 20, 1875, in Warsaw, Russia (now Warszawa, Poland)
Arrived N.Y. May 1, 1899, from Hamburg, Germany
Married Ernestine Lena Moses/Morris on June 1, 1903, in New York, New York
Died December 11, 1950, in Phoenix, Arizona; buried Beth El Cemetery, Phoenix

Max and Ernestine moved to Tacoma three years after their marriage. His sister, Regina Kantoff, followed in 1908. Max's brother Ben came in 1909. A younger sister, Frieda Offerman, came in 1911. A fifth sibling, Hannah, and her husband, Harry Greenbaum, lived briefly in Tacoma after fleeing Germany in 1938. While in Tacoma Max ran a secondhand clothing store on Commerce. He was an incorporator of Talmud Torah in 1908. However he and his brother, Ben, both went bankrupt in 1912. Max served six months in jail for fraud after he confessed to hiding merchandise from the receiver. Max and Ernestine lived the next thirty years in Great Falls, Montana, before retiring to Arizona in 1945. They adopted a daughter, Nellie Bess, while in Montana.

Signature from 1902 New York Declaration of Intention

Name Index

G

214

Made in the USA
Las Vegas, NV
12 July 2022